VILLAGE NAMES
OF
MYSORE DISTRICT

SPECIAL PNSI SERIES

VILLAGE NAMES OF MYSORE DISTRICT

(An Analytical Study)

Prof. D. Javare Gowda

GYAN

Published by

Gyan Publishing House
5, Ansari Road
Daryaganj, New Delhi-110002
Phone: 011-47034999, 9811692060
E-mail: books@gyanbooks.com

Distribution Network
gyanbooks.com
India, USA, Canada, UK, Australia, France

ISBN : 978-81-212-4189-2 (PB)
First Published, 1862

2nd Impression 2020

Printed at: Gyan Press, Delhi.

The book at your disposal is the edition of an old book originally published long back. The Text quality of this book may not be at par as compared to our other books but many readers approached us to reprint this important book so that it could satiate their hunger. We request all the readers of this book to help us to improve its quality by providing the necessary text of those pages which are not properly visible. Your valuable support in this case will be highly appreciated and acknowledged and our future readers will be benefitted immensely.

PREFACE

It is a matter of great pride to place before the world of scholars the special issue of **Village Names of Mysore District** by **Prof. D.Javare Gowda** brought out on the occasion of the nineteenth conference. This work richly deserves my sincere thanks to him for this excellent research work in the field of Onomastics. This analytical study is the first of its kind in the field of Place - Names study. Being a pioneer scholar in the field, his encouragement has given a fillip to the society to take up the Dictionary on Place and Personal Names. Dr. K.V.Ramesh, another veteran scholar in the field of Onomastics has completed successfully the sample survey of the Dictionary of Place - Names of five taluks of Mysore district in Karnataka.

I express my warm and sincere thanks to Prof. D.Javare Gowda, Dr. K.V. Ramesh, Shri Madhav N.Katti and Dr. Y.Balagangadhara Rao for their valuable guidance in promoting Onomastic studies.

I am deeply beholden to Sri Jetley and Sri Suresh. Asian Educational Services. New Delhi who have shouldered the labour of printing and publishing of this volume. I also take this opportunity to express on behalf of the members of the society and on my own behalf our sincere thanks to Asian Educational Services, New Delhi for the agreement entered into with the Place Names Society of India, Mysore in getting this special volume and the Endowment lectures series published.

I thank M/s. Comptek Computer Systems, Mysore for the neat execution and the timely completion of composing this work through D.T.P.

Mysore-5
1-12-1998

M.D. Sampath
Secretary and Executive Editor
Place Names Society of India

A STUDY OF VILLAGE NAMES OF MYSORE DISTRICT

INTRODUCTION

Man would practically have remained a brute but for his wonderful faculty of naming things around him and concepts that originate in his mind. The thinking ability and expansion of knowledge would not have been possible but for this great gift conferred upon him by nature. Naming in one form or the other is said to be the earliest of all intellectual activities and attainments. It is, therefore, correctly assessed that language is all names. It is also true that names endow concreteness clarity, definiteness to everything, objects, ideas, thoughts and the sensory perceptions under the seen. A man's name and even that of an animal or plant or place is his or its signboard to the world. Every name is dynamic and goes on acquiring more and more meaning and significance by constant use, regulated by cultural and scientific advancement. Take for example, names like Vālmīki, Christianity, Islam, Hinduism, Marxism, the Buddha, Lenin, Gāndhi, Swāmi Vivēkānanda, Ambeḍkar, Gaṅgā, Kāvērī and a host of others. They are a great force in the life of any community or country and they gain newer and newer dimensions as time rolls on.

Whether Personal Names (PNS) or toponyms are understood as functional units or identification marks, the fact that they are replete with meanings cannot be dismissed, without endangering the citadels of knowledge. Every place name has an individuality of its own, a personality of its own and a history of its own. The names of rivers like the Ganges, the Thames and the Amazon and of cities such as *Vāraṇāsi*, London, Delhi, Beijing and Tokyo have larger tradition and history than any of the ruling families that histories have witnessed. They have seen the appearance and disappearance of many a great empire and civilisation. One can see an aura of mysterious reality and a halo of sacredness surrounding them.

Historical, cultural and linguistic studies cannot be said to be complete without the application of the results of place name studies.

Even ethnologists, geographers, archaeologists and natural scientists are likely to get solutions to their problems from the study of toponyms. They are said to be the footnotes of history and the fossils of archaeology. They are expressions of intellectual genius and cultural tendencies of the people. They throw a flood of light on the mental attitudes, the speech habits, the customs and manners of the people whose shelters and inspirers they have been. They have been the emblems of rise and fall, and decay of many a people. Sometimes, the mention of a name itself reveals a mass of truth and wonder which cannot be experienced otherwise either by going through a manual or a geography book or a historical document. A great wealth of information relating to history, folklore, geography, ethnology, archaeology and such other kindred disciplines lies embedded in the bosom of each name. There are the rich mines of linguistic materials.

Even from the point of view of national integration, the study of PNS becomes very imperative as it discloses the bond of affinity prevalent among the people of various regions of India, bringing to light many points of cultural and religious contacts. It is possible with the help of the study of PNS to unearth the forgotten chapters of the cultural history of India, the reconstruction of which helps the fostering and strengthening of unity and cordiality among the various ethnic and linguistic groups.

Most of the PNS have witnessed ups and downs during the long course of their existence. Topographical features, political events, economic conditions and religious aspects play a prominent role in determining the destiny of villages, towns and cities. Certain towns like *Taḷakāḍu,* once the capital of the Gaṅgas may sink into insignificance along with the disappearance of the ruling family, while cities like Bangalore may gain world-wide importance as time rolls on. It is also possible that, on account of flood, war, pestilence, drought and various other natural or man made causes, some villages or cities may vanish beyond recognition. At the same time, a number of new villages and cities will spring up with the growth of population and migration. A place name is, by and large, the voice of external souls, the breath of several generations of people, the footprint of civilisation of bygone days, the inviolate record of human history and a great inspiration of mankind.

It is the western countries that recognised the importance of the study of PNS first by giving it a fillip and encouragement as far back as the eighteenth century. It should be said to be credit of the United Nations that it has grasped the value of PNS while appointing, in 1961, a group of experts on the standardisation of geographical names. The Government of India, after obtaining the views of the State governments laid down as early as 1953, certain rules and procedures that are to be followed while changing PNS and determining their correct spellings. The Survey of India and the National Atlas Organisations also are trying to standardise the spellings of toponyms. Epigraphical records, literary works, imperial and state gazetteers, dictionaries, encyclopedias etc., list the villages published by State government departments, census records, resettlement registers, taluk and village survey maps, registers of births and deaths, voters' lists and even the name boards along the roads will serve as useful sources of information with regard to PNS. It is with the help of these sources that the pronunciation, the spelling, the etymology, the semantic value and the history of PNS have to be traced and determined.

Dialectal varieties and colloquial uses account for the multiplicity of spellings and pronunciations. The impact of foreign and neighbourhood languages is likely to affect the spelling systems and pronunciation of a place-name. *Beṅgaḷūru,* for example, has its anglicised pronunciation as Bangalore and its colloquial usage as *Beṅgḷūru.*

Since India came under the influence of various races in prehistoric times and she was subjected to foreign domination during the historical period, they have left their marks in the process of the evolution of PNS, both structurally and semantically. It is possible that some of the PNS have changed in such a way in course of time that their original forms cannot be traced at ali. The evolution of language too has its bearing on the change of PN forms. It is also a known fact that in commemoration of an event or as a memorial to a king or a warrior, or a donor, new names will be substituted in place of old ones.

Sanskritisation and anglicisation are two of the important trends which have caused the change of PNS. It was a fashion among the Hindu kings, perhaps, under the influence of the upper class people to replace the native place name by a Sanskrit name. This replacement is done in two ways viz., by translating the original one into Sanskrit, with the retention of the former semantic value like in *Vēṇupura* in place of *Bidarapaḷḷi* and by coining a new word without any reference to its original meaning as in *Rājarājachaturvēdimaṅgalam* for *Kūḍalūr.* Sanskrit names, however disappear in the long run, since the common man could not digest them.

The advent of Westerners has brought considerable changes in some of the important PNS of India. These changes are mainly orthographical. They could not pronounce the Indian PNS in the same way as the natives since the orthography of English - i.e., the nonphonetic script of the language - and of the Indian languages differ very widely from each other. So they anglicised all the PNS that they came in contact to suit the genius of their own language. Not only the vowel endings are generally dropped, but the entire form is mutilated or distorted, as in Calicut *(Kōzhikōḍe), Rājahmundry (Rājamahēndravaram), Pāṭna (Pāṭaliputra),* Trivandrum (Thiruvananthapuram), *Kānpur (Kaṇhapur < Kṛishnapura),* Chitaldurg (Chitradurga), *Seriṅgapaṭṇam (Śrīraṅgapaṭṭaṇa), Mudhōl (Muduvoḷal), Coorg (Koḍagu),* etc. Sometimes, the original name is completely dropped and a name of their liking is substituted as in Closepet (now *Rāmanagaram*).

The corrupted forms of Sanskrit names are also found here and there as for example, *Agara* for *Agrahāra.* The grammarians, of course, call them *tadbhavas.* This kind of process may be designated as nativisation. The nativisation of English names, such as *Ambaṭṭan* bridge (Madras) for Hamilton bridge too is possible. Such things are rare. While the nativisation of Sanskrit names does not alter the original meaning, the nativisation of English names is likely to modify the meaning, but not always. The same is true of specifics also. There are some specifics and generics which defy any interpretation at present. When all the PNS of South India, nay all the PNS of entire India are studied, it should be possible to find clues to the mysteries which some of these words hide in their bosoms. It is in this background, an attempt is made in this thesis, to study the Village Names (VNS) of Mysore district of the Karnataka State.

Though my interest in the study of PNS/VNS dates back to 1946, I could not pursue the same owing to multifarious activities. In the year 1977 the Place Names Society of India was started with the help of many friends, particularly Dr. G.S.Gai and his colleagues in the office of the Chief Epigraphist, Government of India. I actually took up research work on VNS of the Mysore district, when, by the courtesy of Prof. V.I.Subramoniam, I was invited to be a Senior fellow of the International School of Dravidian Linguistics from 1-2-1979 to 31-1-1980.

I chose the entire Mysore district for my thesis. I was so enthusiastic and ambitious in the beginning that I did not anticipate the multifaceted problems that besiezed me like erected arrows (quills) of porcupine. The district being very vast with eleven taluks,* bordered by these states with three languages, stared me at my face. Within a month of my taking up the job, I came to know that it would not be possible to do full justice in a year to the subject without proper, systematic and comprehensive field work which could not be carried successfully by any one individual without proper assistance. Hence, I had no other go except depending on maps, charts, lists of villages, Gazetteers, inscriptions, reference books, intuition and imagination.

I am quite aware and sure that without field work, interviews, correspondence and discussion with local people, informants and officials, and constant visits to villages whose names do not yield the secrets hidden in their bosom, the investigation is incomplete and the

* It has now been recently bifurcated into two districts viz, Mysore and Chamarajanagar district, the four taluks of Kollegala, Yalanduru, Chamarajanagar and Gundlupet, assigned in the newly formed district.

results are not free from flaws and defects. With slender financial resources at my command, lack of facilities such as good roads and transportation to the places of destination and nonavailability of menial or clerical assistance, I could not visit the villages which posed problems. As a result of these inconveniences, I hasten to confess that this thesis suffers from shortcomings which can be rectified as and when the comparative study of South Indian village names progresses. Yet I feel certain that this challenging task has been carried out with sincerity and a sense of dedication.

It is true that the submission of the thesis to the ISDL was delayed inordinately, for about fourteen years. This unpardonable delay naturally caused worrisome ripples in the mind of the Director of the Institute, Dr. V.I.Subramoniam, a resolute reputed academic disciplinarian who is the architect of the institution. Being confronted with a host of problems, being unable to do field work for want of facilities, my nerves began to rack out of wearisomeness and in the meanwhile I took up another endearing job, viz., the translation of Leo Tostoy's works. It was only after the completion of this sacred duty and persistent persuasion by Dr. Subramoniam, I thought that the completion of the thesis was an obligation from which I could not escape. I took up the work again after a lapse of nearly twelve years. I hope this work will be welcomed by the workers in the field of onomastics, and serve particularly the research scholars in the area of place names, as an incentive. Before I conclude this introduction, I would like to quite a stanza from the old Kannada grammar, *Śabdamaṇidarpaṇa,* authorised by the great grammarian of the 13th century Kēśirāja who addresses the wise people thus:

'Avadharipadu Vibudhar dō-
ṣavidaroḷēnānumuḷḷoḍam priyadim ti-
rduvudu guṇayuktamum dō-
ṣavidūramumāge mechchi kaikoḷvudidam 1-4

The wisemen are requested to take this book to their heart. If there are any flaws in this, they will kindly and affectionately correct them; if it is found flawless and possessed of good qualities, may be it appreciated and received well.' May I commend this aphorism for the consideration of the readers of this book?

I am always an optimist. I hope that the wisdom dawns in the mind of the Government of India, which it will launch the project of the National Dictionary of PNS which might derive benefit from this thesis during course of its preparation.

Before closing this introduction, it is my duty to acknowledge the help derived from the Late Reverend F.Kittel's Kannada-English dictionary while working and processing the semantic study of the village names and the Dravidian Etymological dictionary by T.Burrow and M.B. Emeneau. I will be failing in my duty of I do not convey my gratitude to Dr. K.V.Ramesh who has prepared the sample Dictionary of Indian PNS.

I am extremely grateful to Dr. V.I.Subramoniam, the Honorary Director of the ISDL without whose timely admonitions this work would not have seen the light of the day. I should also thank the ISDL for conferring on me the Senior research fellowship. I am indebted to Dr. K.V.Ramesh, the retired Joint Director - General, Archaeological Survey of India, to Sri M.N.Katti, Director (Epigraphy), Govt. of India and the Chief Epigraphist, Dr. M.D.Sampath, for evincing keen interest while this thesis was in the making. It is they who are fully responsible for publishing this work. My thanks are due to Mr. P.Natarajan, Office of the Director (Epigraphy), an able master craftsman in typing, for preparing a nice manuscript for the press. Last, but not least, I am highly obliged to Asian Educational Series who has willingly published this book.

31-7-1996
Mysore-12

D. Javare Gowda (Dejagow)

ABBREVIATIONS

Arab	Arabic
Br.	Brahmi
CN	Names of commercial importance
Col	Colloquial
DIPN	Dictionary of Indian Place Names
Dir. Par	Directional practice
EN	Names of ethnological bearing
Eng	English
FAN	Names denoting fauna
Fem. ind	Feminine indicator
FLN	Names denoting flora
FN	Foreign Name
FPN	Female Personal Name
Ga	Gadba
Gaz	Gazetteer (Karnataka)
GPN	Names after geographical and physical features
Go	Gondi
H	Hindustāni
HN	Names of historical importance
Kan	Kannaḍa
Kod	Koḍava
Kur	Kurusch
Mal	Malayāḷam
Mhr	Marāṭhi
MN	Miscellaneous names

NK	Naiki
NN	Names after natural phenomena
Nadj	Numerical adjective
Pap	Past participle
Par	Parish
PN	Personal
PRP	Present participle
Suf	Suffix (inflexional increment)
SX	Simplex
Tam	Tamil
Tel	Telugu
Tu	Tuḷu
Vadj	Verbal adjective
< >	Derived from
~	Alternative forms
{ }	Alternative meanings

The alphabetical chart relating to VNS under study is given hereunder

a ā i ī u ū e ē i (ai)

o ō au

k g ṅ

ch j ñ

t ṭh ḍ ṇ

t ṭh d dh n

p b bh m

y r l v ś ṣ s h ḷ

MYSORE DISTRICT IN RETROSPECT

Mysore district is the southernmost district of the present Karnataka State. Before the reorganisation of linguistic States in 1956, the Mysore State was a separate entity with nine districts, ruled by the royal family. After the reorganisation of States, the State lost its separate entity, though the new enlarged State continued to be called Mysore, until it was renamed as Karnataka in 1972. The name Mysore, is therefore, now confined to only one district.

The archaeological researches reveal that the prehistoric man must have been active during the neolithic and megalithic periods in Mysore, as in *T.Narasipūr, Koḷḷegal, Yaḷandūr* and *Chāmarājanagar* taluks, mainly in the river valleys. A fossilised bone of a buffalo was discovered at *T.Narasipūr.* The lone human skeleton discovered at the *T.Narasipūr* site, belonging to the end of the neolithic age with intrusive chalcolithic elements, was of the Mediterranean man, of the same stock as those inhabiting similar sites of Tekkalakōṭa and Piklihal in Raichur district.[1]

The Toḍavas (Toḍa) must have lived in this part of South India, before they were pushed towards the Nilgiri jungles. Buffaloes were and are even now the object of their worship. There are a good number of villages like *Koṇanūr* and *Emedoḍḍi* which are named after buffaloes. The area occupied by the tenders of buffalo must have been called *Erumai Nāḍu* or *Mahishamaṇḍala* which Dipavaṁśa of Aśokan times has mentioned. Ptolemy's (A.D. 130) Punnato has been identified with *Punnāṭa* or *Punnāḍu* in Mysore district. Moreover, the district is very much richer than the other districts of Karnataka in respect of inscriptions and this is a clear evidence of the antiquity of the area.

Even earlier, Mysore witnessed many vicissitudes as an administrative unit. The Gaṅgas, the Chōḷas, the Hoysaḷas, the Vijayanagar rulers, and the Chieftains like Chaṅgālvas and the Pālyagars ruled over the State in different periods of time. Towards the end of the Vijayanagar empire, the royal family of Mysore gained

1. Gazetteer of India, Mysore district, (p.52), Chief Editor, Sūryanāth U.Kāmath.

complete control over the State. Raja Wodeyar made *Śrīraṅgapaṭṭaṇa* his capital in A.D. 1617. After the fall of Tipu, the capital was shifted to Mysore. In the meanwhile the British Commissioners took over the reins of administration and ruled over the State for fifty years between A.D. 1831 to 1881 till it was returned to the royal family.

Mysore district formed part of the *Ashṭagrāma Foujdāri* till it was separated and made into a separate district in A.D. 1862. In 1939, the district was bifurcated into Mysore and *Maṇḍya* districts. *Maṇḍya* district comprises seven taluks viz. *Maṇḍya, Maḷavaḷḷi, Pāṇḍavapura, Śrīraṅgapaṭṭaṇa, Kṛiṣṇarāja Pēṭe, Nāgamaṅgala* and *Maddūr*, while the other ten taluks namely Mysore, *Kṛiṣṇarājanagar, Huṇsūr, Periyāpaṭṭaṇa, Heggaḍadēvana Kōṭe, Guṇḍlupēṭe, Chāmarājanagar, Nañjanagūḍu, Yeḷandūr* and *T.Narasipūr* taluks remain in the Mysore district. After the reorganisation of States in 1956, *Koḷḷegāl* taluk belonging to Coimbatore district of the then *Madras* State was included in the Mysore district.

Physiographically, the district may be classified as partly malnad and partly semi-malnad. It is watered by perennial rivers like Cauvery and Kapini which have been exploited through irrigational facilities. The *Biḷigiriraṅganabeṭṭa* and the Mahadēśwara hills are the primary mountains covered by forests which shelter wild animals like elephants and tigers. The malnad area is rich with flora and fauna.

The district lies between 11°50' and 12°50' North latitude and 75°45' and 77°45' East longitude. It is bounded on the north by Bangalore, *Maṇḍya* and *Hāssan* districts, on the south by the *Caṇṇanore* district of Kerala and *Udhagamaṇḍalam* district of *Tamil Nāḍu,* on the east and south-east by Salem and Coimbatore district of Tamil Nadu, on the west by *Koḍagu* district and the *Wynād* districts of Kerala.

The area of the district is about 11,954 Sq.km. It consists of eleven taluks, 13 towns, `641 inhabited and 196 uninhabited villages as per the 1981 Census report. Of these taluks, *Koḷḷēgal* happens to be the largest with an area of 2,787 Sq.km, while *Yeḷandūr,* the smallest with an area of 263 Sq.km. It may be mentioned that there are slight variations in the taluk-wise number of villages as per revenue records and 1981 Census records, as for example, *Chāmarājanagar* and *Guṇḍlupete* taluks noted 188 and 190, 159 and 161 villages respectively.

The important religions found in the district are Hinduism, Islam, Christianity and Jainism. The Hindus are again divided into many castes, cults and tribes. People belonging to various sects of Hinduism are the followers of Sankaracharya, Basavanna, Ramanujacharya and Madhwacharya, and they worship Vishṇu, *Mahēśwara* and Brahma as well as their consorts. *Hanumān* and *Gaṇēśa* are worshipped alike by all people irrespective of caste or creed. Goddess Śakti is the most popular deity, especially among the rural folk and is worshipped in various names like *Gujjāramma* in *Koḷḷēgāla, Kittūramma* in *Kittūr, Huliyūramma* in *Kyātanahaḷḷi. Grāmadēvata* is the general appellation for these deities.

Kannada has been the mother tongue of about 84% of the population of the district. People who have Urdu, Tamil, Telugu, Malayāḷam and Koḍava languages as their mother tongues form a minority and almost all of them understand and speak Kannada. The tribal population number sixty thousand. They are *Kāḍu Kurubas, Jēnu kurubas* and *Sōligas.*

The total number of villages in each taluk is listed below. The list is prepared on the basis of the 1981 Census. Forest beats and bechirak villages are not included in this list. Small variations in number as between survey settlement records, census figures and the list of villagespublished by the Kannada Culture department have been noted. This variation, however, does not affect the present study of PNS.

	Taluk	Hobaḷi	No. of Villages
1.	*Chāmarājanagara*	*Chāmarājanagar*	39
		Haradanahaḷḷi	37
		Harve	39
		Santēmāranahaḷḷi	42
		Chandakavāḍi	33
		Total	190

2. *Guṇḍlupeṭe*	*Guṇḍlupeṭe*		37
	Bēgūru		38
	Terakaṇāmbi		38
	Hangaḷa		48
		Total	161
3. *Heggaḍadēvana Kōṭe*	*Heggaḍadēvana Kōṭe*		66
	Hampāpura		61
	Saragūru		50
	Kandalike		50
	Antarasante		55
		Total	282
4. *Huṇsūru*	*Huṇsūru*		32
	Biḷikere		69
	Hanagōḍu		72
	Gāvaḍagere		37
		Total	210
5. *Koḷḷegāla*	*Koḷḷegāla*		19
	Pālya		19
	Hanūru		18
	Rāmapura		16
	Lokkanahaḷḷi		15
		Total	87
6. *Krişṇarājanagara*	*Krişṇarājanagara*		29
	Hebbāl		24
	Chunchanakaṭṭe		37
	Sāligrāma		30
	Mirle		23
	Hosa agrahāra		33
		Total	176
7. *Mysūru*	*Mysūru*		29
	Varuṇa		41
	Jayapura		45
	Elawāla		39
		Total	154

8. *Nañjanagūḍu*	*Nanjanagūḍu*		41
	Hullahaḷḷi		61
	Chikkainachatra		25
	Biligere		25
	Kavalande		36
		Total	188
9. *Piriyapaṭṭaṇa*	*Piriyapaṭṭaṇa*		55
	Haranahaḷḷi		60
	Beṭṭadapura		40
	Rāvandūru		46
		Total	201
10. *Tirumakūḍalu-narasipura*	*Tirumakūḍalanarasipura*		28
	Bannūru		26
	Sōsale		40
	Taḷakāḍu		21
	Mūgūru		17
		Total	132
11. *Yaḷandūru*	*Yaḷandūru*		14
	Agara		12
		Total	26

CLASSIFICATION OF VILLAGE NAMES BASED ON SPECIFICS

Classification is the first and foremost requisite in the systematic study of any branch of knowledge. This is especially true of the study of VNS/PNS. The causes of the origin and the evolution of PNS are both simple and complex, variegated and sometimes mysterious. Classification is one of the means by which the complexities could be solved and the mysteries unravelled. The mental attitude and the cultural background of the people that named the particular place could be made out through the application of this method of classification which throws light on the significance which each PN connotes. But the classification of PNS is generally confronted with numerous problems and difficulties which defy easy solution. The primary difficulty that one has to face is the non-intelligibility of the content or the significance of PN beyond doubt. The dictionaries are, of course, a great help in ascertaining the significance of PNS, but they have their own limitations. Dictionaries in general, do not make use of PNS as their source material and even when words similar to or identical with PNS are recorded therein, the meanings given under each word may not be so exhaustive as to help to understand the content of PNS fully and clearly.

A dictionary, however reputed or scholarly, cannot be all comprehensive and exhaustive. It has its own limitations. It cannot record all the words and all the shades of meaning connoted by each word. Moreover, a living language expands itself every minute, gobbles up new words, idioms and forms together with hitherto unknown diversified senses so that it is impossible for any extraordinary scholar - surveyor to have access to them and bring them into the body of the dictionary. By its very nature it is imperfect and becomes outmoded by the time it is published. Though it could be a good guide to the student of place names, he cannot entirely depend upon it in finding out solutions to the problems he is confronted with.

Many a word has more than one meaning or connotation. It becomes very difficult, therefore, to determine the exact meaning of the intended PN. The identification of the original form of the PN itself will be beset with many difficulties.

The above problems may have to be borne in mind while undertaking the classification of VNS. Different scholars have classified VNS variously, based on the criteria they have adopted for themselves. Though their classification is satisfactory from their point of view, the variety and the enormity of VNS of a particular locality entail a different pattern of classification. However, the adaptation of other types of classification, wherever necessary is not ruled out.

I. VNS after individual names
   i. Originators of villages (First settlers)
   ii. Persons known for their social service, valour and philanthropy

II. VNS of religious and puranic importance
   i. Names of gods and goddesses
   ii. Names of saints, sages, priests and religious leaders
   iii. Puranic heroes and events
   iv. Names after philosophical ideas
   v. Names after religious events and institutions
   vi. Names after temples
   vii. Celestial bodies and occurrences

III. VNS of historical significance
   i. Royal dynasties
   ii. King, queens and princes
   iii. Military men and ministers
   iv. Epithet of kings and queens
   v. Subordinate and feudal chiefs and dignitaries
   vi. Official designations
   vii. Historical events such as war, coronation, royal sojourns etc.

IV. VNS of ethnographical bearing
   i. Races
   ii. Tribes
   iii. Castes and professions
   iv. Families and relations
   v. Customs and beliefs

V VNS derived from geographical and physical features
   i. Habitations named after valleys, mountains, mounds, rocky belts etc.
   ii. Villages named after water resources such as rivers, ponds, tanks etc.

VI. Villages denoting flora
   i. Trees, plants, creepers, grasses, shrubs etc.
   ii. Gardens and forests

- iii. Flowers and leaves
- iv. Grains, pulses and other agricultural products

VII. Villages denoting fauna

- i. Animals, both wild and domestic
- ii. Birds
- ii. Reptiles

VIII. Names after Natural phenomena

- i. Directions and days
- ii. Rains, clouds, thunders etc.
- iii. Metals
- iv. Colours
- v. Numbers

IX. VNS of commercial importance

- i. Ports
- ii. Business centres
- iii. Industrial Establishments
- iv. Factories

X. Miscellaneous VNS

- i. Repetitive VNS
- ii. Names which distinguish between the new and old villages of the same name
- iii. Names indicating different sizes of villages of the same name
- iv. Names of villages signifying sentiments, aesthetic senses or superstitions.

While classifying these VNS, the first unit of each name, namely the specific is generally taken into consideration, since the classification based on generics is dealt with elsewhere i.e., under the head 'suffixes'.

Hence it is likely that the same name may occur in two places, viz, both in the chapter dealing with classification and in the chapter dealing with generics or suffixes.

The VNS in the classified lists are arranged talukwise.

1. Village names after individual names

This classification looks very simple at the first sight. But it is beset with serious problems and complications. This complication is due to the fact that one and the same name looks like an ordinary individual name or a historical name or a religious name simultaneously. Nanjanagūḍu, for instance, is a famous religious centre as far as the people of Karnataka are concerned and they know that the town is named after the presiding deity, Nanjuṇḍēswara. For others 'Nanja' may sound as a historical or any other ordinary name. When there are two villages of the same name, one of them may signify a historical name, and the other a religious name.

Even with respect to the ordinary names, it is difficult to say exactly whether the person after whom the place is named is an originator or a social worker, or an adventurer or a philanthropist. These limitations may be kept in mind while going through this classification.

Mysore Taluk

Ayyajjayyanahuṇḍi, Aregowḍanahaḷḷi, Ālanahaḷḷi, Inamuttanahaḷḷi, Kanakanahaḷḷi, Kallūru Naganahaḷḷi Kāvalu, Kāḍanahaḷḷi, Kyātammanahaḷḷi, Kuṇṭanahaḷḷi, Kuḍanahaḷḷi, Kenchalagūḍu, Kōchanahaḷḷi, Gujjagowḍanahaḷḷi, Guḍamādanahaḷḷi, Gumachanahaḷḷi, Chaṭṭanahaḷḷi, (*Chaṭṭa* means a disciple also), *Chāmahaḷḷi, Chikka Kāṭūru, Chikkanahaḷḷi, Chōranahaḷḷi, Chōḷēnahaḷḷi, Chowḍahaḷḷi, Javanahaḷḷi, Jeṭṭihuṇḍi,* (Jetti may even indicate a profession), *Jōganahaḷḷi, Dēvagaḷḷi, Dēvanūru, Doḍḍamāragowḍanahaḷḷi, Nāganahaḷḷi, Nāgavāla, Nāchanahaḷḷi, Nāḍanahaḷḷi, Pillahaḷḷi* (pilla may mean small also), *Puṭṭegowḍanahuṇḍi, Baraḍanapura, Bommēnahaḷḷi, Maraṭi Kyātanahaḷḷi, Mārasettihaḷḷi, Mallahaḷḷi, Maṇḍanahaḷḷi, Mādahaḷḷi, Mādapura, Mādhavagere, Māragowḍanahaḷḷi, Mārabaḷḷi, Yaraganahaḷḷi, Yāchagowḍanahaḷḷi, Rāmaṇahaḷḷi, Lakshmīpura, Vīranagare, Syādanahaḷḷi, Seṭṭināyakanahaḷḷi, Sarkāri Uttanahaḷḷi, Siddalingapura, Sōganahaḷḷi, Hemmanahaḷḷi.*

Krişṇa Rāja Nagar Taluk

Ankanahaḷḷi, Arjunahaḷḷi, Aichanahaḷḷi, Kanaganahaḷḷi, Kaḷḷi Mudnahalli, Krişṇarājanagara, Kākanahaḷḷi, Kāmēnahaḷḷi, Kāḷēnahaḷḷi,

Kūchanahaḷḷi, Kenchanahaḷḷi, Gandanahaḷḷi, Gaḍuganahaḷḷi, Gummanahaḷḷi, Gowḍēnahaḷḷi, Chikkanāyakanahaḷḷi, Chīranahaḷḷi, Chennamgere, Dōrnahaḷḷi, Dammanahaḷḷi, Degganahaḷḷi, Narchanahaḷḷi, Nāṭanahaḷḷi, Nāḍapanahaḷḷi, Nijaganahaḷḷi, Baṭagahaḷḷi, Basavarājapura, Bīchanahaḷḷi, Bīmahaḷḷi, Benaganahaḷḷi, Bommēnahaḷḷi, Madhuvanahaḷḷi, Manuganahaḷḷi, Mallahaḷḷi, Manchanahaḷḷi, Muṇḍiganahaḷḷi, Mādahaḷḷi, Māyigowḍanahaḷḷi, Māragowḍanahaḷḷi, Māḷanāyakanahaḷḷi, Munjanahaḷḷi, Yaremanuganahaḷḷi, Yalemuddanahaḷḷi, Rāmapura, Lakkikuppe, Lāḷanahaḷḷi, Lāḷandēvanahaḷḷi, Venkaṭāpura, Saūkanahaḷḷi, Sādanahaḷḷi, Siddāpura, Sugganahaḷḷi, Sōmanahaḷḷi, Soutanahaḷḷi, Hanumanahaḷḷi, Hangra Bōyanahaḷḷi, Huraḷi Kāmanahaḷḷi, Honnēnahaḷḷi.

Koḷḷegāla Taluk

Uddanūru, Kanḍeyana Pāḷaya, Kōtanūru, Ganganadoḍḍi, Gangādharana Kaṭṭe, Gowḍahaḷḷi, Channalinganahaḷḷi, Jakkanahaḷḷi, Timmarājapura, Dāsanapura, Bhadrayyanahaḷḷi, Bairanatta, Madhuvanahaḷḷi, Managahaḷḷi, Rāmapura, Lakshmīpura, Liṅgaṇapura, Lokkanahaḷḷi, Siddayyanapura, Singanallūru, Seṭṭiaḷḷi.

Guṇḍlupēṭe Taluk

Amīrahosahaḷḷi, Ankahaḷḷi, Agatagowḍanahaḷḷi, Kaṅiyanapura, Kaligowḍanahaḷḷi, Kasavanūru, Garaganahaḷḷi, Chāmanahaḷḷi araṇya, Chikaṇāpura, Chirakanahaḷḷi, Chennamallipura, Dundāsanapura, Nāranāpura, Parvatanapura, Pasaiyanapura, Panjanahaḷḷi, Puttanapura, Basavāpura, Bāchanahaḷḷi, Beṭṭadamādahaḷḷi, Bommanahaḷḷi, Bommalāpura, Bogganapura, Bhīmanahaḷḷi, Maguvanahaḷḷi, Mādapaṭṭaṇa, Māyanāyakanahaḷḷi, Yaḍavanahaḷḷi, Rāghavāpura, Rāmayyanapura, Lakkīpura, Vīranapura, Savakanahaḷḷi, Siddayyanapura, Sinḍanapura, Seṭṭahaḷḷi, Sōmanahaḷḷi, Honakahaḷḷi, Honnegowḍanahaḷḷi, Hongahaḷḷi.

Chāmarājanagara Taluk

Ankanahaḷḷi, Seṭṭipura, Karinanjanapura, Kāḍahaḷḷi, Kāḷanahuṇḍi, Kūtanapura, Kempanapura, Kētanapura, Kētahaḷḷi, Kokkanahaḷḷi, Kottaganahaḷḷi, Ganganūru, Govindavāḍi, Channappanapura, Chāmarājanagara, Channipuradamōḷe, Chowḍahaḷḷi, Jyōtigowḍanapura,

Timmegowḍanapāḷaya, Dēvarājapura, Nanjarājapura, Nanjahaḷḷi, Nanjēdēvanapura, Puṭṭanapura, Puṇajanūru, Baṇḍigowḍanahaḷḷi, Bommanahaḷḷi, Bhujaganapura, Malladēvanahaḷḷi, Malleyyanapura, Mādāpura, Mūkanapālya, Yeraganahaḷḷi, Rēchambaḷḷi, Liṅgaṇapura, Vīraṇapura, Venkaṭayyanachatra, Sappayyanapura, Santemāranahaḷḷi, Siddayyanapura, Singanapura, Sōmanapura, Sōmasamudra, Hāraganapura, Honnagowḍanahaḷḷi, Honnahaḷḷi, Honganūru.

Tirumakudal-Narasipura Taluk

Ankanahaḷḷi, Ādibeṭṭanahaḷḷi, Kannāyakanahaḷḷi, Krișṇarājapura agrahāra, Kāchanahaḷḷi, Kuṇtanahaḷḷi, Kempanapura, Channanjavaḍeyanapura, Chāmanahaḷḷi, Chikkalakshmīpura, Danāyakanapura, Doḍḍalakshmīpura, Nāgalagere, Naragyātanahaḷḷi, Nanjyāpura, Nāgalagere, Bīḍanahaḷḷi, Bommanahaḷḷi, Bommanāyakanahaḷḷi, Mādavāḍi, Mādāpura, Mādēgowḍanahuṇḍi, Māragowḍanahaḷḷi, Māranapura, Mudukanapura, Menasinakyātanahaḷḷi, Yaraganahaḷḷ Yāchanahaḷḷi, Rāmanāthapuradahuṇḍi, Rāmēgowḍanapura, Seṭṭihaḷḷi, Hanumanāḷu, Hunaganahaḷḷi.

Nanjanagūḍu Taluk

Aḍakanahaḷḷi, Īswaragowḍanahaḷḷi, Kaṇṭhirāyanapurada Amrutamahal kāvalu, Kāmanahaḷḷi, Kāḷadēvanahaḷḷi, Kāḷanahaḷḷi, Kāḷahaḷḷi, Chāmanamādanahaḷḷi, Chāmalāpura, Chikkayyanachatra, Chinnambaḷḷi, Chennapaṭna, Chunchēnahaḷḷi, Taraganahaḷḷi, Dāsanūru, Dyāvēgowḍanapura, Dugganahaḷḷi, Dēvērammanahaḷḷi, Dēvarasanahaḷḷi, Dēvarāyana Seṭṭipura, Nāgaṇāpura, Bhōgavālu Vaḍeyanapura, Madhuvanahaḷḷi, Mallahaḷḷi, Mallāpura, Mākanapura, Mādanahaḷḷi, Mādahaḷḷi, Mādāpura, Muddanahaḷḷi, Yēchagaḷḷi, Yēchaguṇḍala, Rājūru, Rāmapura, Rāmaseṭṭipura, Rāyagowḍanahaḷḷi, Vīradēvanapura, Seṭṭahaḷḷi, Hadanūru Oḍeyanapura, Hanumanapura, Hāraganapura.

Piriyāpaṭṭaṇa Taluk

Ankanahaḷḷi, Ālanahaḷḷi, Īchanahaḷḷi, Uttēnjahaḷḷi, Aichanahaḷḷi, Aitanahaḷḷi, Kāmanahaḷḷi, Kāḷetimmanahaḷḷi, Keḷaganahaḷḷi, Kowlanahaḷḷi, Gaḷaganakere, Ganganakuppe, Guḍibadranahosaḷḷi, Guḍḍenahaḷḷi, Channēnahaḷḷi, Chāmarāyakōṭe, Chiṭṭanahaḷḷi,

Chowḍanahaḷḷi, Javanikuppe, Jōganahaḷḷi, Tīmakapura, Tirumalāpura, Nāganahaḷḷi, Piriyāpaṭṭaṇa, Bhūvanahaḷḷi, Bhōganahaḷḷi, Manuganahaḷḷi, Manchadēvanahaḷḷi, Māchadēvanahaḷḷi, Muddēnahaḷḷi, Mūkana Kāvalu, Rājāpura, Lakshmīpura, Liṅgāpura, Sangara Seṭṭihaḷḷi, Seṭṭihaḷḷi, Harave Mallarāja Paṭṇa, Haritapura, Halaganahaḷḷi, Honnēnahaḷḷi.

Yaḷanduru Taluk

Yangaiyana Keremole.

Huṇasūru Taluk

Aṇṇarāyanapura, Ankanahaḷḷi, Adiganahaḷḷi, Uyigoṇḍanahaḷḷi, Kari muddanahaḷḷi, Kallūbuchanahaḷḷi, Kādēmanugaṇahaḷḷi, Kuḍinīrumuddanahaḷḷi, Kempanahaḷḷi, Kāmagowḍanahaḷḷi, Gāngēnahaḷḷi, Gāvaḍagere, Guḍiseṭṭihaḷḷi, Gerasanaḷḷi, Gōvindanahaḷḷi, Gowrikere, Channasōge, Chikkaḍiganahaḷḷi, Chikkabīchanahaḷḷi, Chikkāḍanahaḷḷi, Chikyātanahaḷḷi, Tippalāpura, Dāsanapura, Daitanakere Kāvalu Doḍḍakāḍanahaḷḷi, Doddabichanahaḷḷi, Nāḍappanahaḷḷi, Piṇṇi Kyātanahaḷḷi, Ballēnahaḷḷi, Bastimādanahaḷḷi, Billēnahosahaḷḷi, Bījaganahaḷḷi, Bīratammanahaḷḷi, Bīranahaḷḷi, Bommalāpura, Bōḷanahaḷḷi, Bharatavāḍi Mānaganahaḷḷi, Manuganahaḷḷi, Manchabōyanahaḷḷi, Mādahaḷḷi, Mādaḷḷi, Mādāpura, Māragowḍanahaḷḷi, Māranahaḷḷi, Mūkanahaḷḷi, Mūḍaganūru, Maidanahaḷḷi, Yalachanahaḷḷi, Rangayyanakoppalu, Rāmēnahaḷḷi, Rāyanahaḷḷi, Rangēnakoppalu, Lāḷanakere, Vaḍalimanuganahaḷḷi, Vīranahosahaḷḷi, Śravaṇanahaḷḷi, Saṇṇēnahaḷḷi, Sabbanahaḷḷi, Singamāranahaḷḷi, Sindēnahaḷḷi, Seṭṭihaḷḷi, Sōmanahaḷḷi, Hagaranahaḷḷi, Harinahaḷḷi, Handanahaḷḷi, Narikyātanahaḷḷi, Hulaganahaḷḷi, Husainapura, Honnēnahaḷḷi.

Heggaḍadēvanakote Taluk

Āyyanapura, Ankanahaḷḷi, Ankāpura, Ālanahaḷḷi, Kaṇayanahuṇḍi, Kanakanahaḷḷi, Kannēnahaḷḷi, Kandēgowḍanapura, Krisṇarājapura, Kākanakōṭe Kāvalu, Kyātanahaḷḷi, Kenchapura, Kenchanahaḷḷi, Konegowḍanahuṇḍi, Kollēgowḍanahuṇḍi, Kōḍichāmanahaḷḷi, Guḍuvanahaḷḷi, Gowḍamāchanāyakanahaḷḷi, Channaguḍi, Changadanahaḷḷi, Chāmanahaḷḷi, Chāmalāpura, Chikkabairanakuppe, Chōṭanahaḷḷi, Chowḍahaḷḷi, Jompanahaḷḷi, Thimmanahosahaḷḷi,

Dāsanapura, Doḍḍabairanakuppe, Nanjanāyakanahaḷḷi, Nāgarahaḷḷi, Nāyakanahuṇḍi, Nemmanahaḷḷi, Bāchagowḍanahaḷḷi, Bīchanahaḷḷi, Būdanūru, Būpanahaḷḷi, Beḷaganahaḷḷi, Beḷaganahuṇḍi, Bairanapura, Bommalāpura, Bhīmanahaḷḷi, Manuganahaḷḷi, Marubaguṭṭanapura, Mallarājapura, Mallahaḷḷi, Manchanahaḷḷi, Manchēgowḍanahaḷḷi, Manchanahaḷḷi, Māchanāyakanahaḷḷi, Mārchanahaḷḷi, Mādāpura, Muddanahaḷḷi, Muddayyanahuṇḍi, Rājēgowḍanahuṇḍi, Liṅgaṇahaḷḷi, Śambhugowḍanahaḷḷi, Siddāpura, Singapaṭṭaṇa, Siranahuṇḍi, Haḷemanchanahaḷḷi, Hunaganahaḷḷi, Heggaḍadēvanakōte.

II. Village Names of religious and puranic importance

Some of the VNS which come under this category are misleading. They could either be personal names or names of gods and goddesses. It is very difficult to make a distinction between them unless salutary, definite and incontrovertible evidence is available. Basavanapura which occurs frequently in some of the taluks under study may indicate either the name of a person or the name of the sacred animal or the great religious reformer of the twelfth century. The same difficulty presents itself in respect of *Hanumanālu* of TNP taluk, Hanumanapura of Nanjangud taluk and *Hanumanahaḷḷi,* of KRN taluk. This explanation holds good in respect of both religious and puranic names.

Most of the names of gods and goddesses are either Śaivite or Vaishṇavite, suggesting that these two sets had a dominating influence in this part of the State. Names of local minor gods and goddesses, in other words folk deities occur rarely in VNS. Perhaps, this is because these deities were not held in respect by those responsible for naming the villages. Names influenced by Jaina or *Vīraśaiva* religion are very few in number, meaning thereby that these two religions did not make deep dent into the religious life of the people of this area.

i(a) The following VNS have Śaivite elements, though it is not unlikely that some of them might have been influenced by *Vīraśaiva* religion.

Ankanāthāpura (Heg), *Iḍiganāthapura araṇya* (Koḷ), *Irēdēvanahaḷḷi* (TNP), *Kandāgāla (Guṇ), Kandagālā* (Heg), *Kandēgāla* (PP), *Kallināthapura* (Mys), *Kumārabiḍu* (Mys), *Kailāsapura* (PP),

Komāranahaḷḷi (Yel), *Gangādharanakaṭṭe* (Koḷ), *Goravanapura* (TNP), *Chāmuṇḍibeṭṭa* (Mys), *Chikkanandi* (Heg), *Joḍibasavanapura* (TNP), *Tāṇḍavapura* (Nan), *Triyambakapura* (Heg), *Gangādharabasavanahaḷḷi* (PP), *Nanjanagūḍu* (Nan), *Nanjēdēvanapura* (PP), *Nandiguṇḍa* (PP), *Nandināthapura* (Heg), *Nandināthapura* (KRN), *Nandipura* (PP), *Pasupati* (KRN), *Basavanaaraṇya* (PP), *Basavana ēṇi* (PP), *Basavana Kōṭe* (Heg), *Basavapura* (Heg), *Basavanapura* (Guṇ), *Basavanapura* (CRN), *Basavanahaḷḷi* (Nan), *Basavanahaḷḷi* (PP), *Basavanahaḷḷi* (TNP), *Basavanahaḷḷi* (Mys), *Basaveṭṭi* (CRN), *Basavaṭṭige* (Guṇ), *Basavāpaṭṇa* (KRN), *Basavāpura* (PP), *Binakanahaḷḷi* (Guṇ), *Benakanahaḷḷi* (TNP), *Benaganahaḷḷi* (PP), *Byrāpura* (Guṇ), *Byrāpura* (Heg), *Malladevanahaḷḷi* (CRN), *Mahadēswaramale* (Koḷ), *Liṅgaṇapura* (PP), *Liṅgahaḷḷi* (Heg), *Liṅgāpura* (Nan), *Liṅgāmbudhi* (Mys), *Vīradēvanapura* (Guṇ), *Śambhupura* (CRN), *Śivapura* (PP), *Śivapura* (Guṇ), *Sambarabaḷḷi* (KRN), *Siddalingapura* (Mys), *Subrahmaṇyapura* (Mys), *Sōmanātapura* (TNP), *Sōmēswarapura* (Heg), *Hirenandi* (Heg).

i(b) VNS after *Vaiṣṇava* gods

Kaṇṇūru (Koḷ), *Kriṣṇāpura* (Yel), *Kriṣṇāpura* (Huṇ), *Kriṣṇāpura* (Huṇ), *Kriṣṇāpurada kāvalu* (KRN), *Kriṣṇāpurada kāvalu* (Heg), *Kriṣṇarājapura* (Heg), *Gōpālapura* (Heg), *Gōpinātha araṇya* (Koḷ), *Gōvindanahaḷḷi* (Huṇ), *Gōvindavādi* (CRN), *Nāranapura* (Guṇ), *Narasipur* (Koḷ), *Nārāyanapura* (KRN), *Biḷigirirangaswāmi beṭṭa* (Yel), *Mādhavagere* (Mys), *Muttārāyana hosahaḷḷi* (Huṇ), *Rangaṇapura* (Huṇ), *Ranganāthapura* (TNP), *Rangasamudra* (TNP), *Rāmapaṭṇa* (Huṇ), *Rāmanāthahuṇḍi* (Yel), *Rāmanāthapuradahuṇḍi* (TNP), *Rāmapura* (Koḷ), *Rāmapura* (Huṇ), *Rāmapura* (TNP), *Rāmapuri* (Mys), *Rāmpura* (CRN), *Rāmasamudra* (Huṇ), *Lakṣhmipura* (Koḷ), *Venkaṭapura* (KRN), *Srīrangapura* (Huṇ), *Srīrāmadēvanahanta* (KRN), *Srīrāmanahaḷḷi* (Heg), *Srīrāmapura* (Huṇ), *Srīrāmapura* (Mys), *Srīrāmapura* (KRN), *Hanumanapura* (CRN), *Hanumanapura* (Nan), *Hanumanthapuradanāla* (Huṇ), *Hanumana haḷḷi* (KRN), *Hanumanāḷu* (TNP).

It is very likely that some of the names like the ones listed above may have had their origin after the temples have been located in those places. *Nanjanagūḍu* and *Biligirirangaswāmi beṭṭa* may be cited as examples. *Nanjuṇḍēśwara* and *Rangaswāmi* are the presiding deities of the respective places which are named after them. Whether a certain place has acquired its name after a particular temple or God has to be ascertained from various available sources or after visiting the place concerned. There is a general belief that whenever a place gets its name after a temple, the temple should have existed earlier than the place. Two possibilities may be posited in this situation. Firstly, the people who inhabited that place must have brought with them their family or clan god, must have enshrined and been worshipping the same before they could erect a moderate or a lofty building. They may have built up the village in the name of the God they adored. This is one possibility, but a remote one. The two VNS that occur to my mind immediately in this connection are Mangalore and Mumbai. It is said that these two places take their names after *Mangaḷādēvi* and *Mumbādēvi* respectively. Who are these goddesses? *Mangaḷā* may be identified with *Pārvati*. What about the other goddess? It may be argued that all such names ultimately refer to only one goddess, i.e., the mother of the universe and they are various appellations of one and the same supreme mother. The real fact seems to be that they may have been folk goddesses at the time of the establishment of the village. We find such goddesses in almost all the villages. There is no village without a *grāmadēvata*. This *grāmadēvata* is called by various names, such as *Māramma, Chowḍamma, Bisalamma, Paṭaladamma, Daṇḍina Māramma* etc. The two goddesses mentioned above may have been likewise the village deities. These deities must have at a later date, acquired the village names as their appellatives. This tendency of naming the village gods and goddesses may be borne in mind while dealing with such names.

i(c). Though *Vīraśaivism* is an offshoot of Śaivism, it differs from the latter from the point of view of religious and philosophical aspects. In this district one will come across a few VNS which are distinctly *Vīrasaivite*. *Āyarahaḷḷi* (Mys), *Ayyanapura* (Heg), *Ayyarabīḍu* (PP), *Ayyarahaḷḷi* (Huṇ), *Ayyarahaḷḷi* (Guṇ), *Iyyanahaḷḷi* (CRN), *Oḍeyanapura* (Guṇ), *Channayāvaḍērapura* (TNP), *Tammaḍahaḷḷi* (PP), *Tammaḍahaḷḷi* (CRN), *Tammaḍipura* (TNP), *Tammaḍihaḷḷi* (Huṇ), *Bhōgavāḷu Vaḍeyarapura* (Nan), *Vaḍērahaḷḷi* (Heg), *Vaḍērahosahaḷḷi* (Huṇ), *Vaḍērahosahaḷḷi* (Huṇ), *Vaḍērahosahaḷḷi jungle* (PP), *Sappayyanapura* (CRN), *Sīlavantapura* (Guṇ), etc.

i(d). There are very few names which are named after Jaina tradition.

Jinahaḷḷi (Huṇ), *Jinnahaḷḷi* (Heg), *Bastipura* (CRN), *Bastipura* (Koḷ), *Mallināthapura* (Huṇ), *Vastiliṅgaṇapura* (Guṇ), *Śravaṇanahaḷḷi* (Huṇ).

Here the VN, *Vastiliṅgaṇapura* is rather a peculiar one. Vasti indicates that it must have been a Jaina settlement. Later on, a Saivite name may have been inserted. It is also likely that Linga may be a prominent person of the village.

III. Village names after puranic heroes, saints and events

i. *Agastyapura* (TNP), *Arjunahaḷḷi* (KRN), *Ilvāla* (Mys), *Kāmagere* (Koḷ), *Kāmanaḷḷi* (PP), *Kāmanahaḷḷi* (Nan), *Daityanakere Kāvalu* (Huṇ), *Parasurāmapura* (Nan), *Bharatawāḍi* (Huṇ), *Yamagumbha* (Huṇ), *Rāvandūru* (PP), *Lakshmaṇapura* (Nan).

Some of these names like Kāma, Bharata, Arjuna may be human individuals.

ii. VNS after religious ideas.

There is only one name in this district: Dharmapura (CRN)

iii. VNS after celestial bodies and occurrences

Sūrahaḷḷi (Nan).

iv. Certain VNS indicate gods in general. They are common to all religious sects

Dēmahaḷḷi (CRN), *Dēpura* (PP), *Dēvagaḷḷi* (Mys), *Dēvagahaḷḷi* (Huṇ), *Dēvanūr* (Mys), *Dēvanūru* (Nan), *Dēvarahaḷḷi* (Huṇ), *Dēvarahaḷḷi* (Guṇ), *Dēvarahaḷḷi* (Yel).

v. There is only one VN which is the combination of both Vaishṇava and Saiva deities.

Jōḍihariharapura (Nan).

IV. VNS of historical importance

The naming of places after kings, queens, ministers and other historical personages is a common feature in Karnataka, as well as the entire Indian subcontinent. The birth of a prince or any important event in the life of a king such as victory in a war, his birth anniversary or his visit to a certain place or his ascension to his throne are generally celebrated by naming the particular place after the name. *Jayachāmarājapura* (the former *Seṭṭihaḷḷi*) in *Chikkanāyakanahaḷḷi* taluk is one such case. Thus the study of VNS is likely to throw a flood of light on history and allied subjects.

i. VNS after royal dynasties

Gangavāḍi (CRN).

ii. VNS derived from kings, queens, princes, ministers and military chiefs.

Uttamachōḷapura (Koḷ), *Kriṣṇarājanagara* (DRN), *Kriṣṇarājapura* (Heg), *Kriṣṇarājapura agrahāra* (TNP), *Chāmarājanagara* (CRN), *Chāmarājakoṭe* (PP), *Chāmalāpura* (KRN), *Chāmalapura* (Nan), *Tippalāpura* (Huṇ), *Tirumalāpura* (PP), *Dēvarājapura* (CRN), *Dēvalāpura* (CRN), *Dēvalāpura* (Heg), *Dēvalāpura* (Guṇ), *Dyāvalāpura* (Mys), *Nanjarājapura* (CRN), *Narasamangala* (CRN), *Narasāmbudhi* (Nan), *Nāgalagere* (TNP), *Bommalāpura* (Huṇ), *Bommalāpura* (Guṇ), *Mallarājapura* (Heg), *Rāghavāpura* (Guṇ), *Rājapura* (PP), *Rājanabiḷugali* (PP), *Śāmalāpura* (Heg), *Hariyālapura* (Heg), *Harilāpura* (PP), *Madhavamantrikaṭṭe* (TNP).

iii. VNS after subordinate and feudal chiefs and also famous dignitaries.

Of the names given below it is difficult to distinguish between feudal chiefs and dignitaries. Some of them may have also been the names of kings and ministers. Therefore, it has not been possible to establish very clearly the distinction among these classes of people, until adequate historical or epigraphical evidences are available.

Aṇṇarāyapura (Huṇ), *Alapanāyakanahaḷḷi* (PP), *Kaṇṭhīrayanapura* (Nan), *Kāḍamāchnāyakanahaḷḷi* (Heg), *Kannāyakanahaḷḷi* (TNP), *Kāladevanahaḷḷi* (Nan), *Chikkanāyakanahaḷḷi* (KRN), *Ḍaṇāyakanahaḷḷi* (TNP), *Nanjanāyakanahaḷḷ* (Heg), *Nandirājapura* (CRN), *Nāyakanahuṇḍi* (Heg), *Basavarājapura* (KRN), *Bommanāyakanahaḷḷi* (TNP), *Manchadēvanahaḷḷ* (PP), *Māchadēvanahaḷḷ* (PP), *Māchanāyakanahaḷḷi* (Heg), *Māyanāyakanahaḷḷi* (Guṇ), *Mārchahaḷḷi*

(Heg), *Māḷanāyakanahaḷḷi* (KRN), *Laḷandēvanahaḷḷi* (KRN), *Haravemallarājapaṭṭaṇa* (PP), *Heggaḍadevanakōṭe* (Heg).

There are certain VNS whose identity cannot be established beyond doubt. These names may be attributed to common men or chieftains or even to kings. *Rāyanahaḷḷi* (Huṇ), *Būpanahaḷḷi* (Heg), *Seṭṭanāyakanahaḷḷi* (Mys) and *Timmarājapura* (Koḷ) are such names. It is possible that *Chōḷanahaḷḷi* (Mys) and *Uttamachōḷapura* (Koḷ) may have been named after Chola kings or chieftains. Arasinakere (Mys) may have been founded by one of the members of the Mysore royal family. *Vijayaśrīpura* (Mys) very possibly concerns itself with a historical event, such as success in war or some auspicious occurrence in the Mysore royal family. It is said that *Karkala mādahaḷḷi* (Guṇ) is the variant form of *Karikālamādahaḷḷi.* If this conjecture is correct, it can be said that this name is connected with the Chola king *Karikāla,* who might have conquered this part of the district and ruled over it for a shortwhile. The identification of *Śakadēvanapura* (Mys) is possible only when historical and other additional evidences are available.

iv. VNS having ethnological/sociological bearing

A fairly good number of places derive their names from castes. Names derived from races, tribes, families and customs are absent in this region. It may be noted that there is a tendency on the part of the people belonging to different castes to live separately. Thus denoting that the society is an exclusive one. The castewar classification of names is given below:

a) Okkaligas

Okkaḷigere (TNP)

b) Kumbārās

Kumbāraguṇḍi (CNR), *Kumbārahaḷḷi* (Mys), *Kumbārahaḷḷi* (Nan).

c) Kurubas

Kurubaḷḷi (KRN), *Kurubarahaḷḷi* (Mys), Kurubarahosahaḷḷi (Huṇ), Kurubūru (TNP).

d) Kongas

Kongahaḷḷi (Nan), *Kongahaḷḷi Kāvalu* (Nan), *Kongahaḷḷi Rāja Amritamahal Kāvalu* (), *Kongarahaḷḷi* (Koḷ).

e) Gollas

Gollanahaḷḷi (Heg), *Gollarahosahaḷḷi* (PP), *Gollūru* (Heg), *Gollēnabīḍu* (Heg).

f) Bēḍas

Bēḍarapura (CRN), *Bēḍamudulu* (CRN), *Bēḍarahaḷḷi* (TNP), *Byāḍrabiḷuguḷi* (PP), *Byāḍarahaḷḷihanta* (KRN), *Byādrahaḷḷi* (KRN).

g) Brahmans

Hārupura (TNP), *Hārupura* (Nan), Haruvanapura (Koḷ), *Hārōpura* (Heg), *Hārōhaḷḷi* (Huṇ), *Hārōhaḷḷi* (Mys).

h) Māḍigas

Māḍaragaḷḷi (Mys), *Māḍigahaḷḷi* (TNP), *Māḍarahaḷḷi* (TNP), *Māḍarahaḷḷi* (Guṇ).

i) Vaḍḍas

Oḍḍarapāḷya (Heg), *Oḍḍarahosahaḷḷikāḍu* (PP), *Kāḍavaḍḍaraguḍi* (Huṇ), *Gejjayanavaḍḍaraguḍi* (Huṇ), *Chikkavaḍḍaraguḍi* (PP), *Chikkavaḍḍaraguḍi* (KRN), *Doḍḍavaḍḍaraguḍi* (PP), *Doḍḍavaḍḍaraguḍi* (KRN), *Vaḍḍagere* (Guṇ), *Vaḍḍabāḷu* (Huṇ), *Vaḍḍanahosahaḷḷi* (Guṇ), *Vaḍḍaraguḍi* (Heg), *Vaḍḍarahaḷḷi* (Huṇ), *Vaḍḍarahaḷḷi* (Guṇ), *Vaḍḍarahaḷḷi* (CRN), *Vaḍḍarahosahaḷḷi* (PP).

The above list indicates that the number of villages deriving their names from the community of *Vaḍḍas* is newer than any of the other villages founded on the basis of castes. *Bēḍas* and *Gollas,* though the names of villages after them are very small, come next only to *Vaḍḍas.* The number of villages acquiring their names after Kurubas, Brahmans, *Kumbārs* and *Maḍigas* are four, five, three and three respectively. *Suttūr* (Nan) which according to some scholars, seems to have been derived from the original name *Srōtriyūr* may also be taken to be a Brahman name. *Agrahāra* (Huṇ) and Agara (Yel) also are undoubtedly Brahman villages which were endowed to them by kings in view of their services. There are three villages which give a sense of *Marāṭha* inhabitation: *Ārēnahaḷḷi* (PP), *Ārēpāḷya* (Koḷ) and *Ārēpura* (Guṇ). *Āreyas* are supposed to be *Marāṭhas.* The word itself seems to be derived from the word *Ārya.* *Vājamangala* (Mys) and

Gāṇiganūru (Yel) are the two villages whose names can be connected with goldsmiths and oil mongers respectively. The only two villages connected with the fishermen community are *Paḍuvārahaḷḷi* (Mys) and *Toreyanakāṭūru* (Mys). 'ri' in *Parivāra* (another name for Bestas) has changed into 'ḍu' in *Paḍuvārahaḷḷi.* Nagarthas are a sect of merchant community which is responsible for the name of *Nagarthahaḷḷi* (Mys). There is only one village named after washermen i.e. *Agasanahuṇḍi* (Heg). *Goravanahaḷḷi* (TNP) is of doubtful origin. The derivation of the word itself is not very clear. It is possible to derive it from the word 'Guru'. A sect of Kurubas who are a group of wandering religious mendicants are called goravas. It is very likely that this village may have acquired its name from this community. *Heḷavana Maṭha* (TNP) is named after *Heḷavas,* who are a community of wandering ministrels. *Kukkarahaḷḷi* (Mys) and *Kuttaraṭṭi* (Nan) may have been the abode of people belonging to the communities bearing identical names. There are only two villages viz. Okkalagere (TNP) and *Gāvaḍagere* (Huṇ) named after Vokkaligas, though they constitute a big chunk of the population in this region. *Gangavāḍi* (CRN) and *Kongarahaḷḷi* (Koḷ) are the only two villages which represent ancient royal dynasties, viz. Gangas and *Kongāḷvas.* The word Konga has, of late, degenerated into a caste.

This is in short, the sociological scenario found in the Mysore district. It is really interesting. There is only one village, perhaps founded by people speaking a language other than Kannada, i.e., Telugu. The Village, *Telugaramasahaḷḷi* (Heg) is situated in a remote corner of Karnataka, far away from Andhra Pradesh. The Telugu speaking people who migrated to this region must have founded a hamlet of their own in the beginning into which other people must have found their way in course of time. The study of these places reveals the facts that Vaḍḍas, Bedas and Gollas would not mix with other castes but build their own villages. But it is found later on these villages being gradually occupied or dominated by people other than Vaḍḍas, Bēḍas or Gollas. In some of these villages, the people representing these castes are not seen at all. This fact clearly indicates that Vaḍḍas, Bēḍas and Gollas retain the characterstics of wandering nomads. It is also likely that they may have been ousted by the upper class people. The same argument cannot be advanced with regard to the remaining villages named after various castes. These castes are service oriented guilds and the people belonging to these castes will have to live with other people who require their services. Hence Agasas, Kumbaras, Gaṇigas etc., are not likely to live exclusively for themselves. In spite of the fact that the original inhabitants of a village may have been Agasas or Kumbaras, it must have been inhabited by other castes in course of time. Take for example, *Paḍuvārahaḷḷi* and *Kumbārakoppalu* which are now situated in the middle of the Mysore City. *Parivārs* must have been the original inhabitants *Paḍuvārahaḷḷi.* Today, they form a minority group in the village. The same explanation is true of *Kumbārakoppalu* also. It can be concluded, therefore, that exclusive villages for serving caste people such as named above are very rare. For reasons other than those alluded to above, the Brahmans also do not live exclusively in a village where other caste people are absent. Even in Agraharas which are supposed to have been possessed solely by Brahmans, other caste people are allowed to live. It is the duty of the other caste people to serve the Brahmans who treat them as their serfs.

The ethnological study of VNS of this region helps one to arrive at the following conclusions.

1. People belonging to nomadic groups do not generally live in a place permanently.

2. The people belonging to serving castes do not ordinarily live in a village exclusively for themselves.

3. Even if a certain village has been established by a certain caste people, other dominant communities of the area gradually have infiltrated into it.

4. When people belonging to an upper class or a majority caste infiltrate in large numbers into a village founded by lower class people, it is possible that the original people might migrate to other places.

5. One will not come across a village named after a dominant community such as Vokkaligas or Lingayaths, (with the exception of a few) since they live in almost all the villages.

6. Villages named after Scheduled Caste people also are very rare, though they are found in almost every village. They live separately in the outskirts of the village.
7. There is no case of linguistic minorities establishing a village exclusively for themselves except a few, very rare ones.

V. VNS derived from geographical and physical features

i. Habitations named after valleys, mountains, mounds and rocky belts.

Arepura (Guṇ), *Uppinamōḷe* (Yel), *Eḍuru* (CRN), *Eryūru* (Guṇ), *Kaggunḍi* (PP), *Kalkere* (PP), *Kalkuṇike* (Huṇ), *Kalkunda* (Nan), *Kalkōḍu* (Heg), *Kallahaḷḷi* (Guṇ), *Kallahaḷḷi (Mys), Kallahaḷḷi* (Nan), *Kallahaḷḷi* (Huṇ), *Kallahaḷḷi* (KRN), *Kallaḷḷi Kāvalu* (Huṇ), *Kallapura* (Nan), *Kalluru nāganahaḷḷi* (Mys), *Karlapura* (Nan), *Kuṇigallu* (Heg), *Kuppalūr* (Mys), *Kundagere* (Guṇ), *Kunduru* (Heg), *Kuppahaḷḷi* (KRN), *Kuppe* (KRN), *Kuppekūḷaghaṭṭa* (Huṇ), *Kuppegāla* (Mys), *Kuppehanta* (KRN), *Kupya* (TNP), *Kūrgallu* (PP), *Kebbepura* (CRN), *Kemmaṇṇapura* (Mys), *Koppa* (PP), *Koppalu* (TNP), *Gaṭṭavāḍi* (Nan), *Gaṭṭavāḍipura* (Nan), *Gaḍiguḍḍada Kāvalu* (TNP), *Gariguḍḍadakāvalu* (PP), *Guḍḍadamaṭha* (CRN), *Channakalla Kāvalu* (PP), *Chikkare* (PP), *Chikkakundūru* (Heg), *Taggalūru* (Guṇ), *Tarikallu* (Huṇ), *Tarikallu* (PP), *Tarikallu* (Yal), *Tippūru* (Huṇ), *Tippūru* (KRN), *Diṇḍahaḷḷi* (KRN), *Dinnahaḷḷi* (Koḷ), *Banḍaḷḷi* (Koḷ), *Būdititṭu* (CRN), *Būdambaḷḷi* (CRN), *Būdipaḍaga* (CRN), *Būdihaḷḷi* (TNP), *Beṭṭada Kāvalu* (PP), *Beṭṭadapura* (CRN), *Beṭṭadabīḍu* (Heg), *Beṭṭada Tunga* (PP), *Beṭṭadahaḷḷi* (Heg), *Beṭṭadahaḷḷi* (CRN), *Beṭṭahaḷḷi* (KRN), *Beṭṭahaḷḷi* (TNP), *Beṭṭahaḷḷi* (Guṇ), *Beṭṭahaḷḷi Kāvalu* (KRN), *Beṭṭahunḍi* (Heg), *Beddadapura* (Heg), *Benagallu* (PP), *Beḷagunda* (PP), *Bylakuppe* (PP), *Bylaguppe* (Guṇ), *Maṇalūru* (Nan), *Maraḍipura* (TNP), *Maraḍiyur* (PP), *Maraḍūru* (PP), *Maraḷūru* (Nan), *Maleyūru* (CRN), *Maleyūru* (Heg), *Maleyūru Kāvalu* (Heg), *Maḷalagadde* (Heg), *Maḷalavāḍi* (Mys), *Māḷūru* (CRN), *Maḷḷūru* (Koḷ), *Mēṭikuppe* (Heg), *Mēlukōṭe* (Heg), *Mēlūru* (CRN), *Mēlūru* (KRN), *Mēlmāḷa* (CRN), *Yaḍapura* (CRN), *Yaḍahaḷḷi* (TNP), *Yaḍahaḷḷi* (Mys), *Yaḍahaḷḷi* (Heg), *Yariyūru* (Guṇ), *Yariyūru* (Yal), *Yaḍiyūr* (CRN), *Rāsimaraṭi Kāvalu* (PP), *Lalitādripura* (Mys), *Vaḍḍagalpura* (CRN), *Haḷḷadakallahaḷḷi* (Huṇ), *Haḷḷada Koppalu* (Huṇ), *Haḷḷadapura* (Nan), *Husukūru* (Nan).

It may be noted here that the villages coming under this category are found in large numbers in the hilly tracts of this region.

ii. VNS after water resources such as rivers, ponds, tanks, confluences etc.

Kaṭṭepura (Heg), *Kaṭṭepura* (CRN), *Kaṭṭemanuganahaḷḷi* (Huṇ), *Kaṭṭemaḷalavāḍi* (Huṇ), *Kaṭṭe Huṇasūru* (Heg), *Kaṭṭehuṇḍi* (Heg), *Kāvēripura* (TNP), *Kūḍalūru* (TNP), *Kūḍlāpura* (Nan), *Kūḍlūru* (CRN), *Kūḍlūru* (Huṇ), *Keriyūru* (Yal), *Keriyūru* (Huṇ), *Kerehaḷḷi* (CRN), *Kesarekere* (PP), *Koṇada haḷḷi* (TNP), *Koḷagere* (TNP), *Kōḍiugane* (CRN), *Kōḍimūle* (CRN), *Kōḍihaḷḷi* (PP), *Kōḍihaḷḷi* (Guṇ), *Guṇḍlupēṭe* (Guṇ), *Chikkakereyūru* (Heg), *Tirumakūḍalu Narasipura* (TNP), *Toravaḷḷi* (Guṇ), *Toravaḷḷi* (Heg), *Dadadahaḷḷi* (KRN), *Daḍadahaḷḷi* (Mys), *Daitanakere Kāvalu* (Huṇ), *Doḍḍakere Kāvalu* (Heg), *Doḍḍakereyūru* (Mys), *Dōrasamudra* (Heg), *Bakrehaḷḷada kāvalu* (KRN), *Biḷikere* (Huṇ), *Biḷikere Kāvalu* (Huṇ), *Biligere* (Nan), *Maḍuvinabīḍu* (CRN), *Mūlehoḷe araṇya* (Guṇ), *Yeḍatore* (KRN), *Yaḍatore* (Heg), *Yaḍatore* (TNP), *Vaḷagere* (Nan), *Vaḷagerehaḷḷi* (KRN), *Sagarakaṭṭe* (Mys), *Sindhuvaḷḷi* (Mys), *Sūḷekere Kāvalu* (Huṇ), *Hālakere* (PP), *Hoḷesālu* (TNP), *Hoḷehuṇḍi* (Heg).

VI. Places denoting flora

i. Trees, plants, creepers, grasses, thorns and shrubs contribute in a large measure in the naming of villages.

Attaḷḷi (TNP), *Attiguppe* (Huṇ), *Attigōḍu* (PP), *Araḷikaṭṭe* (CRN), *Araḷikumari* (PP), *Araḷipura* (CRN), *Alagōḍu* (TNP), *Avarekāyiguḍḍada Kāvalu* (PP), *Aḷalakuppe* (KRN), *Aḷalūru* (PP), *Alakere* (Yal), *Ālattūru* (Nan), *Āladūru* (CRN), *Ālambūru* (Nan), *Ālahaḷḷi* (Koḷ), *Ālūru* (CRN), *Ibbajāla* (Nan), *Immāvu* (Nan), *Īchūru* (PP), *Uganiya* (Koḷ), *Uganedahuṇḍi* (CRN), *Uganeya* (Nan), *Uddibāgūru* (TNP), *Uddūru* (Huṇ), *Ummattūru* (Huṇ), *Ummattūru* (CRN), *Elachigere* (Nan), *Kaggala* (KRN), *Kaggalipura* (CRN), *Kaggalibōre Kāvalu* (KRN), *Kaggalūru* (Nan), *Kaṭṭehunasuru* (Heg), *Kallipura* (Guṇ), *Kallipura* (CRN), *Kārepura* (Nan), *Kārya* (Nan), *Kirenelli* (PP), *Kirijāji* (Huṇ), *Koḍasige* (Guṇ), *Gajjiganahaḷḷi* (Nan), *Garikekaṭṭe Kāvalu* (Heg), *Guḷuvinattiguppe* (KRN), *Gobbaḷi Kāvalu* (PP), *Gōḷūru* (Nan), *Gōlūru* (Heg), *Jālahaḷḷi* (Nan), *Tammanēraḷe* (Nan), *Toṇḍālu* (Huṇ), *Diṇḍagāḍu*

(PP), *Nāgavalli* (CRN), *Nāgahaḷḷi* (Mys), *Nellitāḷupura* (Guṇ), *Nērḷe* (Heg), *Bejjaḷalearaṇya* (Koḷ), *Badanakuppe* (Heg), *Nērale (Mirli)* (Nan), *Nēralakuppe* (Huṇ), *Nēralekuppe* (PP), *Badanaguppe* (CRN), *Badanavālu* (Nan), *Badanahaḷḷi* (Nan), *Bannahaḷḷi* (TNP), *Bannikuppe* (KRN), *Bannikuppe* (Huṇ), *Bannitālapura* (Guṇ), *Bannisārige* (Yal), *Bannūru* (Nan), *Bannūru* (TNP), *Baḷḷahaḷḷi* (PP), *Baḷḷipura* (CRN), *Basalāpura* (PP), *Bāgūru* (Guṇ), *Bāgūru* (TNP), *Bāgūru* (Nan), *Bidaragūḍu* (Nan), *Bidarahaḷḷi* (Heg), *Beṭṭatāvarehuṇḍi* (Heg), *Beṇḍagaḷḷi* (Nan), *Bemmatti* (PP), *Belavatta* (Mys), *Bēgūru* (PP), *Bēgūru* (CRN), *Bēgūru* (Heg), *Bēvinatāḷapura* (CRN), *Bēvinahaḷḷi* (TNP), *Bēvinahaḷḷi* (KRN), *Byāḷūru* (Koḷ), *Byālūru* (Nan), *Mākōḍu* (PP), *Māgaḷḷi* (PP), *Mādalavāḍi* (CRN), *Māmbaḷḷi* (Yal), *Māvanūru* (KRN), *Māvinahaḷḷi* (Mys), *Māvinahaḷḷi* (TNP), *Mutagūru* (PP), *Muḷḷūru* (Nan), *Muḷḷūru* (Huṇ), *Muḷḷūru* (Heg), *Muḷḷūru* (Koḷ),

Yalachagere (CRN), *Yalachaṭṭi* (Guṇ), *Yalachahaḷḷi* (Mys), *Yalchaḷḷi* (Nan), *Yalemattūru* (Heg), *Yalehuṇḍi* (Heg), *Lakkasōge* (Heg), *Lakkikuppe* (KRN), *Lakkipura* (Guṇ), *Lakkūru* (Guṇ), *Lakkūru* (Heg), *Lakkūru* (Huṇ), *Lakkere* (Guṇ), *Vadaneguppe* (Nan), *Saṇabinakuppe* (PP), *Saṇabinaguppe* (KRN), *Sampigepura* (Guṇ), *Sīgavāḍi* (Heg), *Sīgavāḷu* (KRN), *Sīgūru* (PP), *Sīgetore Kāvalu* (PP), *Sigōḍi* (Guṇ), *Sujjalūru* (TNP), *Hanagōḍu* (Huṇ), *Hanasōge* (Huṇ), *Hangrepura* (CRN), *Hanchipura* (Heg), *Hanchipura* (Guṇ), *Hanchitāḷapura* (CRN), *Hattavāḷu* (Nan), *Haraḷahaḷḷi* (Huṇ), *Haraḷahaḷḷi* (PP), *Haralahaḷḷi* (PP), *Haraḷu Kōṭe* (CRN), *Haraḷe* (Heg), *Halasūru* (Heg), *Halasūru* (PP), *Hāgalahaḷḷi* (CRN), *Huṇasanāḷu (Huṇiseneḷalu)* (Nan), *Huṇasavāḍi* (PP), *Hāgalahaḷḷi* (TNP), *Huṇasinapura* (Guṇ), *Huṇasūru* (Huṇ), *Huṇasūru* (Heg), *Huṇasūru* (TNP), *Huṇasekuppe* (PP), *Huṇisekuppe* (Heg), *Huṇasekoppalu* (PP), *Huṇasēla* (Heg), *Hullahaḷḷi* (Nan).

ii. VNS denoting gardens and forests.

Kāḍahaḷḷi (CRN), *Kānūru* (PP), *Tōpinapeṭlu* (KRN), *Banahaḷḷi* (CRN).

iii. VNS derived from flowers and leaves:

Elemāḷa (Koḷ), *Kirijāji* (Huṇ), *Yelehaḷḷi* (Nan), *Yelehuṇḍi* (Heg), *Sampigepura* (Guṇ), *Hūkunda* (Guṇ), *Hūvinakoḷa* (Heg).

iv. VNS originated on the basis of grains, pulses and other agricultural products.

Akihaḷibēgūrugrāma (Guṇ), *Sakkare* (KRN), *Huraḷipura* (Heg).

Before passing on to the other items of classification, it is worthwhile to note here that, barring a very few, the plants on the basis of which the villages acquire their names are all those grown in non-forest areas. It may be mentioned that such of the trees which grow abundantly in a certain place may have been responsible for being chosen as the names of villages. It is also a fact that those places are well known for the produce of such trees or the trees grown there are of good breed.

VII. VNS influenced by fauna

i. PNS signifying animals.

Ānegaṭṭi (Heg), *Ānechākūru* (PP), *Ānemāḷa* (Heg), *Ānevāḷu* (PP), *Karaḍihaḷḷi* (CRN), *Karahaṭṭi* (Nan), *Kurihuṇḍi* (Nan), *Kōṇanapura* (Nan), *Kōṇanahosahaḷḷi* (Huṇ), *Kōṇanūru* (Nan), *Koṇasūru* (PP), *Gūḷipura* (CRN), *Gōhaḷḷi* (Huṇ), *Gohaḷḷi* (Mys), *Chikkakāṭi* (Guṇ), *Chikkanandi* (Heg), *Tagarapura* (Koḷ), *Turuganūru* (TNP), *Tōravaḷḷi (Turuvaḷḷi)* (Nan), *Danagere* (Koḷ), *Baḷḷūru* (KRN), *Mysūru* (Mys), *Suṇḍavāḷu* (PP), *Handiguḍḍada Kāvalu* (PP), *Hasuvina Kāvalu* (PP), *Hirik-āti* (Guṇ), *Hirenandi* (Heg), *Hulikura* (Heg), *Hulikura Kāvalu* (Heg), *Huligaṇamaraḍi* (Guṇ), *Hullāṇa* (Guṇ), *Hullēṇahaḷḷi* (Huṇ), *Hullēpura* (Koḷ), *Hullēpura* (Guṇ), *Hullēpura* (CRN), *Hullebōre Kāvalu* (KRN), *Hullēmāḷa* (Heg), *Hullēmāḷa* (Heg), *Hullēhaḷḷi* (Huṇ), *Hullehosūru* (KRN), *Hōtanahaḷḷi* (Nan).

ii. VNS signifying birds

Kōgilavāḍa (PP), *Kōgilūru* (KRN), *Chilakavāḍi* (Koḷ), *Chilkunda* (Huṇ), *Navilūru* (Nan), *Navilūru* (PP), *Navilūru* (Huṇ).

When a certain species of animals or birds is found in larger numbers at the time of the establishment of a particular village, the village takes the name of the animal or the bird. It could also be conjectured that it gets the name of an animal only when the latter is related to it in a special way, by being an extraordinary place where a good breed is produced. Wild animals also contribute their mite in the naming of villages. Generally such villages are the haunting places for those animals.

VIII. VNS after natural phenomena

They play some role in the christening of the villages.

i. The directions towards which the villages are situated contribute to the naming process. VNS related to week days also are found. This is perhaps due to the fairs which were held on those days.

Kaḍakoḷa (Mys), *Kaḍegadde* (Heg), *Paḍagalapura* (CRN), *Paḍavala agrahāra* (Nan), *Paḍavalamarahaḷḷi* (Nan), *Paḍukōṭe* (Heg), *Paḍukōte Kāvalu* (Heg), *Paḍugūru* (Heg), *Baḍaga* (Heg), *Mūḍagūni* (Heg), *Mūḍanakōḷu* (CRN), *Mūḍalakuppe* (KRN), *Mūḍala* (Mudla) *agrahāra* (CRN), *Mūḍlapura* (CRN), *Mūḍalabīḍu* (KRN), *Mūḍalahosahaḷḷi* (CRN), *Mūḍahaḷḷi* (Nan), *Mūḍalapura* (Huṇ), *Mūlepeṭlu* (KRN), *Megaḷapura* (Mys), *Mēlūru* (PP), *Mēlūru* (KRN), *Yaḍakoḷa* (Mys), *Yaḍahaḷḷi* (Mys), *Sōmavārapēte* (CRN).

Note: Paḍavala may mean a vegetable called snake gourd.

ii. Villages are named after minerals which are found in plenty in a particular locality. Either the mines concerning particular minerals must have existed long ago or it should be possible to find out the particular mineral if excavated.

Upinahaḷḷi (Nan), *Uppinahaḷḷi* (Nan), *Kānchanahaḷḷi* (CRN), *Kānchinakere* (KRN), *Chikkahonnūru* (PP), *Jōḍihonnūru* (TNP), *Tagaḍūru* (Nan), *Doḍḍahonnūru* (PP), *Doḍḍahonnūru Kāvalu* (PP), *Māṇikyapura* (Mys), *Muttūru* (PP), *Sōnahaḷḷi* (Huṇ), *Sōnahaḷḷi* (Heg), *Honnāpura* (PP), *Honnūru* (Mys), *Honnūru* (Yal), *Honnūrukuppe* (Heg).

It is possible that Muttūru in PP taluk may have acquired its name from the existence of a large number of Muttuga trees.

iii. Natural colours are also a source of VNS. But they are very small in number.

Kappasōge (Nan), *Nīlasōge* (TNP).

iv. There are a few village names which signify numbers.

Panchavaḷḷi (PP), *Mummaḍi Kāvalu* (PP), *Hadināru* (Nan).

IX. VNS of Commercial importance

Trade and commerce are also taken into consideration while giving names to villages or towns. Business constitutes the predominating factor in the process of naming the villages where taxes are also collected.

Sunkadahaḷḷi (PP), *Haradanahaḷḷi* (CRN), *Haradanahaḷḷi* (Huṇ), *Haradanahaḷḷi* (KRN); *Haradanahaḷḷi* (Nan), *Haradūr* (PP).

In the village name *Haradanahaḷḷi,* Harada refers to a tradesman. Some of the VNS classified under 'minerals' (VIII, ii) such as *Uppinahaḷḷi Chikkahonnūru* may have acquired those names because of the trade in respect of a particular mineral.

The village name *Seṭṭihaḷḷi* is found in almost all parts of Karnataka. The word *Seṭṭi* derived from the Sanskrit word *Śrēṣṭi* means a person who is engaged in business or trade. Therefore *Seṭṭis* carrying business or trade must have originally lived in such villages. *Seṭṭi* is also the name of a caste. Whether they continue to carry on their professional trade or not, they inherit their surnames from their forefathers. In course of time, even when these people eschewed their business, they must have continued to live there. Even when they migrate to some other places or when people belonging to other communities dominate the village, the names of the villages remain unchanged.

It is also likely that the villages with the suffix *'paṭṭaṇa'* such as *Kunnapaṭṇa* (Heg) and Haravemallaraja *paṭna* (PP) may have been places of commercial importance.

X. Miscellaneous VNS

The classification of VNS on the basis of specifics is indeed an intricate problem. The source of VNS are unlimited. A systematic, comprehensive and rigid classification comprising all the connotations and denotations that the myriad VNS imply is next to impossibility. Hence it is considered desirable for the present to bring the remaining items of VNS under this group

i. The practice of naming a new village after an old one is in vogue every where. The person or persons leaving the old village and founding the new one would like to retain the old name out of love, respect and sentiment. The old name may be retained also in order to perpetuate a certain tradition or the name of a person to honour which or whom the old one is given. There is a danger in bringing all such similar names together under this group, for the simple reason that the two similar names may denote two different persons. This sort of complication will continue to exist until conclusive and incontrovertible evidence is available.

Many places acquiring their names after similar or varied sources are also repeated, though one need not be a copy of the other. The circumstances under which one place gets a certain name may be present in the case of other places too. To cite an example, *Hosahaḷḷi,* simply means a new village. The founder or the first inhabitant may not have worried himself about the naming of the village. It so happens that the people of the neighbouring villages may have called the same as the new village for purposes of identification. *Hosahaḷḷi* as a place name is found largely in KRN, TNP, Heg and Huṇ. taluks

Rāmēnahaḷḷi is repeated twice in Huṇ taluk, *Heggavāḍi* twice in CRN taluk and Pura twice in Heg taluk. Pura is found in a changed form Hura in Nan taluk. KRN and Heg have each a place called *Siddāpura. Ālanahaḷḷi* is found both in Mysore and KRN taluks and Abbūru in Huṇ and PP taluks. There are two places with the same name, *Hārohaḷḷi* in Mys taluk. Heg, TNP and Huṇ have each a place with the same name, *Huṇsūru.* The PN *Kallhaḷḷi* occurs thrice in Nan, Huṇ and Mys taluks. *Mādāpura* which may be either a personal name or a saint's name finds itself in three places of Mys, TNP and Huṇ taluks. CRN and TNP has one *Kūdlūru* each.

Similarly places such as *Kappusōge, Mēgaḷapura* and *Chikkahaḷḷi* indicating colours, physical features and size may also get repeated. Examples of such repetitions may be many. Suffice it to say that the repetition of VNS is a common feature.

Kottagāla (Heg), *Kottagāla* (Huṇ), *Kottagāla* (TNP), *Korla-hosahaḷḷi* (PP), *Gollara-hosahaḷḷi* (PP), *Hangaḷa-hosahaḷḷi* (Guṇ), *Hammarahosahaḷḷi* (Guṇ), *Haḷayūru* (PP), *Haḷayūru* (KRN), *Haḷepura* (Huṇ), *Haḷepyāte Kandapura* (PP), *Haḷebīḍu* (Huṇ), *Haḷemirle* (KRN), *Haḷeyūru* (Heg).

ii) Generally prefixes are used to distinguish new and old villages. The prefix 'Hiri' signifies both size and age.

Hirikyātanahaḷḷi (Huṇ), *Hiriyūru* (TNP), *Hirihaḷḷi* (Heg), *Hirekāṭi, Hirēnandi* (Heg), *Hirēbēgūru* (CRN), *Hirēmaḷali* (PP), *Hosa-agrahāra* (KRN), *Hosakōṭe* (Nan), *Hosakōṭe* (TNP), *Hosakōṭe* (Mys), *Hosakōṭe* (KRN), *Hosakōṭe* (Huṇ), *Hosakōṭe* (Heg), *Hosapura* (Guṇ), *Hosapura* (Nan), *Hosapura* (TNP), *Hosamālangi* (Koḷ), *Hosaviḍu* (Nan), *Hosahaḷḷi* (KRN), *Hosahaḷḷi* (CRN), *Hosahaḷḷi* (Heg), *Hosahaḷḷi* (Mys), *Hosahaḷḷi* (PP), *Hosahaḷḷi* (TNP), *Hosahuṇḍi* (Mys), *Hosahoḷalu* (Heg), *Hosūru* (Heg), *Hosūru* (Guṇ), *Hosūru* (KRN).

It is interesting to note that the villages bearing the prefix 'hosa' (new) are larger in number than those bearing the prefix *'haḷeya'* (old). *Haḷemanchanahaḷḷi* (Heg) and *Haḷemagge* (Heg) do not have their counterparts (Hosa), though *Manchanahaḷḷi* and Magge are available.

iii. Names consisting of prefixes indicating different sizes of villages concerned.

Chikkakavalande (Nan), *Chikkakāṭi* (Guṇ), *Chikkakāḍanahaḷḷi* (Huṇ), *Chikkakamarahaḷḷi* (PP), *Chikkakānya* (Mys), *Chikkinduv-/aḍi* (Koḷ), *Chikkakundūru* (Heg), *Chikkakeriyūru* (Heg), *Chikkatuppūru* (Guṇ), *Chikkanandi* (KRN), *Chikkanēriḷe* (PP), *Chikkabīchanahaḷḷi* (Huṇ), *Chikkabelalu* (PP), *Chikkabēgūru* (CRN), *Chikkabainakuppe* (Heg), *Chikkamālāpura* (Koḷ), *Chikkalakṣhmihaḷḷ* (TNP) *Chikkavaḍḍaraguḍi* (KRN), *Chikkahanasōge* (KRN), *Chikkahabbūru* (Huṇ), *Chikkahaḷḷi* (Mys), *Chikkahuṇsūru* (Huṇ), *Chikkahomma* (Nan), *Doḍḍakamaravaḷḷi* (PP), *Doḍḍakavalande* (Nan), *Doḍḍakāḍanahaḷḷi, Doḍḍakeriyūru* (Heg), *Doḍḍatippūru* (Guṇ), *Doḍḍanērle* (PP), *Doḍḍabēchanahaḷḷi* (Huṇ), *Doḍḍabeḷālu* (PP), *Doḍḍabairanakuppe* (Heg), *Doḍḍamōḷe* (CNR), *Doḍḍalakṣmīpura* (TNP), *Doḍḍavaḍḍaraguḍi* (KRN), *Doḍḍaharave* (PP), *Doḍḍahuṇsūru* (Huṇ), *Doḍḍahebbūru* (Huṇ), *Doḍḍahomma* (Nan), *Doḍḍahosūru* (PP), *Doḍḍinduvāḍi* (Koḷ), *Hirekāṭi* (Guṇ), *Hirenandi* (KRN).

It may be pointed out here that the villages whose prefixes signify big and small are generally found in one and the same taluk. Sometimes one of the two small and big villages is found missing. For example, *Chikkakundūru* in Heg does not have its counterpart *Doḍḍakundūru.* Perhaps, *Kundūru* may have to be considered as its counterpart as it is bigger than *Chikkakundūru*. *Doḍḍapura* (TNP), *Doḍḍamōle* (CRN), *Doḍḍaharave* (PP), and *Hirimaḷali* (PP), do not have their counterparts, not even prefixless names. The villages having their names as pura, *Mōḷe, Māḷali* and Harave are found in other taluks, but not in the nearby places. The places with size indicators are ordinarily very near each other. Although *Chikkahaḷḷi* (Mys), *Chinnahaḷḷi* (Heg), *Hirihaḷḷi* (Heg), *Hiriyūru* (TNP), and *Kurugūru* (PP) indicate the size of the villages, corresponding counterparts are not anticipated. *Hebbāḷu* (KRN) is a compound word comprising *Hiri* + *Haḷu*. Likewise, *Hebbasūru* (KRN) seems to be a compound of *Hiri* + *Hosūru* (?)

iv. VNS signifying sentiments, aesthetic sense and moral values.

Nallūru (CRN), *Nallūru* (Heg), *Mangaḷa* (Guṇ), *Mangaḷa* (CRN), *Mangaḷūru* (Nan).

Such names are very rare. Sometimes if becomes very difficult to determine whether such names as *Mēlūru* (KRN) could be brought under this group or under the group indicating geographical features.

CLASSIFICATION OF VILLAGE NAMES BASED ON GENERICS

A VN normally consists of two components. They are called specifics and generics. A specific is a component which differentiates one village from the other. It is a name peculiarly or particularly assigned or suited to an individual place. In a sense, it is called a proper name. Generally it suggests the special features or characteristics of a settlement. It also indicates as to why that particular name was given to a certain village. Attiguppe (CRN) for example was named so, because Ficus racemosa Lin trees grow three abundantly. The second component, viz, generics signifies the sort of habitation, marked by general characteristics. In Attiguppe (Atti + Kuppe) the first element is the specific and the second, the generic. They are also called adjectival and substantial elements respectively by some scholars. But the use of prefixes and suffixes for these words does not seem to be satisfactory in view of their acepted grammatical meanings. Though Atti in the above example looks like qualifying the second element Kuppe, it functions like a proper name. Therefore, the terms specific and generic are extensively made use of for the present.

There are certain villages which contain more than two elements, as in *Chikka Bīchana haḷḷi* (Huṇ). Chikka here is certainly an adjective, functioning likewise. There are also instances of village names with only one word or element such as Harave (CRN). Such names will be studied at the appropriate places. In this chapter, generics will be dealt with in detail.

The generics are amenable to classification. All the generics are grouped under ten heads:

I. Generics which indicate habitation:

Ambaḷe, Ūru, Kēri, Grāma, Doḍḍi, Natta, Pāḍi, Pura, Puri, Bīḍu, Bīḍi, Vāda, Vāḍi, Haṭṭi, Haḷḷi, Hāḍi, Huṇḍi.

II. Generics which denote rocks, hills, mounds, forests etc.:

Aranya, Are, Kallu, Kāḍu, Kunda, Kuppe, Kumari, Koppalu, Kōḍu, Guṇḍa, Guṇḍla, Ghaṭṭa, Tiṭṭu, Beṭṭa, Maraḍi, Male, Māḷa.

III. Generics which indicate water resources:

Ambi[2]*, Ambudhi, Kaṭṭe, Kūḍalu, Kere, Koḷa, Kōḍi, Guṇḍi, Tore, Nāla, Mōḷe, Vāti*[3]*, Samudra, Hoḷe.*

IV. Generics which denote the tupes of the soil, location or other geographical features:

Āḷu, Kāvalu, Gadde, Bāḷu, Vāḷu, Sāl, Hanta, Hāḷu.

V. Generics denoting relation, caste and kindred things:

Agara, Agrahāra, Guḍi, Chatra, Mangaḷa, Maṭha.

---

2. A place situated at the foot of a hill (GPTEK - Raghupal Bhat Kemtur), A boat (KED).
3. Bank of a river (PSI) could it be Āvati as found in Amarāvati, Vēdāvati etc?

VI. Generics which indicate trading centres:

Nagara, Paṭṭaṇa (Paṭṇa), Pēṭe, Sante.

VII. Generics which signify forts and military centres:

Kōṭe, Pāḷya.

VII. Generics which signify forts and military centres:

Kōṭe, Pāḷya.

VIII. Generics indicating flora and fauna:

Āla, Kāṭi, Jāji, Jāla, Nandi, Nelli, Nērale, Māvu, Magge, Mūlangi.

IX. Miscellaneous generics:

Acchi[4], *amāni, Ēṇi*[5], *Kuṇike, Gāṇa, Gumbha, Tale, Bāgilu, Bele, Mūle, Vaṭṭa, Soḍlu, Sōge.*

X. Generics whose meanings cannot be deciphered beyond doubt at present:

Abbāgilu[6], *Kāla*[7], *Guḷi*[8], *Chatta*[9], *Thara, Peṭlu*[10], *Beḷalu*[11], *Maṇḍlu, Vaṭṭi, Vattige, Vara, Vāḷu.*

It may be noted here, with the exception of few Skt. words like *Pura, Puri, Grāma, Samudra, Ambudhi, Agrahāra, Chatra, Nagara, Maṭha* etc., almost all of them are Kannada words or words of Drn. origin. There are a very few words like Agara which are the corrupt forms of Skt. words.

The generics of the entire district are arranged in the alphabetical order and analysed.

---

4. Mother (KED).
5. Could it be derived from Ēṇu which means a border, an edge?
6. Abbe + Bāgllu (?) Abbe means a thorny plant from which ocasionally pens are made by school boys (KED).
7. Kāla means a water course, a channel (KED): a hill, bottom of a hill (GPTEK): Kāla in Skt. means time.
8. Could it be a variant of Kuli, a Killer.
9. Has this anything to do with Chatte which means flat, level land?
10. The plant Cida mauritiana herit (KED).
11. Compare the words Beḷala, Beḷavala (KED), could it be Bḷalu?

-agara

This occurs in Yel Taluk and is a settlement of Brahmans. This is understood to have been found in the 10th century A.D. This is a corrupted form of the Skt word *Agrahāra > Aghrāra > Agrāra > Agara.*

-agrahāra

Agrahāras are villages assigned mainly to Brahmans for their maintenance. Vide Agara. Like Agara, Agrahāra is also sometimes used as a free PN without any specific.

Agrahāra (Huṇ), *Paḍavala agrahāra* (Nan), *Mūḍla agrahāra* (CRN), *Hosa agrahāra* (KRN).

-acchi

It means mother according to KED

Ponnacchi (Koḷ)

-aṭṭi

This is a variant form of *Haṭṭi.* The initial H is elided. *Paṭṭi* is the oldest form of *Haṭṭi.* P changes into H phoneme by about the 11th century A.D. It means a cow stall, sheepfold, hamlet, village. See -*haṭṭi/-paṭṭi.*

Yalachaṭṭi (Guṇ)

-atti

It means the red-wooded big tree or country fig tree. Hatti (cotton) may also be reduced to Atti after losing its aspirateness.

Abbaḷatti (PP), *Muttatti* (TNP).

-amāni

What is in change or under the immediate care of a collector on the part of the Government.

Nallūru amāni (Guṇ), *Vijayapura amāni* (Guṇ).

-ambaḷe

Ambala, ambila, ambela are its variants. It means the court-yard of a temple, specifically an open shed or hall where public affairs are discussed (GPTK). In Tamil ambalam means open space for the use of public, village assembly for transacting village affairs.

Ambaḷe (Yal)

-ambi

Ambi means a small boat, ship in Tamil and a boat in Kannada. The last vowel *i* changes into *e*.

Terakaṇāmbi (Guṇ).

-ambudhi

It is a Skt. word which means water receptacle.

Lingāmbudhi (Mys), *Vallāmbudhi* (KRN).

-āṇa

?

Hullāṇa (Guṇ), Could it be *Hullevana* > *Hullevaṇa* > *Hullāṇa?*

-ādi

Vat (< *ādi*) the Skt. affix is added to nouns to show possession. It signifies an abode also. Morphophonemically it takes the forms *Vati, Āvati.*

Bhōga + vati becomes Bhōgavati. Further in Kannada Vati is reduced to ādi; Bhōgādi (Mys).

-araṇya

This is a Skt. word which means a wood, a forest. A village situated in or near a forest

Mēṭikuppe araṇya

-are

The cognates in Tam., Kod., Tel. respectively are arai, ar and rāyi, the meaning of which are rock, grinding stone, flat rock, stone etc. The initial ṟ of OK changes into r in MK.

Chikkare (PP), *Bekkare* (PP), *Macchare* (Heg), *Hallare* (Nun).

-āra/-vāra

Āra is a corrupt form of the Skt. word *āgāra* which means a dwelling place. But vara is said to be the corrupted form of the Skt. word pura (Chidanandamurthy); and *āhāra* (Kalaburgi). See Marga II-PP 531-534.

Haluva	+	ara	TNP
Hala	+	vara	

-āra, āre

Āra could be derived from the Skt. word *Āgāra. Āre* means shoemaker's knife, shrub, a Mahratta man. These meanings do not hold good in this context.

Ambalāre (PP), *Jiyyāra* (Heg)

-āru

The Drn. numeral six. OK form is *āṟu*

Hadināru (Nan)

āla

It means a banyan tree and is found in Tam., Mal. and Kod.

Mariyāla (CRN), *Haḍiyāla* (Nan), *Horeyāla* (Guṇ)

-āḷu

See *hāḷu*

-ike/ige

An affix used in the formation of nouns, especially neutral nouns. *Koḍasige* (Heg) is the corrupted form of the Skt. word *Kuṭajaka,* in which case ka becomes ge. *Koḍasige* is also written as *Koḍesige* which alters the meaning. An example of ike is *Kandalike* (Heg). -*ike* could be derived from *-key* which means field. *Koḷavige* (Huṇ), *Hejjige* (Nan), *Hemmige* (TNP), *Hemmige* (Huṇ), *Hairige* (Huṇ; Heg).

-ugane

It is a woody creeper

Uganiya (Koḷ), *Kōdiugane* (CRN)

-ūru

Haḷḷi is the generic of nearly thirty per cent of the VNS of this district. *ūru* is the next biggest generic which is common to almost all the Drn. VNS. The scholars are of the opinion that this is the oldest generic which perhaps was used in the beginning without any prefix or suffix to denote any settlement. They connect it with the ancient Babylonian city of Ur. According to them, *Wippūr,* the seat of Mesopotamian culture has ūr as its generic.[12] Whatever it is, the different forms of *ūr* are found in all the Drn. languages from the very beginning of their existence.

Some scholars seem to think that *ūr* is derived from pura, the Skt. word. According to them, there is an elision of the first consonant phoneme 'p'. *Ura* then becomes *ūru.* This is nothing but wild imagination. It may have been otherwise. Pura may have been the Sanskritised form of *ūru - ūru,* which according to Drn. scholars comes from the root *ir,* to exist or from *ur* to dwell. For Drn. cognates the DED (pp 36-37 - item No. 407; and p.55 - item No. 608) may be consulted.

Mysūru taluk

Ānandūr, Udbūr, Kāṭūr, Kuppalūru, Gurūr, Chikkāṭūr, Talūr, Torina Kāṭūr, Dēvanūr, Doḍḍakāṭūr, Maddūr, Muḷḷūru, Maisūru.

Krişṇarājanagara taluk

Aḍagūru, Abbūru, Kundūru, Kestūru, Kōgilūru, Kōlūru, Tippūru, Baḷḷūru, Māvattūru, Māvanūru, Muṇḍūru, Mēlūru, Saragūru, Haḷayūru, Hullehosūru, Hebsūru, Hosūru.

Koḷḷēgal taluk

Kaṇṇūru, Chennūru, Doḍḍa Ālattūru, Beḷattūru, Māvatūru (Araṇya), Saragūru, Singanallūru, Hanūru.

Guṇḍlupēṭe taluk

Aṇṇūru, Ālattūru, Kaḍabūru, Kasavanūru, Kuttanūru, Kelasūru, Chikkatuppūru, Taggalūru, Dāribēgūru, Doḍḍatuppūru, Nallūru

12. The Bible comes alive, p. 260 by Sri Charles Merston.

amānikere, Paḍugūru, Bēgūru, Maddūru, Muḍugūru, Yariyūru, Lakkūru, Huttūru, Hosūru.

Chāmarājanagara taluk

Ālūru, Āldūru, Ummattūru, Kiragasūru, Kullūru, Kūḍlūru, Kestūru, Gaṇaganūru, Chikkabēgūru, Jannūru, Teḷanūru, Nallūru, Naralūru, Puṇajūru, Maliyūru, Mēluru, Yaḍiyūru, Yalakkūru, Saragūru, Suttūru, Hiribēgūru, Hebbasūru, Honganūru.

Tirumakūḍalu Narasipura taluk

Akkūru, Uddibāgūru, Kaliyūru, Kiragasūru, Kukkūru, Kusubūru, Kūḍlūru, Koḷatūru, Turaganūru, Bannūru, Bāgūru, Maleyūru, Mūgūru, Sujjalūru, Hiriyūru, Huṇasūru, Heggūru, Honnūru, Hyākanūru.

Nanjanagūḍu taluk

Ariyūru, Ālattūru, Ālambūru, Kaggalūru, Kadabūru, Kaṇēnūru, Kāṭūru, Kugallūru, Koṇanūru, Gōḷūru, Tagaḍūru, Tāyūru, Teḷanūru, Dāsanūru, Dēbūru, Dēvanūru, Navalūru, Bannūru, Bāgūru, Mangalūru, Maraḷūru, Muḷḷūru, Rājūru, Saragūru, Suttūru, Hādanūru, Husakūru.

Piriyāpaṭṇa taluk

Aḍagūru, Abbūru, Aḷalūru, Aichūru, Kānūru, Kittūru, Kirangūru, Kiragūru. Kuḍakūru, Koṇasūru, Chowkūru, Doḍḍahonnūru, Doḍḍahosūru, Navalūru, Bēgūru, Beḷatūru, Maraḍiyūru, Maradūru, Muttugūru, Muttūru, Mēlūru, Sīgūru, Habbaṭūru, Haradūru, Halasūru, Haḷeyūru Hegatūru.

Yaḷandūru taluk

Kestūru, Yaḷandūru

Huṇasūru taluk

Abbūru, Uddūru, Ummattūru, Kirangūru, Kūḍlūru, Kerūru, Kellūru, Chikkahuṇsūru, Chikkahebbūru, Tippūru, Doḍḍahejjūru, Doḍḍahebbūru, Doddahuṇsūru, Nellūru, Nēgatūru, Beṭṭadūru, Beḷatūru, Maradūru, Marūru, Muduganūru, Muḷḷūru, Mailambūru, Mōdūru, Rāvandūru, Lakkūru, Siriyūru, Heggandūru.

Heggaḍadēvanakōṭe taluk

Agattūru, Aṇṇūru, Udabūru, Kaṭṭehuṇsūru, Kaḍasūru, Kaḷasūru, Kaṇiyanahuṇḍihosūru, Kittūru, Kundūru, Keḷasaragūru, Kōṇanālattūru, Guṇḍattūru, Gōḷūru, Chākkūru, Chikkakundūru, Chikkakeriyūru, Doḍḍakeriyūru, Nallūru, Būdanūru, Beḷattūru, Bēgūru, Majjūru, Moḷeyūru, Yalamattūru, Lakkūru, Saragūru, Hādanūru, Halasūru, Hoḷeyūru, Huṇsūru, Husagūru, Hegganūru, Hosūru.

-ele

Ele means leaf. *Yeradele* (Nan). Whether it is *yaradale* or *taragele* is not certain, since different versions of the same name are available.

ēṇi

Ēṇi means a ladder. Another word *ēṇ* or its variant *eṇu* is used in the sense of edge, border or point. In Tamil *ēṇ* or *ēṇi* indicate boundary, limit

The vowel *ē* is augmented sometimes by *-y*

Basavana yēṇi (PP)

-ēru

Its original form is *ēru* which means to rise, to increase, to ascend, to climb. It's variant forms in other languages are: *ēru* (Tam.), *ēruka* (Mal.), *ēruni* (Tu.), *ētaniu* (Tel).

Kudēru (CRN) - *Kudiha + ēru* : The last three phonemes of the specific are elided in the combination.

-kaṭṭe

Kaṭṭe means a dam. Its variants in other Drn. languages are: *Kaṭṭi* (Ta), *Kaṭṭe* (Kod.), *Kaṭṭa* (Tu.), *Kaṭṭa* (Tel.), *Kaṭṭa* (NK.), *Kaṭṭṭā* (Ga.).

Araḷikaṭṭe (CRN), *Gangādharanakaṭṭe* (Koḷ), *Garikekaṭṭe* (Heg), *Nyānekaṭṭe* (Guṇ), *Puradakaṭṭe* (Heg), *Sāgarakaṭṭe* (Mys).

-kal/-kallu

Kal whose primary meaning is stone is found in all the Drn. languages, in various forms: *kal* (Tam.), *Kal, kallu* (Mal.), *kal* (Ko.), *kalli* (Kod.), *kallu* (Tu.), *kallu* (Tel.), *kel* (Pa.), *khal* (Br.)

The initial surd generally changes into sonant in the intervocalic position

Karikallu (PP), *Kūrgallu* (PP), *Channakallu* (PP), *Tarikal* (Huṇ), *Tenakallu* (Heg), *Benagalu* (PP), *Hinkal* (Mys).

The final consonant gets doubled when a vowel is added to it. Sometimes, doubling does not occur as is in the last example.

-kavalande

Kaval + anje > Kavalande (?) which means a bifurcated branch of a river. For anje, see GPTK

Chikkakavalande (Nan), *Doḍḍakavalande* (Nan)

-kanchi

It means a kind of lime; also smallness

Alaganchi (Heg). An old village famous for lime trees

-kāki

It means crow, and is found in all the Drn. languages in varied forms. *Kākkai* in Tam. and Tel. In this context, it means a common herb or a half shrub, with red, yellow or black berries.

Kengāki (CRN)

-kāṭi

It signifies bison.

Hirekāṭi (Huṇ)

-kāḍu

It means a forest or a jungle in all the Drn. languages. A jungle has a name. The name is derived from the particular kind of trees thereon. When a jungle is cleared of the existing trees to make it a suitable place for human habitation, the former name is sometimes retained. *Dinḍagādu* (PP) for example is a jungle where *Diṇḍiga,* the tree Anogeissus latifolia is grown. The village founded in that area is called *Diṇḍagāḍu.* Though *Taḷakāḍu* (TNP) has *kāḍu* as its generic, the local folk tale gives a different story connecting its origin to *Tala* and *Kāḍa.*

-kāla/-kālu/-gālu

It seems to be the variant of *kāluve* which means a stream (PNSI). It is also said to be the variant of mangala (for details, see mangala).

Kenegāla (PP), *Kandāgāla* (TNP, PP, Heg, Guṇ), *Karigāla* (Heg), *Kuppēgāla* (Mys), *Kottēgāla* (Heg, Huṇ), *Kōḷagāla* (Heg), *Guṇḍēgāla* (Koḷ), *Goṇatagāla* (Nan), *Nilangāla* (PP), *Bidagāla* (Heg), *Satyagāla* (PP), S*āṇigāla* (CRN).

-kāval/-kāvalu

Kaval is derived from the root *ka* which jeans to preserve, shelter, watch, guard, ward off, rescue, wait for. It is found in almost all the Drn. languages: *Kāppu, kāval* (Tam.), *kāvu* (Mal.), *kāvi* (Ko.), *kāvalu* (Tu.), *kāvali* (Tel.), *khāpus* (Kur.). *Kāvạl* in Kannada is also used in the sense of a place where cattle are tended. The name ends with the consonant as well as vowel.

Ālambāḍi kāval (KRN), *Āspatre kāval* (Huṇ), *Avarekāyibeṭṭada kāval* (PP), *Uddūru kāval* (Huṇ), *Karōhaṭṭi kāval* (Nan), *Kallahaḷḷi kāval* (Huṇ), *Kāṭnāḷu kāval* (KRN), *Koṭṭige kāval* (Huṇ), *Kriṣṇapurada kāval* (Heg), *Garikekaṭṭe kāval* (Heg), *Gariguḍḍada kāval* (PP), *Gāḍiguḍḍada kāval* (Nan), *Gobbaḷi kāval* (PP), *Channakallu kāval* (PP), *Chilkundada kāval* (Huṇ), *Jammanēraḷe kāval* (Nan), *Tarikal kāval* (Huṇ), *Tippūru kāval* (Huṇ), *Daityanakere kāval* (Huṇ), *Doḍḍakere kāvalu* (Huṇ), *Doḍḍahejjūru kāval* (Huṇ), *Doḍḍahonnūru kāval* (PP), *Navilkōḍi kāval* (PP), *Nilavāgil kāval* (Huṇ), *Panjahaḷḷi kāval* (Huṇ), *Paḍukōte kāval* (Heg), *Biḷikere kāval* (Huṇ), *Bīranahaḷḷi kāval* (Huṇ), *Beḷaganahaḷḷi kāval* (Heg), *Beṭṭada kāval* (PP), *Beṭṭadahaḷḷi kāval* (KRN), *Maṭada kāvalu* (KRN), *Mādahaḷḷi kāval* (Huṇ), *Mummaḍi kāval* (PP), *Mēṭikuppe kāval* (Heg), *Moḷeyūru kāval* (Heg), *Yarahaḷḷi kāval* (Heg), *Yelehuṇḍi kāval* (Heg), *Rāsimaraṭi kāval* (PP), *Satyagāl kāval* (PP), *Sīgetore kāval* (PP), *Sūḷekere kāval* (Huṇ), *Hanagōḍbōre kāval* (Huṇ), *Handiguḍḍa kāval* (PP), *Hasavina kāval* (PP), *Haḷēbīḍu kāval* (Huṇ), *Hulikere kāval* (Heg), *Hullebōre kāval* (KRN), *Hussainpura kāval* (Huṇ), *Heṇṇegere kāval* (Heg), *Hebbāḷu kāval* (KRN), *Hosavāḍu kāval* (Nan).

Kaval sometimes presupposes the existence of a village in the vicinity after which it takes its name. Hence there will be more than one generic attached to these places.

-kuṇike

It has various meanings: a hollow, a cavity, a loop, a noose, a corner etc. In this context it means a cavity.

Kallukuṇike (Huṇ)

-kuppe/-koppa/-koppalu

Kuppe means a heap, a pile, a dung hill. It is found in almost all the Drn. languages: *Kuppam* (Tam.), *kuppa* (Mal.), *kip* (Ko.), *kuppe* (Tu.), *kuppa* (Tel.), *kuppa* (Pa.), *kupa* (Kui.).

Koppal/Koppalu means a heap, a small hamlet (perhaps on a raised ground). *Kuppu* which means to jump, hump etc., seems to be the root of these generics and also *koppa*. *Koppa* and *kuppe* serve as free forms of PN.

Attikuppe (Huṇ), *Attiguppe* (Huṇ), *Aḷalakuppe* (KRN), *Kanchugārakoppal* (KRN), *Karṇakuppe* (Huṇ), *Kuppe* (KRN), *Koppa* (PP), *Koppalu* (TNP), *Ganganakuppe* (PP), *Gāṇiganakoppal* (TNP), *Guḷuvina-attiguppe* (KRN), *Chagachikuppe* (Heg), *Javanakuppe* (PP), *Yeluginakuppe* (PP), *Doḍḍabairanakuppe* (Heg), *Nūralakuppe* (Heg), *Nēralakuppe* (Huṇ), *Nēraḷakuppe* (PP), *Pārekoppalu* (Huṇ), *Badanakuppe* (Heg), *Bannikuppe* (KRN), *Bannikuppe* (Huṇ), *Bailakuppe* (PP), *Masaṇakuppe* (Heg), *Mudikuppa* (KRN), *Mūḍlakoppal* (KRN), *Mēṭikuppe* (Heg), *Ragalakuppe* (Heg), *Rangayyanakoppalu* (Huṇ), *Lakkikuppe* (KRN), *Saṇabinakuppe* (PP), *Habbanakuppe* (Huṇ), *Haḷḷadakoppal* (Huṇ), *Huṇasekuppe* (Heg), *Huṇasekuppe* (PP), *Huṇasekoppalu* (PP), *Hebbalaguppe* (Heg), *Hebbāḷukoppalu* (KRN).

-kumari

Kumari in Tam. simply means cultivation in hills. In Kan it means a piece of ground in a jungle, on which the trees are cut down and burnt, whereafter it is cultivated for one or two years only. It exists in Tu. in the form of *kumēru* which means a waste land cleared for cultivation. The only one village with this generic is *Aralikumari* (PP).

-kura

It is probably the corrupted form of the Skt. word khura which means hoof.

Hulikura (Heg).

-kunda/-kundi

It means a pillar of bricks. In Tulu, it means a pillar or a post. it is found in Telugu also. Kunda in Kan, signifies an earthern pot wherein domestic decorative plants are reared. In Skt. it means a kind of jasmine. According to *Sirigannaḍa arthakōśa* by Shivarama Karanth, it also means a small hillock. The initial 'k' of the generic changes into 'g' in the intervocalic position.

Kallukunda (Nan), *Kiragunda* (PP), *Chilkunda* (Huṇ), *Nandigunda* (Nan), *Biḷagunda* (PP), *Beḷagunda* (Nan).

-kūḍalu/-kūḍlu/-gūḍlu

Kūḍu is the root from which *kūḍal* or *kūḍalu* is derived. *Kūḍal* generally means a junction. It is mainly used to mean a confluence of more than one river. In spoken language, the final vowel is dropped, and as in the case of all consonant ending words, it takes the vowel 'u' at the end as in *kūḍlu.* As already indicated elsewhere, the initial surd changes into sonant in the medial position.

Tirumakūḍlu (TNP), *Hinḍagūḍlu* (Huṇ)

-kūḍu/-gūḍu

Gūḍu is a variant of *Kūḍu* which is used both as a verb and a noun. When it is a verb, it means joining, assembling, happening etc. When it is a noun, it means a nest, fowl house, lodging, cottage. This is common to almost all the Drn. languages.

Nanjanagūḍu (Nan)

-kere

It is a very common generic. A common phenomenon is that people used to establish villages in the vicinity of some kind of water resources. They would even put embankment across small streams so that they might get sufficient water supply during the dry season. There would, therefore, be an artificial or natural tank or pool or pond by the side of a village. Hence, no village without a water resource can be conceived of.

Generally a tank is named after a man who is responsible for its construction or after a person whose name is intended to be perpetuated. A tank is likely to be named after a person who live nearby.

The initial surd gets sonantised in the intermediary position.

Variants of kere in various Drn. cognate languages are noted here: *ceṛu, ciṛai* (Tam.), *cira* (Mal.), *ker* (Ko.), *kere* (Kod.), *kere* (Tu.), *ceruvu* (Tel.), *Cēr* in Tam. means to join together, shut, close, store up, to control.

Arakere (KRN), *Arsanakere* (Mys), *Ukkalagere* (TNP), *Kaggere* (KRN), *Kanchinakere* (KRN), *Kāṇikere* (CRN), *Kallukere* (Huṇ), *Kilagere* (Guṇ), *Kilagere* (CRN), *Kundakere* (Guṇ), *Kesarakere* (PP), *Kōṭekere* (Guṇ), *Gaḷigekere* (KRN), *Gavadagere* (Huṇ), *Goḷaganakere* (PP), *Gowḍikere* (Huṇ), *G.Channamgere* (KRN), *Jābagere* (Huṇ), *Taṭṭekere* (Huṇ), *Daṇḍikere* (Mys), *Duddagere* (PP), *Daityanakere* (Huṇ), *Doḍḍakere* (Heg), *Doḍvaḍḍakere* (PP), *Dorekere* (Huṇ), *Nāgalagere* (TNP), *Nālūru amānikere* (Guṇ), *Biḷagere* (Nan), *Biḷikere* (Huṇ), *Biḷigere* (Huṇ), *Baṇṇegere* (Heg), *Bhaṇḍikere* (CRN), *Haṭṭakere* (Heg), *Mādhavagere* (Mys), *Malaganakere* (Huṇ), *Musikere* (Heg), *Meṭṭakere* (KRN), *Yelachagere* (CRN), *Yelachagere* (Nan), *Lāḷanakere* (Huṇ), *Vaḍagere* (Yal), *Vaḍḍagere* (Guṇ), *Vaḍḍargere* (PP), *Vaḷagere* (Nan), *Vīrangere* (Mys), *Sūḷekere* (Huṇ), *Haḷḷikere* (Huṇ).

-kēri

It is found in almost all the Drn. languages: *Cēri* (Tam.) = town, village, street; *cēri* (Mal.) = assemblage, street; *kēri* (Kod.) = hamlet; *kēri* (Tu.) = street. In Kan. its primary meaning is street.

Chikkavaḍḍara kēri (PP)

-koṭhāra

It is a corrupted form of the Skt. word *Kōsṭhāgāra* which means a granary, a store room, a treasury.

Heggoṭhāra (CRN)

-koḷa

Koḷa means a pond, a lake. Its variants in the other Drn. languages are: *Kuḷam* (Tam.), *kuḷam* (Mal.), *kuḷa* (Tu.), *koḷanu* (Tel.). That it has been derived from Skt. *kūla* cannot be accepted. Sometimes *ḷ* changes itself into *ṇ*.

Kaḍakoḷa (Mys), *Tuppadakoḷa* (Huṇ), *Yeḍakoḷa* (Mys)

-kōṭe

Kōṭe means a wall round a town; a fort, a stronghold. It is the place wherein the king generally lived with all his paraphernalia. The word is available in all the major languages of the Drn. group: *Kōṭṭai* (Tam.), *kōṭṭa* (Mal.), *kōṭe* (Tu.), *kōṭe* (Tel.).

Kōṭe is said to have originated from the Skt. word, *kōttah*. Whether it has been borrowed from Skt. or by Skt. from the Drn. languages requires thorough examination. *Kēśiraja,* a grammarian of the 13th century says, in his grammar Śabdamaṇidarpaṇam, that *kōṇṭe* (the variant of *kōṭe*) is common to both Skt. and Kan. and calls it Samasamskrita (*Sūtra* 312).

Kākanakōṭe (Heg), *Chāmarāyanakōṭe* (PP), *Jāganakōṭe* (Heg), *Paḍukōṭe* (Heg), *Basavanakōṭe* (Heg), *Mēlkōṭe* (Heg), *Suḷekōṭe* (PP), *Heggaḍadēvanakōṭe* (Heg), *Hosakōṭe* (Mys), *Hosakōṭe* (TNP), *Hosakōṭe* (Nan).

-kōḍi

It is used in the sense of a passage to carry off excess of water, outlet of a tank. The word occurs in Tam. also.

The village which is situated round about such an outlet, adopts it as its generic.

When the preceding consonant is a nasal, the surd gets sonantised.

Tengōḍi (Guṇ), *Navilkōḍi* (Kaval) (PP)

-kōḍu

In almost all the languages of the Drn. family, it means a horn, a tusk, a bunch, a branch. In Tel. it is used in the sense of rivulet also. But in Kan. it signifies a point, a peak, or top of a hill, in addition to the above.

Intervocalic 'k' changes into 'g'

Attigōḍu (PP), *Kallukōḍu* (Heg), *Kenchalagōḍu* (Mys), *Doḍḍamaragōḍu* (TNP), *Paḍnakōḍu* (CRN), *Bidaragōḍu* (Nan), *Mākōḍu* (Huṇ), *Mudnakuḍu** (CRN), *Varakōḍu* (Mys), *Sulgōḍ+* (PP), *Hanagōḍu* (Huṇ), *Hosa alagōḍu* (TNP).

* *ō* in *kōḍu* changes into 'u', thus becoming *kuḍu*

\+ The last vowel is elided.

-gaṭṭa/ghaṭṭa

The grammarian, Kittel maintains that it is tatsama. It means a mountain range. In Marāthi, it is *ghaṭa.* In Skt. it means a landing place, steps on the side of a river, leading to the water. It is used in this sense also in Kan. Since Kittel says, it is a *tatsama* (which is common both to Kan. and Skt.) it may be reasonably guessed, it is a native word as far as Kannada is concerned.

The equivalent of *gaṭṭa* in Mal. is *khaṭṭam,* in Tel, *ghaṭṭa* (Item No. 96 in PNSI).

The initial 'g' seems to have been aspirated owing to the influence of *Marāthi.*

Ānegaṭṭa (Heg), *Kuppekoḷagaṭṭa* (Huṇ), *Nāgaraghaṭṭa* (Huṇ)

-gaṭṭi

The different forms of *gaṭṭi* in other Drn. languages are *kaṭṭi, keṭṭi* (Tam.), *kaṭṭa* (Mal.), *gaṭṭi* (Tel.), *gaṭṭi* (Tu.).

It means strong, ability, lump, solid.

Ānegaṭṭi (Heg).

-gadde

Its earliest forms are *gaḷde* > *garde,* meaning paddy field. In Tam. and Mal. its equivalent is *kaḷani,* in Ko, *gad.* A village surrounded by paddy field acquires this generic.

Kāḍegadde (Heg), *Maḷalagadde* (Heg).

-gāṇa

Gāṇa signifies an oil mill, a sugar-cane press or mill. The village which possesses an oil mill gets that name.

Kulagāṇa (CRN)

-grāma

This is one of the very few generics taken from Skt. It means a village, hamlet, race, community, collection (of anything). The Skt. generics are not so widely used as Kan. or Drn. generics, though generics like *grāma* are popular.

-guḍi/-guḍilu

It means house, temple; *kuḷi* is another form of *guḍi.* Kittel says, it is a corrupted form of *kuṭi.* DED gives its variants in Drn. languages: *kuṭi* (Tam.), *kuḍi* (Kod.), *guḍi* (Tu.), *guḍi* (Koḷ.), *guḍi* (Pa.), *guḍi* (Ga.). From these examples, it may be stated that *guḍi* is a Drn. word (vide DED, item No. 1379)

Kāḍuvaḍḍaraguḍi (Huṇ), *Gejjayana Vaḍḍaraguḍi* (Huṇ), *Chikkavaḍḍaraguḍi* (KRN), *Doddavaḍḍaraguḍi* (KRN), *Māguḍilu* (Heg), *Vaḍḍaraguḍi* (Heg.)

It is interesting to find that this generic is used in connection with particular caste.

-Guṇḍi/-Guṇḍa

Gundi is used in the sense of a hole, a pit, a hollow. Some scholars seem to suggest that it is a synonym of *Kuṇṭe* which means a pond. A pond is not a pit. *Guṇḍi,* of course, is related to *Guṇi* or *Kuṇi. Guṇḍi* is noticed in other. Drn. languages also: *kaṇṭam* (Tam.), *kuṇṭam* (Mal.), *kuṇḍi* (Kod.), *kuṇḍa* (Tu.), *Guṇṭa* (Tel.). It is also compared with Skt. *kuṇḍa.*

Kaggunḍi (PP), *Kumbāragunḍi* (CRN), *Goragunḍi* (KRN), *Channagunḍi* (Heg).

-Gunḍlu/-Gunḍla

This generic consists of two elements viz. *gunḍu + lu.* It may be even *Gunḍa + lu. Gunḍa* means roundness, hollowness and deepness. Perhaps, the latter one is appropriate here. *lu* means that place, or to be fit or proper. *Gunḍlu* is the name of a river also which flows in Nan and Guṇ taluks. *Gunḍu* means a mass, a heap; round stone.

Yachegunḍlu (PP)

-Gumba

It means a pot, the nave of a wheel. It is a corrupted form of the Skt. word *Kumbha.*

Yamagumba (Huṇ), *Yeṇagumba* (CRN)

-gūli

Perhaps it is the variant of *kuli/guli* which means a killer.

Hasugūli (Guṇ).

-chatra

The word *chatra* is used in two senses: One, in the sense of an umbrella, and the other, in the sense of a house or a place of refuge. Actually it is the corrupt form of two words chatra and satra of Skt. S (the sibilant of Skt.) is palatalised in Kan. In Kan. it means a place of refuge, a choultry, or a halting place for travellers or strangers. It signifies also a building or spot reserved for distribution of food to Brahmanas and mendicants. In the beginning a Satra may have been erected in an unpopulated spot. Later on, people must have built residential quarters around these institutions which were religious in nature.

Gungrālachatra (Mys), *Chikkānyachatra* (Nan), *Venkaṭaiyanachatra* (CRN).

-jaṭṭi

Jaṭṭi in Kan. means a wrestler. This does not seem to be appropriate here. *Chaṭṭu, chaṭṭa* which mean flatness or levelness may be more appropriate. *Chaṭṭa* is the Tu. equivalent.

Kāḍajeṭṭi (Nan)

-Jāti

Jasminum grandiflorum is the botanical equivalent of this word which is derived from the Skt. word *jāti*.

Kirijati (Huṇ)

-Jāla

Jāla in Skt. means a net, a cobweb, a lattice, a collection, a cover, the sky, the tree Nauclea kadamba. *Jāla,* the Kan. word means the wild thorny Acacia arabica. Here the word is taken in this sense.

Ibbajāla (Nan).

-tale

It means head, or upper most. *Talai* in Tam. means head, top, end, tip, hair. It has its equivalents in all the Drn. languages: *tare* (Tu.) *tala* (Tel.), *tal* (To.), *tal* (Koḷ.).

Haradale (PP)

-taḷale

Taḷal means new leaf, young shoot. It's another variant is *taḷir.* In Tam. and Mal., its equivalent is *taḷir.*

Taḷale (Guṇ).

-tiṭṭu

It means rising ground, bank, elevation, hillock, and is found in almost all the Drn. languages: *Tiṭṭai* (Tam.), *tiṭṭa* (Mal.), *tiṭ* (Ko.), *diḍḍu* (Tu.), *tiṭṭa* (Tel).

Būditiṭṭu (CRN)

-tunga

It is a Skt. word, meaning high, elevated, lofty, prominent.

Rāmanāthatunga (PP)

-tore

Tore is a small stream. In ancient days, people used to establish habitations on the banks of the rivers or streams. Usually the names of the rivers were transferred to the villages. Or the villages used to be called by names suggestive of physical features of the rivers. In Tam. *tore* is used in many senses, including river.

Yeḍatore (KRN), *Yaḍatore* (TNP)

The principle of sonantisation works here also, as elsewhere.

-daḍa

It is a corrupted form of the Skt. word *taṭa* which means a bank, a shore.

Geradaḍa (KRN)

-doḍḍi

Fence, yard, pound, enclosure, small village, stable etc. are the meanings of this generic. originally, there may have been very few enclosures meant for cattle only. By and by, it must have been developed into a residential place. It must have been a small hamlet or even an appurtenance to a big village.

Ganganadoḍḍi (Koḷ.)

-nagara

Nagara is a popular Skt. word which means a city or town. The quantitative content of population determines whether a particular place is a village or a town or a city. Generally, only a trading or industrial centre attracts more and more people. By and by, the original concept of *paṭṭaṇa* and *nagara* is lost and any place, big or small is called by this designation.

Krisṇarājanagara (KRN), *Chānarājanagara* (CRN)

-natta

This is a Tam. generic, not fount in Kan. Tel. also has used this. It means town, village.

Byranatta (Koḷ.)

nandi

Nandi means joy, delight, a son; the bull on which Siva rides; a large timber tree with white bark. It is difficult to determine its meaning in this context. It may indicate either flora or fauna.

Chikkanandi (Heg), *Hirenandi* (Heg)

-nāḷa

A water channel. It is a corrupted form of the Skt. word *nala* or *naḷive*

Kaṭṭemaḷalavāḍināla (Huṇ), *Gōvindanahaḷḷināla* (Huṇ), *Siriyūrunāla* (Huṇ).

-nelli

It is the Drn. word meaning a popular tree. The sane name occurs in many of the languages of this group. The botanical name is Phylanthus emblica.

Kiranelli (PP).

-nēraḷe/nērḷe

It is a common tree with purple berries, *Eugeniajambolana Iam, Nēral* and *nēril* are the original forms of *nerile.* Its variant forms are *nīṛalu, nīrale, nīrle, nēral, nērlu, nērale.* *ṛ* goes out of use in both middle and modern Kan. when the penultimate vowel is dropped in spoken language; it becomes *nērḷe.* The dental *l* changes into *ḷ.*

Chikkanērḷe (PP), *Thammanērḷe* (Nan), *Doḍḍanērḷe* (PP)

-paṭṭaṇa/-paṭṇa

Kittel derives this term from the Skt. word *Paṭṭaṇa,* Caldwell opines that this is a Drn. word. It means a city or town. It is usually a business centre. Śambha Jōshi derives it from the verbal root *'paḍu'* which is used in the sense of settling down or to sink. Many scholars favour the Drn. origin of this word. In Tam. and Tel., *Paṭṭiṇam/ paṭṭaṇam* means a maritime town. In Tu., it means, a coastal town. In Kan. it means any small town.

The phonological changes are that the intermediary ṭ and a are elided, especially in spoken dialect, the resultant form being *paṭṇa.*

Kunnapaṭna (Heg.) *Channapaṭṇa* (Nan), *Periapaṭṇa* (PP), *Basavapaṭṇa* (KRN), *Mādapaṭna* (Guṇ), *Singapaṭṇa* (Heg), *Haravemallaraja paṭṇa* (PP).

-paḷeya/-pāḷya

Kittel opines that it could be connected with *pāli* or *pālya* or *pāḍi*. It is even possible that *paḍu* may be the verbal root from which it could be derived. It may even be associated with *paḷḷi*. In Tam. *pāḷayam* means army, war-camp, village surrounded by hillocks. In Tu., *pāḷya, pāḷyc* means army, halting place. In Tel. it is *pāḷemu*. In Kan. it means an encampment, a camp, a settlement, a hamlet. The term which was used formerly in connection with army camp came to be used later on in relation to any settlement.

Timmegowḍanapāḷya (CRN), *Baṇḍipāḷya* (Mys), *Mūkanapāḷya* (TNP).

-pura/-puri

Pura is a Skt. word. It is used widely in all parts of India and in all regional languages. Of all generics of Skt. origin, this is the only one which is more extensively used than others in Kan. Pura and its variant normally signify a city. But this meaning is sometimes forgotten when it forms part of Kan. VNS. It is used to mean simply a village or a settlement.

The initial p- becomes -v- in a compound.

Among the taluks taken up for the study, -pura is more widely used in CNR than in any other taluks

Mysore taluk:

Kallināthapura, Kīḷanapura, Kemmaṇṇapura, Gujjagowḍanapura, Gōpalapura, Dāripura, Dyāvalapura, Baraḍanapura, Māṇikyapura, Mādapura, Mēgalapura, Lakshmīpura, Lalitādripura, Śakadēvanapura, Siddalingapura, Subrahmaṇyapura, Sōmēswarapura, Vijayaśrīpura.

Krisṇarājapura taluk:

Chāmalāpura, Nārāyaṇapura, Bailāpura, Rāmpura, Venkaṭapura, Sanyāsipura, Siddāpura, Srīrāmapura, Hampāpura.

Kollēgāla taluk:

Ajjipura, Uttamasōḷapura, Timmarājapura, Dāsanapura, Rāmapura, Lakshmīpura, Lingaṇapura, Siddyyanapura, Hampāpura.

Guṇḍlupēṭe taluk

Arepura, Kaṇiyanapura, Kaḷḷipura, Kebbepura, Kelasūrupura, Kellupura, Guruvanapura, Chikkanapura, Chennamallapura, Tōḍipura, Triyambakapura, Dundāsanapura, Dēpapura, Dēvalapura, Dēsipura, Nāraṇapura, Paramapura, Parvatanapura, Pasaiyanapura, Puṭṭanapura, Basavāpura, Bogganapura, Bommalapura, Bhaṇḍipura, Mālāpura, Māyanāyakanapura, Rāghavapura, Ramaiyanapura, Lakkipura, Vaḍiyanapura, Vastilingapura, Vijayapura, Vīranapura, Sampigepura, Siddāpura, Sindanapura, Sīlavantapura, Sōmanapura, Hangaḷapura, Hanchipura, Haḷḷadapura, Huṇasinapura, Huṇḍipura, Hullepura, Hosapura.

Chāmarājanagara taluk:

Ankanaseṭṭipura, Achchaṭṭipura, Aṭṭuguḷipura, Ammanapura, Aināpura, Kaggalipura, Kanagālapura, Kaṭṭepura, Karinanjapura, Kaḷḷipura, Kaḷalipura, Kebbepura, Kempanapura, Kētanapura, Kottanapura, Gāḷipura, Gūḷipura, Channappanapura, Chāṭipura, Jōtigowḍanapura, Dēvarajapura, Dēvalāpura, Doḷḷipura, Nanjedēvanapura, Nandirājapura Puṭṭanapura, Baḍagalapura, Baḍagalupura, Basavaṇapura, Basavāpura, Bastipura, Benḍarapura (?), Beṭṭadapura, Bevinatāḷupura, Bokkepura, Bōgapura, Bhujagnapura, Manchaguṇḍipura, Mallayyanapura, Mallāpura, Masagapura, Masaṇapura, Mūḍalapura, Yeḍapura, Lingaṇapura, Vagarapura, Vīranapura, Voḍḍagālapura, Sappayyanapurà, Singanapura, Sindayyanapura, Śivapura, Seṭṭipura, Sōmanapura, Śrīrangāpura, Hangarepura, Hanchitāḷapura, Hanumanapura, Haraganapura, Hullepura, Heggavāḍipura, Hosapura.

T. Narasipura taluk

Agastyapura, Kallipura, Kempanapura, Kētupura, Kriṣṇarājapura (agrahara), Chikkalakṣhmipura, Ḍaṇayakanapura, Tammaḍipura, Tirumakuḍlu-narasipura, Doḍḍapura, Ḍoḍḍalakṣmipura, Nanjāpura, Basavanapura, Bhairapura, Mādāpura. Māranapura, Mudukanapura, Ranganāthapura, Rāmēgowḍanapura. Lakṣmīpura, Vijayapura, Śivegowḍanapura, Sōmanāthapura, Hosapura.

Nanjanagūḍu taluk

Kakwāḍipura, Kānipura, Kārepura, Karlapura, Kariapura, Kūḍlāpura, Kōṇanapura, Krişṇāpura, Gaṭṭawāḍipura, Goddanapura, Chāmalapura, Dyāvegowḍanapura, Nandiguṇḍapura, Narasipura, Nāganapura, Nellitāḷupura, Basavanapura, Mākanapura, Mādāpura, Mallāpura, Rāmapura, Rāmaseṭṭipura, Lakṣhmaṇapura, Vīradēvanapura, Sinduvaḷḷipura, Hādanūru-voḍeyanapura, Hanumanapura, Hampāpura, Haragaṇapura, Haḷepura, Hārupura, Hosapura.

Piriyapaṭṇa taluk

Ailāpura, Kambipura, Kailāsapura, Kōmaḷapura, Charapura, Timakāpura, Tirumalāpura, Dēpura, Nandipura, Nāraḷāpura, Basalāpura, Beṭṭadapura, Mallināthapura, Rājapura, Lakṣmipura, Lingāpura, Sanyāsipura, Harilapura, Haḷepētekandapura.

Yaḷandūr taluk

Krişṇāpura

Hunsuru taluk

Annarāyanapura, Uḍuvepura, Kamplāpura, Krişṇapura, Tipplāpura, Dāsanapura, Dharmapura, Benkipura, Bommalāpura, Mādāpura, Mallināthapura, Mūḍlāpura, Vāranchigurupura, Haḷepura, Husēnapura.

Heggaḍadēvanakōṭe taluk

Ankapura, Aiyanapura, Kaṇḍegowḍanapura, Kārāpura, Kebbepura, Krişṇarājapura, Chaṭagatipura, Chāmalāpura, Taṇḍasipura, Dāsanapura, Dēvalāpura, Dyāvalāpura, Nanjanāthapura, Nandināthapura, Narasipura, Pura, Bairapura, Bomblāpura, Mallarājanapura, Mādāpura, Mārabhugutanapura, Lakṣhmaṇapura, Siddāpura, Siddāpura, Suṇḍēpura, Soḷḷēpura, Syantanapura (?), Hanchipura, Hampāpura, Hariyālapura, Huraḷipura, Heggaḍapura.

-peṭlu

It is the name of a plant whose botanical name is Sida mauritiana herit. It's other variant is *peṭṭalu.*

Mūlepeṭlu (KRN)

-*pēṭe*

Pēṭe means an emporium, a mart, a market town, a place of sale, a long street of shops in a town. It is likely that it may have been borrowed from *Marāṭhi pētha pēnṭha.* It is found in almost all the major languages of the Drn. family. It is *pēṭṭai* in Tam., *pēṭṭa* in Mal., and *pēṇṭa* in Tel. The verbal root from which *paṭṭi, paṭṭana* and *pāḍi* are derived, i.e., *paḍu* could be associated with *pēṭe* also. Sometimes the final vowel is lost due to foreign influence.

Guṇḍlupēṭe (Guṇ), *Sōmavārapēt* (CRN).

-*bāgilu*

Bāgilu denotes gate, doorway. Its variant forms are *bāgil, bāgal, bākal.* Its ancient form is *vāyil.* Its variant forms in the other Drn. languages are: *vāyil, vāyal* (Tam.), *vāṭel* (Mal.), *bākilu* (Tu.), *vākili* (Tel.)

In compounds 'b' becomes 'v' *Niluvāgilu* (Heg), *Niluvāgilu* (Huṇ), *Hiṭṭe Hebbāgalu* (PP)?

-*bāḷu/-vāḷu/-vālu*

Bāḷu may perhaps be derived from the root *bāḷ* which means to live, to live prosperously. The variant of bāḷ whose connotation is to live, to subsist, to make a livelihood. One of the noun forms of *bālu* is *bāḷe* which means cultivation of soil. It is in this sense the present generic is used. The old Kan. *ḷ* changes into *ḷ* in middle Kan. *Bāḷu,* therefore, means cultivated land. b- changes into -v- in the intervocalic position.

Ānivāḷu (PP), *Āswāḷu* (TNP, PP), *Induvāḷu* (TNP), *Kāṭavāḷu* (Heg), *Bīravāḷu* (Heg), *Būdabāḷu* (Koḷ), *Voḍḍambāḷu* (Huṇ), *Sīgavāḷu* (KRN), *Sunḍawāḷu* (PP), *Syābāḷu* (KRN), *Haginavāḷu* (Nan), *Hatwāḷu* (Heg), *Hebbāḷu* (Mys), *Hebbāḷu* (KRN), *Honḍarabāḷu* (CRN).

-*biḷugali/-beḷugali*

-*bīḍu*

Bīḍu is found in almost all the Drn. languages both as a generic and a free form, with its variants. It means settlement, habitation, house, camp, halting place, uncultivated waste land. Its equivalent in Tam., Mal. and Tel. is *Vīḍu* and *būḍu* in Tu.

The phonological change generally noticeable in this generic is that the initial -b changes into -v- in the intervocalic position

Ayarabīḍu (PP), *Gollanabīḍu* (Heg), *Beṭṭadabīḍu* (Heg), *Bhīmanabīḍu* (Guṇ), *Maḍuvinabīḍu* (CRN), *Mūḍlubīḍu* (KRN), *Haḷebīḍu* (Huṇ), *Hosavīḍu* (Nan).

-bīdi

Bīdi is supposed to have been derived from the Skt. word *Vīdhi*. It means a street, a lane, a row. A village comes into existence along with its street which acquires some name. Later on, the street name is applied to the village also

Chandrabīḍu (Mys). This is an incongruous compound, i.e. *Arisamāsa*.

-beṭṭa

Beṭṭa means hill or mountain. One Pn which has *beṭṭa* as generic is actually situated on the hill.

Chāmuṇḍibeṭṭa (Mys)

-bele

It means price, cost. It's Tam. counterpart is *Vilai,* and Tel., *Vela.*

Hāgadabele (CRN)

-besage

With its variant form besuge, it means soldering and the root of the ear (KED). It also means a cot-like thing, on which pots are arranged in the kitchen.

Chikkabesage (Heg)

-byāḷaḷu

Bayal > Byāl + āḷu. See *āḷu*

Chikkabyālāḷu (PP), *Doḍḍabyālāḷu* (PP)

magge

Maggu or magge means bud. *Moge* means a fertile, yellowish soil. Magge could be derived from either of these two words.

Magge (Heg), *Haḷemagge* (Heg)

-maṭha

This is a Skt. word which signifies a hut, a cottage, a residence of a company of ascetics, a residence of a guru, a school.

Heḷavaramaṭha (TNP)

-mattaru

A measure or quantity of land

Yalemattaru (Heg)

-matti

It is the name of a timber tree, *Vaṭica robusṭa* stend. It is Arjuna in Skt.

Bemmatti (PP): Beḷ + matti

-male

Male is a synonym of *beṭṭa.* It is a Drn. word. The cognates in the other Drn. languages are: *malai* (Tam.), *male* (Kod.), *male* (Tu.), *mala* (Tel.), *Mālē* (Ke.).

Aḷagumale (Alagumūle) (Koḷ)

-maḷali

It is a small fish, called also *maḷḷi. Maḷali Vasanthakumar* says that this word is found in *Rāghavanka,* a poet of the 13th century A.D.

Chikkamaḷali (PP), *Maḷali* (KRN), *Maḷali* (Heg)

-mangaḷa/-mangala

Mangala is a Skt. word. It means good fortune, success, auspiciousness, prosperity, bliss: Any happy event, any festive occasion, anything tending to a lucky issue, a good omen. Villages that end with the generic *mangala* are akin to *agrahāras,* granted by kings to Brahmans. *Mangaḷa* villages were formerly conferred on Brahmans well-versed in vedas. This custom comes into existence during the reign of the Chola kings. Even after the Brahmans abandoned these villages, the appendages remain intact. The concept of *mangaḷa* is discussed in Epigraphia Indica, Vol. XXV (pp. 75-76). Villages with this generic are also found in *Tamil Nāḍū* and *Andhra Pradesh,* besides *Karṇāṭaka.* Mangala is exclusively used as a village name also.

Narasamangala (CRN), *Mangala* (Guṇ), *Mangala* (CRN), *Vājamangala* (Mys).

-māvu

The word means mango which again is of Drn. origin. It is *mā* in Tam. and Mal., *mānge* in Kod., *māvi* in Tel., *māmri* in NK.

Places where special varieties of mango are available or where it is grown in large quantities are named after this tree. The same argument holds good in respect of all places which bear the names of animals and plants.

Immāvu (Nan), *Toremāvu* (nan), *Huḷimāvu* (Nan).

-māḷa

It means a plain or an extended tract of land.

Āne māḷa (Heg), *Mēlmāḷa* (CRN), *Yalemāḷa* (KRN), *Vaḍakinamāḷa* (Heg), *Hullemāḷa* (Heg).

-mudlu

The meaning is not clear. Could it be a variant of *muttalu* which means environing, surrounding (DED).

Byāḍamudlu (CRN)

-mūle

Mūle signifies a corner, an angle; a point of compass. Its equivalents in other Drn. languages are: *mūlai* (Tam.), *mūla* (Mal.), *Mūl* (Ko.), *mūle* (Tu.), *mūla* (Tel.).

Mugatanamūle (Heg).

-mūḷe/-mōḷe

Mōḷe, according to Kittel, is a small hole (made by crabs etc) in the banks of rice fields or tanks. It also means a pile or heap. In rural areas, it is used in the sense of a small spring also. There is no equivalent in other Drn. lang DED gives *muṟai* as the Tam. equivalent.

Kōḍimōḷe (CRN), *Doḍḍamōḷe* (CRN).

-vaṭṭige

Paṭṭige > haṭṭige means an abode. -p- and -h- of *pattige > hattige* change into -v- in compounds.

Basavaṭṭige (Nan).

-vatta

It is a corrupted form of the Skt. word patre which means leaf.

Belavatta (Mys)

-pāḍi/-vāḍa/-vāḍi-vāḍila

There are the variant forms of one and the same generic which is derived from a verbal root *'paḍu'*. *Paḍu* means to occur, happen, acquire, a place of refuge. Of these four variants *-pāḍi* is the earliest. p- changes into -v-. Later on v- continues to stay in the initial position also. These generics signify a settlement or a habitation. p- changes into -b- sometimes, specially when it is preceded by a nasal.

In Tam., *Pāḍi* means town, hamlet, pastoral village. In Kod. it means a hut of a Kuruba. *Pāḍu* in Tel. means a village.

Amachavāḍi (CRN), *Amachavāḍi* (Mys), *Arakalawāḍi* (CRN), *Ālawāḍi* (Guṇ), *Irasavāḍi* (CRN), *Undavāḍi* (Huṇ), *Kaṭṭevāḍi* (Huṇ), *Kaṭṇavāḍi* (CRN), *Kaṇidavāḍi* (CRN), *Kamaravāḍi* (CRN), *Kāravāḍi* (Heg), *Kaḷalavāḍi* (Mys) *Kaḷastavāḍi* (Mys), *Kāgalavāḍi* (CRN), *Kottavāḍi* (Huṇ), *Kottalavāḍi* (CRN), *Kōgilavāḍi* (PP), *Gangavāḍi* (CRN), *Gaṭṭavāḍi* (Nan), *Gōvindavāḍi* (CRN), *Chandakawāḍi* (CRN), *Toṭṭavāḍi* (TNP), *Toṇḍavāḍi* (Guṇ), *Nīlavāḍi* (PP), *Bankavāḍi* (Heg), *Banagavāḍi* (TN), *Bannavāḍi* (Guṇ), *Baraḍavāḍi* (Huṇ), *Balachavāḍi* (Guṇ), *Bāṇasavāḍi* (Guṇ), *Bisalavāḍi* (CRN), *Beṇḍaravāḍi* (Guṇ), *Beṇḍaravāḍi* (CRN), *Beḷachalavāḍi* (Guṇ), *Beḷavāḍi* (Guṇ), *Beḷavāḍi* (Mys), *Bērambāḍi* (Gun), *Maḷalavāḍi* (Huṇ), *Maḷalavāḍi* (Mys), *Mādavāḍi* (TNP), *Mādalavāḍi* (CRN), *Muttalavāḍi* (TNP), *Vundavāḍi* (Mys), *Singavāḍi* (Guṇ), *Singavāḍi* (Heg), *Huṇasavāḍi* (PP), *Heggavāḍi* (CRN), *Heggavāḍi* (Guṇ), *Hongalavāḍi* (CRN), *Hoḷalavāḍi* (Nan).

-vāla/-vāra

It means tail in Skt. It may be conjectured that it is a variant of vāra (vide āra).

Ilwāla (Mys), *Nāgavāla* (Mys), *Bīrvāla* (Heg).

-vāḷa/-vālu

Vāḷa is an affix for the formation of masculine nouns in the sense of possession. *Vāḷa* is derived from *vaḷa.*

Biravāḷa (Heg).

-vēdi

There is no certainty about the exact style of the generic - whether it is *vēdi,* or *vidhi,* or *vīdhi.* The name as a whole is an incongruous compound. Further investigation is needed.

Iruvēdi (Heg)

-samudra

This is one of a very few Skt. words. used as generic in Kan. VNS. Sometimes its form is distorted and the changed form reads as sandra. *Sandra* is, however, not found in the VNS of this area.

Samudra means an ocean or a sea. But in these VNS it signifies any embankment, however big or small.

Rangasamudra (TNP), *Rāmasamudra* (CRN), *Sōmasamudra* (CRN)

-sante

It means an assemblage, a mass, a gathering of buyers and sellers, a fair, or a market. Scholars are of the opinion that it is derived from the Skt. word samstha. It requires investigation.

Antarasante (Heg)

sārige

A field which is plain and oblong is called *sārige.*

Bannisārige (Yal)

-sāl/-sālu

It signifies a continuous line, a row, a furrow, a mass, a multitude. It is found in other Drn. languages in slightly modified forms. *Cāl* (Tam., Mal.), *Sōl* (To.), *Cālli* (Kod.), *Sālu* (Tul.), *Cālu* (Tel.). In Tel. it means a grove or a track.

Hoḷesāl (TNP). It means a row of houses on the bank of a stream.

-soḍlu

Soḍlu means lamp. Various forms of *Soḍlu* viz. *Soḍar, Soḍaru, Soḍalu* are also in vogue. *Soḍal* seems to be the earliest form which is derived from the verbal root *suḍu* = to burn. *-al* is the nominal suffix. When the end vowel is added, the penultimate vowel is elided. The verbal root *suḍu* with all its derivations are available in all the Drn. languages.

Kirasoḍlu (Huṇ), *Hejjoḍlu* (Huṇ).

-sōge

Sōge means leaf of palms; a peacock's feather. *Tōkai*. its equivalent in Tam. has the following meanings: tail of peacock, plantain stem: *Tōka* (Mal.). *Tōke* (Ko.). Another form of *sōge* in Kan. is *tōke*. The existence of peacocks in abundance is the reason for naming certain VNS as such.

Kōḍasōge (Guṇ), *Channasōge* (Huṇ), *Tumbasōge* (Heg), *Nīlasōge* (TNP), *Lakkasōge* (Heg).

-haṭṭi/-paṭṭi

Paṭṭi of OK becomes *haṭṭi* in the MK period. *Paṭṭi* which is derived from *paḍu* to lie, to settle, which means cow stall, sheepfold, hamlet, is found in all the Drn. languages. In the intermediary position -h becomes -v-.

Kakkarahaṭṭi (Nan), *Karahaṭṭi* (Nan), *Kurihaṭṭi* (Nan), *Duggahaṭṭi* (Yal). *Hasuvaṭṭi* (TNP).

-hanta

Hanta means a stair, a step or a stage. There seems to be no parallels in other cognate languages. Generally. VNS with *hanta* as their generics are found distributed, where channel system is in existence. The following VNS are found in KRN taluk only.

Kappaḍihanta (KRN), *Kātnālhanta* (KRN), *Kuppehanta* (KRN), *Koluruhanta* (KRN), *Chandagālhanta* (KRN), *Byaḍarahaḷḷihanta* (KRN), *Māvatturuhanta* (KRN), *Hanasōgchanta* (KRN), *Hāḍyada hanta* (KRN).

-harave

It may be posited that it could be derived either from *haravi,* an earthen water vessel or *haravu,* to spread out. The latter seems to be more tenable than the former. It cannot be related to 'arive' which means a plant or cloth.

Doddaharave (PP), *Harave* (CRN), *Harave* (Huṇ)

-haḷḷa

Paḷḷa is the OK form of *haḷḷa.* It means a pit, a hole in the ground, a stream. It is found in all the major languages of the Drn. family. Tam., *paḷḷam* means low level, valley and ditch; Tel. *paḷḷamu* means pit or low ground.

Karaḍihaḷḷa (CRN)

-haḷḷi

More than thirty per cent of VNS have *haḷḷi* as their generics. In old Kannada it was *paḷḷi.* It is supposed to have been derived from the Skt. *paḷḷi.* It is also possible that *haḷi* is a word which the people speaking the Skt. language may have borrowed from Drn. Its primary meaning is a settlement, a hamlet, or a headman's village. It must have acquired many other meanings in course of time, such as hut, house etc. According to caldwell this word, like *paṭṭa* comes from Drn. *paḍu* (KED XX). *H* is sometimes elided in the compounds the initial consonant.

Mysore taluk

Anagaḷḷi, Ayarahaḷḷi, Aragowḍanahaḷḷi, Ālanahaḷḷi, Uttanahaḷḷi, Kammaravaḷḷi, Karakanahaḷḷi, Kallahaḷḷi, Kallūrunāganahaḷḷi, Kukkarahaḷḷi, Kuntanahaḷḷi, Kumbārahaḷḷi, Kurubarahaḷḷi, Kūdanahaḷḷi,

Kōchanahaḷḷi, Kyātamāranahaḷḷi, Guḍamādanahaḷḷi, Gumachahaḷḷi. Gōhaḷḷi, Chaṭṭanahaḷḷi. Chaṭnahaḷḷi, Chāmanahaḷḷi Chikkanahaḷḷi, Chikkaharadanahaḷḷi, Chikkahaḷḷi, Chōranahaḷḷi. Chōḷenahaḷḷi, Chowḍahaḷḷi. Jatagaḷḷi, Javanahaḷḷi, Jōganahaḷḷi, Daṭṭagaḷḷi, Daḍadahaḷḷi, Daḍadakallahaḷḷi, Danagaḷḷi. Dēvagaḷḷi, Doḍḍamāragowḍanahaḷḷi, Nagartahaḷḷi, Nāganahaḷḷi, Nāchanahaḷḷi, Nāḍanahaḷḷi, Nandagaḷḷi, Nuggehaḷḷi, Paḍuvārahaḷḷi, Pillahaḷḷi, Ballahaḷḷi, Basavanahaḷḷi, Bommanahaḷḷi, Byāṭahaḷḷi. Bhugatahaḷḷi, Manḍakaḷḷi, Manḍanahaḷḷi, Marātikyātanahaḷḷi, Mādagaḷḷi, Mādahaḷḷi, Mādaragaḷḷi. Māragowḍanahaḷḷi, Mārabaḷḷi, Mārasеṭṭihaḷḷi, Māvinahaḷḷi, Mēṭagaḷḷi, Mosanabayanahaḷḷi, Yanḍahaḷḷi, Yaraganahaḷḷi, Yalachaḷḷi, Yāchagowḍanahaḷḷi, Yeḍahaḷḷi, Ratnahaḷḷi, Rāmanahaḷḷi. Syāḍanahaḷḷi, Seṭṭanāyakanahaḷḷi, Sātagaḷḷi, Sindavaḷḷi. Hārohaḷḷi, Hunnavaḷḷi. Hūṭagaḷḷi, Hemmanahaḷḷi, Hosahaḷḷi.

Krişṇarājanagara Taluk

Ankanaḷḷi, Aḍaganahaḷḷi, Arjunahaḷḷi, Aichanahaḷḷi, Kanaganahaḷḷi. Kanchanahaḷḷi. Kantenahaḷḷi, Karpūravaḷḷi, Kallahaḷḷi, Kaḷḷimuddanahaḷḷi. Kākanahaḷḷi, Kāmēnahaḷḷi, Kāḷēnahaḷḷi, Kuppahaḷḷi, Kurubahaḷḷi, Kōchanahaḷḷi, Gandenahaḷḷi, Gandhanahaḷḷi, Gāyanahaḷḷi. Guduganahaḷḷi, Gummanahaḷḷi, Chikkanāyakanahaḷḷi, Chibukahaḷḷi. Chīranahaḷḷi, Dammanahaḷḷi, Diḍḍahaḷḷi, Deggavaḷḷi, Doḍḍahaḷḷi. Dōranahaḷḷi, Nātanahaḷḷi, Naḍapanahaḷḷi, Narachanahaḷḷi. Nijaganahaḷḷi. Baṭiganahaḷḷi, Banḍahaḷḷi, Bāchahaḷḷi, Bīchanahaḷḷi, Bīranahaḷḷi. Bīrambaḷḷi, Buvanahaḷḷi, Beṭṭahaḷḷi, Beṭṭiganahaḷḷi. Bēvinahaḷḷi. Bōmmēnahaḷḷi, Byāḍarahaḷḷi, Manchanahaḷḷi, Manuganahaḷḷi, Manḍiganahaḷḷi, Maluganahaḷḷi, Mallahaḷḷi, Mādavanahaḷḷi, Mādahaḷḷi, Māyigowḍanahaḷḷi, Māragowḍanahaḷḷi, Mārchahaḷḷi, Malanayakanahaḷḷi. Muniyanahaḷḷi, Yaramanuganahaḷḷi, Yelemuddanahaḷḷi, Yalladahaḷḷi, Vaḍḍarahaḷḷi, Vaḷagerehaḷḷi. Lāḷanahaḷḷi, Lāḷandēvanahaḷḷi, Sankanahaḷḷi. Sambrahaḷḷi, Sātanahaḷḷi, Sugganahaḷḷi, Sōmanahaḷḷi, Hangrabōyanahaḷḷi. Hanumanahaḷḷi, Haradanahaḷḷi, Hārambaḷḷi, Huraḷikāmēnahaḷḷi, Honnēnahaḷḷi. Hosahaḷḷi.

Koḷḷēgāla taluk

Ikkaḍahaḷḷi, Uttambaḷḷi, Kanchaḷḷi, Kandaḷḷi, Gowḍahaḷḷi, Channalinganahaḷḷi. Chinchaḷḷi, Chengadarahaḷḷi, Jakkaḷḷi. Jakkaṇahaḷḷi.

Tērambaḷḷi, Dantaḷḷi, Baṇḍaḷḷi, Bhadrāyyanahaḷḷi, Manuganahaḷḷi, Madhuvanahaḷḷi, Māṛtaḷḷi, Mōḍaḷḷi, Lokkanahaḷḷi, Seṭṭihaḷḷi.

Guṇḍlupēṭe taluk

Agatagowḍanahaḷḷi, Ankahaḷḷi, Kabbahaḷḷi, Kamarahaḷḷi, Karakalamādahaḷḷi, Kallahaḷḷi, Kaligowḍanahaḷḷi, Kuṇagahaḷḷi, Kōdahaḷḷi, Kuṇagaḷḷi (Koḷ), *Garaganahaḷḷi, Chikkanahaḷḷi, Chirakanahaḷḷi, Toravaḷḷi, Dēvarahaḷḷi, Panjanahaḷḷi, Ballahaḷḷi, Bāchanahaḷḷi, Bāchchaḷḷi, Bēṭṭadamādahaḷḷi, Beṭṭahaḷḷi, Beṇḍagaḷḷi, Bommanahaḷḷi, Managahaḷḷi, Maguvanahaḷḷi, Manchahaḷḷi, Malavaḷḷi, Marihōsahaḷḷi, Masahaḷḷi, Mādahaḷḷi, Mādarahaḷḷi, Māyanāyakanahaḷḷi, Mūkahaḷḷi, Maidānahaḷḷi, Yaḍayanahaḷḷi, Vaḍḍanahosahaḷḷi, Vaḍḍarahaḷḷi, Savakanahaḷḷi, Seṭṭihaḷḷi, Sōmahaḷḷi, Syanāḍrahaḷḷi, Hangaḷahosahaḷḷi, Hadanahaḷḷi, Haḷḷadamādahaḷḷi, Heggaḍahaḷḷi, Hoṇakahaḷḷi, Hongehaḷḷi, Honnegowḍanahaḷḷi.*

Chāmarājanagara taluk

Uttahaḷḷi, Karaḍihaḷḷi, Kanchanahaḷḷi, Kadahaḷḷi, Kuṇachavaḷḷi, Kerehaḷḷi, Kellambaḷḷi, Kētahaḷḷi Kokkanahaḷḷi, Koṭaganahaḷḷi, Kōtambaḷḷi, Chowḍahaḷḷi, Tammaḍahaḷḷi, Dēmahaḷḷi, Dēsavaḷḷi, Nanjavaḷḷi, Bandigowḍanahaḷḷi, Bāṇahaḷḷi, Būdambaḷḷi, Beṭṭahaḷḷi, Bommaṇahaḷḷi, Managaṇahaḷḷi, Malladēvanahaḷḷi, Mādigaḷḷi, Mukkaḍahaḷḷi, Mūkahaḷḷi, Mūḍaluhosahaḷḷi, Muṇachanahaḷḷi, Yanagaḷḷi, Yeragaṇahaḷḷi, Rēchambaḷḷi, Vaḍḍarahaḷḷi, Santemarahaḷḷi, Hamahaḷḷi, Handrakaḷḷi, Haradahaḷḷi, Honnegowḍanahaḷḷi, Honnahaḷḷi, Hosahaḷḷi.

Tirumakūḍalu Narasipura taluk

Ankanahaḷḷi, Attahaḷḷi, Ādibeṭṭahaḷḷi, Kannahaḷḷi, Kannāyakanahaḷḷi, Kayyambaḷḷi, Kāragahaḷḷi, Kuṇṭanahaḷḷi, Kenchanahaḷḷi, Kētahaḷḷi, Koḍagahaḷḷi, Kongahaḷḷi, Kyātanahaḷḷi, Goravanahaḷḷi, Chāndahaḷḷi, Chāmanahaḷḷi, Chikkabūhaḷḷi, Chidaravaḷḷi, Chouhaḷḷi, Narakyātanahaḷḷi, Pillahaḷḷi, Bannahaḷḷi, Basavanahaḷḷi, Binakanahaḷḷi, Bīḍanahaḷḷi, Būdahaḷḷi, Beṭṭahaḷḷi, Bēvinahaḷḷi, Bommanahaḷḷi, Bommanāyakanaḥaḷḷi, Maḍrahaḷḷi,, Mādigahaḷḷi, Māragowḍanahaḷḷi, Māvinahaḷḷi, Meṇasinahaḷḷi, Yaragaṇahaḷḷi, Yāchanahaḷḷi, Yeḍahaḷḷi, Vaḍeyaṇḍanahaḷḷi, Sīhaḷḷi, Seṭṭihaḷḷi, Sēnāpatihaḷḷi, Hiṭṭavaḷḷi, Huṇaganahaḷḷi, Huṇasahaḷḷi, Horaḷahaḷḷi, Hosahaḷḷi.

Nanjanagūḍu taluk

Aḍakanahaḷḷi, Amakahaḷḷi, Īśwaragowḍanahaḷḷi, Uppēnahaḷḷi, Kallahaḷḷi, Kalmahaḷḷi, Kasavanahaḷḷi, Kāmanahaḷḷi, Kāḷadēvanahaḷḷi, Kāhaḷḷi, Kupparavaḷḷi, Kummara (Kumbāra) haḷḷi, Kongahaḷḷi, Kōtanahaḷḷi, Gīkahaḷḷi, Gejjaganahaḷḷi, Gonnana (Gōna) haḷḷi, Chāmanamādanahaḷḷi, Chinnambaḷḷi, Chunchanahaḷḷi, Jālahaḷḷi, Taraganahaḷḷi Toravaḷḷi, Duggahaḷḷi, Dēvarasanahaḷḷi, Dēvīrammannihaḷḷi, Paḍavalamarahaḷḷi, Bankahaḷḷi, Bokkahaḷḷi, Madhuvanahaḷḷi, Mallahaḷḷi, Mādanahaḷḷi, Bankaḷḷi, Mādahaḷḷi, Muddanahaḷḷi, Mūḍahaḷḷi, Meḷḷagaḷḷi, Yaḍahaḷḷi, Yelachahaḷḷi, Yelahaḷḷi, Rāyagowḍanahaḷḷi, Varahaḷḷi, Siramaḷḷi, Sindhuvaḷḷi, Surahaḷḷi, Seṭṭagaḷḷi, Haniyamballi, Handavana (dhuvina) haḷḷi, Hullahaḷḷi, Heggaḍahaḷḷi.

Piriyapaṭṇa taluk

Ankanahaḷḷi, Ālnahaḷḷi, Iṭṭagaḷḷi, Uttēnahaḷḷi, Aitanahaḷḷi, Ayichanahaḷḷi, Kachōnahaḷḷi (jungle), Kavalanahaḷḷi, Kāmanahaḷḷi, Kāletimmanahaḷḷi, Kunnanahaḷḷi, Kutavaḷḷi, Kōḍahaḷḷi, Korlahosahaḷḷi, Gangādharabasavanahaḷḷi, Guḍibhadranahaḷḷi, Guḍḍenahaḷḷi, Guḷēdahaḷḷi, Gollarahosahaḷḷi, Gorahaḷḷi, Chapparadahaḷḷi, Channēnahaḷḷi, Chāvunḍēnahaḷḷi, Chikkamaravaḷḷi, Chētanahaḷḷi, Jōganahaḷḷi, Tōtanahaḷḷi, Tammaḍihaḷḷi, Doḍḍakamaravaḷḷi, Nāganahaḷḷi, Panchavaḷḷi, Pūnāḍahaḷḷi, Basavanahaḷḷi, Bilahaḷḷi, Bōganahaḷḷi, Bhuvanahaḷḷi, Bhūtanahaḷḷi, Manchadēvanahaḷḷi, Manuganahaḷḷi, Mākanahaḷḷi, Muddanahaḷḷi, Mellahaḷḷi, Seṭṭahaḷḷi, Śānbhōganahaḷḷi, Sangaraseṭṭihaḷḷi, Sunkadahaḷḷi, Haraḷahaḷḷi, Harinahaḷḷi, Hāranahaḷḷi, Hiṭnahaḷḷi, Hulaganahaḷḷi, Hosahaḷḷi.

Yaḷandūru taluk

Avalakandahaḷḷi, Komāranahaḷḷi, Gowḍahaḷḷi, Dēvarahaḷḷi, Duyamakandahaḷḷi, Bīchahaḷḷi, Mallaganahaḷḷi, Mellahaḷḷi, Sivakahaḷḷi, Yaragambaḷḷi.

Huṇasuru taluk

Ankanahaḷḷi, Angaṭahaḷḷi, Aḍiyanahaḷḷi, Arēhaḷḷi, Airahaḷḷi, Uyagowḍanahaḷḷi, Uyigowḍanahaḷḷi, Karimuddanahaḷḷi, Kallahaḷḷi, Kāḍemanuganahaḷḷi, Kāmēgowḍanahaḷḷi, Kāḷabōchanahaḷḷi,

Kuḍinīrumuddanahaḷḷi, Kurubarahosahaḷḷi, Kenchēnahaḷḷi, Kempanahaḷḷi, Keḷaganahaḷḷi, Kōḍihaḷḷi, Kōnanāhosahaḷḷi, Gāgēnahaḷḷi, Guḍḍaseṭṭihaḷḷi, Gerasanahaḷḷi, Gōvindanahaḷḷi, Gōhaḷḷi, Challahaḷḷi, Chikkakāḍanahaḷḷi, Chikkyātanahaḷḷi, Chikkabīchanahaḷḷi, Jinahaḷḷi, Tammadahaḷḷi, Dēvanahaḷḷi, Doḍḍakāḍanahaḷḷi, Doḍḍabīchanahaḷḷi, Dyāvarahaḷḷi, Nāgarahaḷḷi, Nāḍappanahaḷḷi, Pinnikyātanahaḷḷi, Ballēnahaḷḷi, Bastimādahaḷḷi, Billarahosahaḷḷi, Bīchaganahaḷḷi, Bīratammanahaḷḷi, Bīranahaḷḷi, Būcha (Bocha) haḷḷi, Bōganahaḷḷi, Bōḷanahaḷḷi, Managanahaḷḷi, Manuganahaḷḷi, Manchabōyanahaḷḷi, Mādanahaḷḷi, Mādahaḷḷi, Māragowḍanahaḷḷi, Māranahaḷḷi, Mūkanahaḷḷi, Muttarāyanahosahaḷḷi, Yalachanahaḷḷi, Rāmenahaḷḷi, Rāyanahaḷḷi, Vaḍimanuganahaḷḷi, Vaḍḍarahaḷḷi, Vīranahosahaḷḷi, Sankahaḷḷi, Saṭṭahaḷḷi, Śambhugowḍanahaḷḷi, Śhivēnahaḷḷi, Śravaṇahaḷḷi, Saṇṇēnahaḷḷi, Sabbanahaḷḷi, Singamāranahaḷḷi, Sindanahaḷḷi, Seṭṭihaḷḷi, Sōnahaḷḷi, Sōmanahaḷḷi, Hagaranahaḷḷi, Haṇḍitavaḷḷi, Handanahaḷḷi, Haradanahaḷḷi, Haralahaḷḷi, Harīnahaḷḷi, Haḷḷadakallahaḷḷi, Hirikyātanahaḷḷi, Honnēnahaḷḷi, Hosahaḷḷi.

Heggaḍadēvanakōṭe taluk

Akkadavanahaḷḷi, Aḍahaḷḷi, Aḷalahaḷḷi, Uyambaḷḷi, Kaṭṭemanuganahaḷḷi, Kanakanahaḷḷi, Kanchanahaḷḷi, Kaṇḍegowḍanahaḷḷi, Kannēnahaḷḷi, Kālambaḷḷi, Kenchanahaḷḷi, Kētahaḷḷi, Kōdichāmanahaḷḷi, Kallegowḍanahaḷḷi, Kōhaḷḷi, Kyātahaḷḷi, Gangaḍahaḷḷi, Gangaḍahosahaḷḷi, Guḍamānahaḷḷi, Gowḍamanchanahaḷḷi, Chanḍahaḷḷi, Channagowḍanahaḷḷi, Chākahaḷḷi, Chākōḍahaḷḷi, Chāmanahaḷḷi, Chinnahaḷḷi, Chillahaḷḷi, Chōṭanahaḷḷi, Chowḍahaḷḷi, Jampahaḷḷi, Timmanahosahaḷḷi, Telugamasana (masa) haḷḷi, Toravaḷḷi, Nanjanāyakanahaḷḷi, Nāganahaḷḷi, Nēmanahaḷḷi, Penjahaḷḷi, Bāchagowḍanahaḷḷi, Bidarahaḷḷi, Bīchanahaḷḷi, Bīrambaḷḷi, Beṭṭahaḷḷi, Beḷaganahaḷḷi, Boppanahaḷḷi, Bhīmanahaḷḷi, Manchahaḷḷi, Manchanāyakanahaḷḷi, Manchegowḍanahaḷḷi, Managanahaḷḷi, Manuganahaḷḷi, Mallahaḷḷi, Masahaḷḷi, Mārchahaḷḷi, Muddanahaḷḷi, Linganahaḷḷi, Vaḍērahaḷḷi, Sankahaḷḷi, Sambhugowḍanahaḷḷi, Sindēnahaḷḷi, Siramahaḷḷi, Sōgahaḷḷi, Sōnahaḷḷi, Haḷemanchanahaḷḷi, Hālanahaḷḷi, Hirihaḷḷi, Hirehaḷḷi, Huṇasahaḷḷi, Hunaganahaḷḷi, Heggaḍahaḷḷi, Hommaragaḷḷi, Horamaraḷi (Horamahaḷḷi) Hosahaḷḷi.

The initial p- of *paḷḷi* in OK changes into h- as in *haḷḷi* in MK. This phonemic change generally conforms to the usual grammatical laws governing the transformation of OK into MK. Other morphophonemic changes are also observed and they appear in the forms noted below:

Vaḷḷi, Gaḷḷi, Gaḷi.

-hādi

Hādi is used in the sense of a road, a way etc. It is derived from the verbal root *pāy* which means to jump over, stepover, cross, jump, leap, advances go.

Nāḍahāḍi (Heg)

-hāḷu/āḷu

Pāḷ which is the earliest form of *Hāḷu* always means ruin, desolation, damage, evil, wasteland, in all the Drn. languages. VNS with this generic are surrounded by cultivated lands. Could it be possible to derive the same from *bāḷu* in which case b- becomes h-? *Hāḷu* at present has to be taken in the sense of wasteland. The aspirate h- tends to change into a- especially in compounds. Thus

pāl > hālu > hāḷu > āḷu

Kāṭnāḷu (KRN), *Kāṭnāḷu* (KRN), *Kirāḷu* (Mys), *Tonḍāḷu* (Huṇ), *Doḷḷāḷu* (Huṇ), *Doḍḍabyāḷāḷu* (PP), *Bavalālu* (Nan), *Vāṭāḷu* (TNP), *Hanumanāḷu* (TNP), *Huṇasanāḷu* (Nan), *Hullehāḷu* (Huṇ).

-huṇḍi

The generic *-pūṇḍi* is found in VNS of *Tamiḷ Nāḍu*. It means a village, a town, a district. (Tam. Lexion, P.2830). It is found in the same form in Tel. also. It sometimes, denotes smaller village appended to bigger villages. Later it became an independent village. In Kan, the initial consonant p- is changed into h- and the first vowel gets shortened.

VNS with this generic occur only in Mysore, Heg, TNP, CRN and Nan taluks. They are found in larger number in Heg taluk than in any other taluk.

Agasanahuṇḍi (Heg), *Ayyajjayyanahuṇḍi* (Mys), *Uganēdahuṇḍi* (CRN), *Kaṭṭehuṇḍi* (Heg), *Kaṇiyanahuṇḍi* (Heg), *Kārehuṇḍi* (Heg), *Kurihuṇḍi* (Nan), *Kōnēgowḍanahuṇḍi* (Heg), *Jeṭṭihuṇḍi* (Mys), *Nāyakanahuṇḍi* (Heg), *Neṭṭakalluhuṇḍi* (Heg), *Puṭṭegowḍanahuṇḍi* (Mys), *Peṭṭehuṇḍi* (TNP), *Beṭṭatāvarehuṇḍi* (Heg), *Maṇegāranahuṇḍi* (Heg), *Mādigowḍanahuṇḍi* (TRN), *Muddayyanahuṇḍi* (Heg), *Yelahuṇḍi* (Heg), *Rājagowḍanahuṇḍi* (Heg), *Rāmanāthapuradahuṇḍi* (TNP), *Śīvanahuṇḍi* (Heg), *Sīmēgowḍanahuṇḍi* (Heg), *Hosahuṇḍi* (Mys), *Hoḷehuṇḍi* (Heg).

-hoḷalu

The OK form of this generic is *poḻal* which means a dwelling place, town, city. Medial -p/-g changes into -v-. Its equivalents in Tam. and Tel. respectively are *poḻil* and *prōlu.*

Hosahoḷalu (Heg).

-homma

PK 'pom' means gold. *Pom > hom > homma*

Chikkahomma (Nan), *Doḍḍahomma* (Nan), *Homma* (CRN)

LINGUISTIC STUDY

The study of Pns contributes a great deal to the linguistic science. Language is a living dynamic force. Change is the law of Life. Language also changes from time to time. Causes are many and varied. Individual pronunciation and idiosyncracies, geographical distance, growth of knowledge, cultural differences, foreign influences are some of the causes which determine the course of language. Kannada is a dynamic language. During the course of two thousand years it has changed a lot. These changes are reflected in Pns also. Important linguistic and grammatical features are recorded here along with appropriate examples.

1. Phonemic variations of *a/ā* and *ā/a.*

Ālavāḍi/Alavāḍi (Guṇ), *Ālagōḍu/Alagōḍu* (TNP), *Ankapura/Ankāpura* (Mys), *Paḍavala agrahāra/Paḍavāla agrahāra* (Nan),

Piriyapaṭṭaṇa/Piriyāpaṭṭana (PP), *Basavapura/Basavāpura* (CRN), *Mallapura/Mallāpura* (Nan), *Mādapura/Mādāpura* (Nan).

2. *(a > ē)*

Nanjadēvanahaḷḷi/Nanjēdēvanahaḷḷi (CRN), *Mallēdēvanahaḷḷi* (CRN), *Manchēdēvanahaḷḷi* (PP)

3. Phonemic alternation of *i/a, i/e*

Kurihaṭṭi/Kurahaṭṭi (Nan), *Tammaḍihaḷḷi/Tammaḍahaḷḷi* (PP), *Bidirahaḷḷi/Bidarahaḷḷi, Seṭṭihaḷḷi/Seṭṭahaḷḷi* (Nan), *Huṇisūru/Huṇasūru* (Heg), *Huṇisehaḷḷi/Huṇasehaḷḷi* (Heg), *Kirinelli/Kirenelli* (PP), *Hirikāṭi/Hirekāṭi, Nēgilapura/Nēgalapura* (Mys), *Hirihaḷḷi/Hirehaḷḷi* (Heg), *Hirikāṭi/Hirekāti* (Huṇ), *Hirinandi/Hirenandi* (Heg), *Hiribēgūru/Hirebēgūru* (CRN), *Hirimaḷali/Hiremaḷali* (PP).

4. Phonemic Variation of *ī/i*

Nīlasōge/Nilasōge (TNP)

5. Phonemic Variation of *ou/a, u/ā, u/o*

Induvāḷu/Indavāḷu (TNP), *Kallupuṛa/Kallāpuṛa* (Nan), *Karlupura/Karlāpura* (Nan), *Kumaranapura/Komaranapura* (Yal), *Kumārabīḍu/Komārabīḍu* (Mys).

6. Phonemic alternation of *e/a, e/i, e/ē, e/ā*

Iṭṭigehaḷḷi/Iṭṭigahaḷḷi (PP), *Toṇḍevāḍi/Toṇḍavāḍi* (Guṇ), *Torevaḷḷi/Toravaḷḷi* (Guṇ), *Doḍḍamalēgōḍu/Doḍḍamalagōdu* (CRN), *Dinnehaḷḷi/Dinnahaḷḷi* (Koḷ), *Badanēvāḷu/Badanavāḷu* (Nan), *Sīgevāḍi/Sīgāvadi* (Heg), *Heggaḍehaḷḷi/Heggaḍahaḷḷi* (Nan, Guṇ, Heg), *Kaḍekoḷa/Kaḍakoḷa* (Mys), *Kōgilevāḍa/Kōgilavāḍa* (PP), *Kereyūru/Keriyūru* (KRN), *Maleyūru/Maliyūru* (TNP), *Yereyūru/Yeriyūru* (Huṇ, Yel), *Heḍeyāla/Heḍiyāla* (Guṇ), *Daṇḍekere/Daṇḍikere* (Mys), *Beṇṇegere/Beṇṇigere* (Heg), *Kārehuṇḍi/Kārēhuṇḍi* (Heg), *Hullēmaḷa/Hellēmāḷa* (Heg), *Kārepura/Kārāpura* (Heg).

7. *uva > ō Hāruvahaḷḷi/Hārōhaḷḷi, Haruvapura/Hārōpura.*

8. Initial front vowels *e-* and *ē-* develop an onglide *y* and the basic vowels *u-, o* and *ō-* change into *v-*.

Eḍahaḷḷi/Yaḍahaḷḷi (Mys), *Eraganahaḷḷi/Yeraganahaḷḷi* (Mys).

A good number of such instances may be quoted: *Yāchagowḍanahaḷḷi* (Mys), *Yaragambaḷḷi* (Yal), *Yariyūru* (Yal), *Yalachanahaḷḷi* (Huṇ), *Yāḍatore* (TNP), *Yalemattaru* (Heg), *Yalehuṇḍi* (Heg), *Yerahaḷḷi* (Heg), *Yāchanahaḷḷi* (TNP), *Yaremanuganahaḷḷi* (KRN), *Yalemudnahaḷḷi* (KRN), *Yaḍavanahaḷḷi* (CRN), *Yelachagere* (CRN), *Yalehaḷḷi* (CRN), *Yēchagaḷḷi* (Nan), *Yēchagundla* (Nan).

Dyāvegowḍanapura (Nan), *Byāḍarabilugali* (PP), *Byālūru* (Nan).

Sometimes *-e* is retained along with *y-* : Eg. *Elachagere/Yelachagere* (CRN), *Kētamānahaḷḷi/Kyātamānahaḷḷi* (Mys), *Bēḍarahaḷḷi/Byāḍarahaḷḷi* (KRN), *Ōjamangala/Vājamangala* (Mys), *Vaḍḍabāḷu* (Huṇ), *Vaḍḍarahaḷḷi* (Huṇ, CRN), *Vaḍḍaraguḍi* (Huṇ), *Vadērahaḷḷi* (Heg), *Vaḍḍagalpura* (CRN), *Vaḷagere* (Nan), *Vaḷagerehaḷḷi* (KRN),

ow changes into *āva*. *Gowḍagere/Gāvaḍagere* (Huṇ).

9. OK. *p* changes generally into *h* in M.K. This rule does not apply to words borrowed from other languages, especially Skt. P. of *Pālahaḷḷi (Pāl < Paul,* axiom name*)* which occurs in Mandya district has not changed into *h*. Here are some exceptions of Skt. words where P has changed into *h*.

Paṇḍitavaḷḷi/Haṇḍitavaḷḷi (PP), *Pura/Hura* (Nan), *Puradahaḷḷi/Huradahaḷḷi* (Guṇ).

This is a common feature in Kannada. The initial *p* of almost all the words of O.K. have changed into *h*. The present *Heggaḍahaḷḷi* (Heg) would have been *Pergaḍapaḷḷi* in O.K.

10. The medial *p* > *v* (see Stanza 77, *Śabdamaṇidarpaṇa*)

Kengavāḍi (Guṇ), *Gaṭṭavāḍi* (TNP), *Beḷachavāḍi* (Guṇ), *Beḷavāḍi* (Guṇ), *Bērambāḍi* (Guṇ), *Mādavāḍi* (TNP), *Sīgavāḍi* (Guṇ), *Huṇasavāḍi* (PP), *Heggavāḍi* (DRN), *Horaḷavāḍi* (Nan).

11. Even after OK. *p*, changed into *h*, the medial *v* remains. It may be posited that *h* changed into *v* in the medial position. It is a matter for investigation whether *v* or *b* replaced *p* before the latter underwent a change for *h*. *Goravaḷḷi* (PP), *Hiṭṭuvaḷḷi* (TNP), *Honnavaḷḷi* (Mys), *Toravaḷḷi* (Guṇ, Nan), *Dēsavaḷḷi* (CRN), *Malavaḷḷi* (Heg), *Hebboḷalu* (KRN), *Hiṭṭuvaḷḷi* (TNP), *Honnavaḷḷi* (Mys).

12. Medial *b* > *v*.

Iṇḍavāḷu (TNP), *Nilavāgilu* (Huṇ), *Sīgavāḷu* (KRN), *Haginavāḷu* (Nan), *Aswāḷu/Asumbāḷu* (Huṇ), *Kaṭṭavāḷu* (Heg), *Badanavāḷu* (Nan), *Hattavāḷu* (Nan), *Hosaviḍu* (Nan), *Kirāḷu (Kiru + bāḷu > Kiruhāḷu)* (Mys).

This change happens generally when two words join together to make a compound.

13. Elision of medial *-y-*, with compensatory lengthening of *c, -yy-* particularly when possessive case suffix *-na* occurs. The principle of compensatory lengthening functions here.

Rāmayya + na + haḷḷi = Rāmēnahaḷḷi (Huṇ), *Rangayya + na + koppalu = Rangēnakoppalu* (Huṇ).

Other examples are: *Ballēnahaḷḷi* (Huṇ), *Saṇṇēnahaḷḷi* (Huṇ), *Siṇḍēnahaḷḷi* (Huṇ, Heg), *Hullēnahaḷḷi* (Huṇ), *Kannēnahaḷḷi, Gollēnabiḍu* (Heg), *Ārēnahaḷḷi* (PP), *Uttēnahaḷḷi* (PP), *Guḍḍēnahaḷḷi* (PP), *Channēnahaḷḷi* (PP), *Chiṭṭēnahaḷḷi* (PP), *Chowḍēnahaḷḷi* (PP), *Muddēnahaḷḷi* (PP), *Kaṇṭēnahaḷḷi* (KRN), *Kōtēnahaḷḷi* (KRN), *Guṇḍēgala* (KRN), *Gowḍēnahaḷḷi* (KRN), *Chunchēnahaḷḷi* (nan), *Honnēnahaḷḷi* (KRN, Huṇ), *Rāmēgowḍanapura* (TNP), *Uppēnahaḷḷi* (Nan), *Honnēgowḍanahaḷḷi* (Guṇ).

14. *-y-* alternates with *ē:*

Vaḍeya + ra + haḷḷi = Vaḍērahalli (Heg).

15. *-ya-* alternates with *ai*

Bayalakuppe/Bailakuppe (PP), *Bayalāpura/Bailāpura* (KRN)

16. OK *ṟ* > *r* This is a common feature of linguistic change in Kannada

Aṟe > Are, Keṟe > Kere, Kiṟu > Kiru etc.

17. Medival *v* changes into *g*

Bēvu + ūru = Bēgūru (PP, Guṇ), *Paḍuva + ūru = Paḍugūru* (Guṇ)

18. *p* is easier than *h* to pronounce; still OK. p. > (MK) *h; -h-* again changes into *-a-:* Eg. *Hosa + haḷḷi > Hosaḷḷi > Osaḷḷi* (Heg)

Other examples : *Attaḷḷi* (TNP), *Kuraṭṭi Hosūru* (Koḷ), *Bannaḷḷi* (TNP), *Billaḷḷi* (Heg), *Mūkaḷḷi* (Guṇ, CRN), *Muttatti* (CRN), *Mēgadaḷḷi* (TNP), *Hanumanāḷu* (TNP), *Hosaḷḷi* (Heg), *Santemaraḷḷi* (CRN).

19. *-h- > -k-, -g*

Kūrgaḷḷi (Mys), *Kongaḷḷi* (Nan), *Kottagaḷḷi* (PP), *Jantagaḷḷi* (Mys), *Daṭṭagaḷḷḷi* (Mys), *Dēvagaḷḷi* (Mys), *Nandagaḷḷi* (Mys), *Maṇḍakaḷḷi* (Mys), *Mangaḷḷi* (Koḷ), *Mādagaḷḷi* (Mys), *Mādaragaḷḷi* (Mys), *Mētagaḷḷi* (Mys), *Hūṭagaḷḷi* (Mys).

20. A few remarks about the phonemes *p, ṟ, v,* and *ḻ*

These phonemes exist only in old Kannada. They lose their identity when old Kannada changes into middle Kannada. *p* becomes *h*. *ṟ* becomes *ḍ* or *r* or *ḷ*. *v* becomes *b* and *ḻ* becomes *ḍ r* or *ḷ*. The lists prepared under the aegis of successive governments do not record the earlier forms of names with the above lost phonemes. Though the phonemes *ṟ* and *ḻ* are completely lost, *p* and *v* are still in use, though in a limited way. Some of the VNS which are mentioned in inscriptions have retained these phonemes and are given below in juxtaposition to the names taken from the list. This arrangement will give clues to the possible origin and historical evolution of some of the VNS. The first column contains the VNS taken from the Government list, the second column VNS gathered from inscriptions and the third, the dates of the inscriptions and the taluks.

Arakalavāḍi	*Aṟakalavāḍi*	CRN 30/1555
Arabīkere	*Arabageṟe*	Koḷ 62/1354
Eḍadore	*Edatoṟe*	TNP 40/1180
Oddagere	*Oḍageṟe*	Heg 36/1197
Kiragasūru	*Kiṟigusūru*	CRN 44/1413
Kiragāsūru	*Kiṟigusūru*	TNP 35/15th century
Kilagere	*Kelligeṟe*	CRN 306/1318
Kudēru	*Kudihēṟu*	CRN 73/1409
	Kudihēṟu	CRN 76/1501
Kurahaṭṭi	*Kuṟahaṭṭi*	Nan 328/1662
Kurubūru	*Kuṟubūru*	TNP 287/1303
Kerehaḷḷi	*Keṟehaḷḷi*	CRN 351275
Kōṭegere	*Kōṭeyakeṟe*	Guṇ 49/1548

Gaḷigekere	*Gaḷigekere*	KRN 104/1597
Chikkahanasōge	*Panasōge*	KRN 23/1100
	Hanasōge	KRN 28/15th century
Tandre	*Tandaṟe*	KRN 80/1492
Tarikallu	*Taṟiyakallu*	Huṇ 24/1162
Talakāḍu	*Taḷaikk-āḍu*	TNP /1289 Tam
		TNP /150/1293 Tam
	Taḷekāḍu	TNP /200/935
Baṇḍigere	*Baṇḍigeṟe*	CRN 263/1316
Badanāḷu	*Vadaṇeguppe*	Nan 328/1662
Bāgali	*Bāḷguḷiyūru*	CRN 114/10th century
Biḷigere	*Biḷigeṟe*	CRN 246/1527
Beṭṭahaḷḷi	*Veṭṭanpaḷḷi*	TNP 84/1179
Bēgūru	*Vēgūru*	Guṇ 14/17th century
Bokkahaḷḷi	*Boggapaḷḷi*	Nan 313/9th century
Maddūru	*Mardūru*	Heg 90/Ganga Śripurusha
Maliyūru	*Malevūru*	Heg 86/1531
		(Perhaps v is a wrong usage)
Mādanahaḷḷi	*Mādanapaḷḷi*	Nan 398/1513
Mirle	*Miṟle*	KRN 94/17th century
	Mirile	KRN 88/1299
	Mirle	KRN 92/15th century
Yaragambaḷḷi	Yeṟagambaḷi	Yal 200/1556
		Yal 202/1512
Yariyūru	*Yeṟeyūru*	Yal 34/16th century
Yeraganahaḷḷi	*Eṟaganahaḷḷi*	CRN 239/1289
Sagaḷḷi	*Sogehaḷḷi*	Heg 135/1107
Haṇḍitavaḷḷi	*Haṇḍitavaḷḷi*	PP 229/16th century
Hangrepura	*Hangaṟepura*	CRN/1605
Hayirage	*Pairage*	Heg 7/1037
Heggavāḍi	*Pergaiyavāḍi*	CRN 85/1242 Tam
Homma	*Poḷma*	CRN 147/1294/
		Date not known
	Homma	CRN 149/1294
Horeyāla	*Hoṟeyāla*	Heg 53/1546
Hosahoḷalu	*Posavaḷalu*	Heg 135/1107
Honnūru	*Ponnūr*	Yal 17/11th Century Tans

The above examples show that these phonemes started changing towards the end of the 11th century and some of them, especially r lingered on till the end of the 15th century. The *p* of proper names does not generally change into *h* except in rare instances. Pura, of course, indicates a habitat; but devoid of anything specific, it is sometimes used as a proper name also. *P* of pura sometimes changes into *h*, making it hura (Nan). There is a rare instance of a Sanskrit word used as VN being changed into *h* as for example, *Panditavaḷḷi/ Haṇḍitavaḷḷi* (PP). There are many VNS wherein the above mentioned phonemes have sunk into oblivion. Since inscriptions or other recorded evidences wherein these VNS occur, are not available, it has not been possible to prove how these changes have come about.

21. Change of *h* into *y* and then *ai*.

Maisūru < *Mayisūru* < *Mahisūru* < *Mahishūru*

22. Change of *h* into *a*

Attaḷḷi (TNP), *Ālanaḷḷi* (PP), *Kallaḷḷikāvalu* (Huṇ), *Kāmanaḷḷi* (PP), *Kāṭnāḷu* < *Kāṭanahāḷu* > *Katanabālu* (KRN), *Kirālu* < *Kirubālu* (Mys), *Kuraṭṭihosūru* (Koḷ), *Kurubaḷḷi* (KRN), *Kētaḷḷi* (Heg), *Kongāḷḷi* (Nan), *Chunchaḷḷi* (Koḷ), *Chowaḍaḷḷi* (Heg), *Jakkaḷḷi* (Koḷ), *Toṇḍāḷu* < *Toṇḍhāḷu* < *Toṇḍe + bāḷu* (Huṇ), *Dantaḷḷi* (Koḷ), *Bannaḷḷi* (TNP), *Baṇḍaḷḷi* (Koḷ), *Basavaṭṭi* (CRN), *Billaḷḷi* (Heg), *Bīranaḷḷi Kāvalu* (Huṇ), *Manchaḷḷi* (CRN), *Mādaḷḷi* (Huṇ), *Mūkaḷḷi* (CRN), *Mōdaḷḷi* (Koḷ), *Yalachaṭṭi* (Mys), *Santemaraḷḷi* (CRN), *Sōgaḷḷi* (Heg), *Sōmaḷḷi* (Huṇ), *Hanumanāḷu* (TNP), *Hosaḷḷi* (Heg).

It may be observed here that *h* is not originally a Dravidian phoneme. It is absent both in Tamil and Malayalam. Owing to the influence of Prakrits, Kannada and Telugu have adopted this phoneme. Since Kannada borrows heavily from Skt. *h* has a place in Kannada alphabet. It is strange that *p* which is easier to pronounce, started towards the close of the tenth century yielding place to *h* which Kannada people cannot aspirate properly. And it is also true that h was deaspirated as soon as it came into existence. Though it is used in writing invariably, even the educated people do not pronounce it properly. It is generally pronounced as *a*. This is not necessarily a feature of euphonic junction; even otherwise, when it is written as *haṭṭi, h* is pronounced in the same way as *h. Heggaḍahalli,* for example, is pronounced as *Heggaḍahaḷḷi.* Even when *haḷḷi* is written as it is, h loses its significance in euphonic junction and a is glued to the final consonant of the first word after eliding its vowel. Thus, though the VNS like *Chowḍahaḷḷi, Javanahaḷḷi* and *Chīranahaḷḷi* are written as they are, they are pronounced as *Chowḍaḷḷi* (Mys), *Javanaḷḷi* (Mys) and *Chīranahaḷḷi* (Mys) only.

23. *ri* changes into *ḍu (r > ḍ)*

Parivārahaḷḷi (Mys) > Paḍuvārahaḷḷi

24. *d > ṭ*

Rāsimaraṭikāvalu (PP)

25. *ḷ* changes into *n* and *anusvāra*

Beṇagallu (PP), *Koṇadahaḷḷi* (TNP), *Kuntūru* (Koḷ)

26. *l > ḷ*

Kalale > Kaḷale (Nan)

27. All VNS consist of two or more elements (words or a word and a suffix). These words and suffixes join together to make it a compound or a euphonic combination. Whether it is a compound or a euphonic combination, morphophonemic changes will take place. The changes will take place in three ways: 1. elision, 2. augment and 3. substitution. In the absence of any morphophonemic change, the words remain separately with hiatus. Since every *VN* falls under anyone of the categories mentioned above, only a few examples are given by way of illustration.

i) Elision: Generally the final vowel of the first member of the compound drops itself while the first vowel of the second member persists.

Akkūru (TNP), *Aḍagūru* (PP), *Aṇṇūru* (Guṇ, Heg), *Abbūru* (PP), *Āladūru* (TNP), *Ichūru* (PP), *Kaggalūru* (Nan), *Kaḍubūru* (TNP, Nan), *Kāṭūru* (Nan), *Kurubūru* (TNP), *Kallūru* (PP), *Koṇasūru* (PP), *Gollūru* (Heg), *Gōlūru* (Nan), *Chikkinduvādi* (KRN), *Chennūru* (KRN), *Yagadūru* (Nan), *Tāyūru* (Nan), *Tippūru* (KRN), *Toṇḍāḷu* (Huṇ), *Doḍḍahosūru* (PP), *Bannūru* (Nan), *Baḷḷūru* (KRN), *Bāgūru* (TNP),

Mangalūru (Nan), *Maraḍūru* (PP), *Marūru* (Han), *Mēlūru* (KRN), *Lakkūru* (Huṇ), *Sīgūru* (PP), *Sūḷeri* (Koḷ), *Halasūru* (Heg), *Huṇasūru* (Huṇ).

ii) **Augment:** Generally *y* occurs as augmentative infix when the last phoneme of the first member of the combination is *i* or *e* and the first phoneme of the second member is *ā* or *u*.

Aṇiyūru (Guṇ), *Kaliyūru* (TNP), *Chikkakereyūru* (Heg), *Maliyūru* (TNP), *Maleyūru* (CRN), *Mariyāla* (CRN), *Yariyūru* (Guṇ), *Siriyuru* (Huṇ), *Haḷeyūru* (Heg), *Horeyāla* (Guṇ).

iii) **Substitution:** The morphophonemic changes of this kind generally occur in compounds i.e., when two words join together. Two types of changes are observed.

(a) Intervocalic surds like *k, t* and *p* get sonantised. (see *Śabdamaṇidarpana,* Stanza 75). *Attiguppe* (Huṇ), *Attigōḍu* (PP), *Ālagōdu* (TNP), *Uḍigāla* (CRN), *Okkalagere* (TNP), *Kaṇagālu* (Huṇ), *Kiragunda* (Nan), *Kundagere* (Guṇ), *Kuragallu* (PP), *Gāvaḍagere (Huṇ), Guṇḍēgāla* (Koḷ), *Chennamgere* (KRN), *Nandigunda* (Nan), *Naragyātanahaḷḷi* (TNP), *Baṭaguppa* (Koḷ), *Badaneguppe* (CRN), *Beṇṇegere* (Heg), *Beḷagunda* (Nan), *Mudigoṇḍa* (Koḷ), *Yamagumbha* (Huṇ), *Voḷagere* (TNP), *Sanabinaguppe* (KRN), *Hebbālaguppe* (Heg), *Heggothāra* (CRN), *Yeḍadore* (TNP), *Kembal* (Nan).

b) Intervocalic *s* changes into *j* + : *Chikkahejjōḍlu* (Huṇ), *Hejjoḍlu* (Huṇ).

There are certain exceptions wherein intervocalic surds do not change into sonants: *Arakere* (KRN), *Bilikere* (Huṇ), *Hosakōṭe* (KRN).

28. Most of the specifics of VNS contain possessive or adjectival meaning from the point of view of generics.[13] Often, the genitive case suffix is joined to the specific. As a result, morphophonemic changes occur while the root and the suffix combine. According to *Śabdamaṇidarpana* of *Kēsirāja* (1280), the possessive case suffix is *a* or *ā* (*Sūtrā* 127). Depending upon the last vowel of specifics,

13. Shasṭi vibhakti or the genitive case indicates relationship - see Sutra 143 of Śabdamaṇidarpaṇa.

connecting phonemes like *-n-*, *-r-* (plural), *-d-* and *-ina-* are used; sometimes *-a* is added to the root without any connectives.

i) *-n-*

Ankanahaḷḷi (KRN), *Ayyanapura* (CRN), *Ālanahaḷḷi* (PP), *Kāḍanahaḷḷi* (Nan), *Kāmanahaḷḷi* (PP), *Kiḷanapura* (Mys), *Kōṇanapura* (Nan), *Kōṇanūru* (Nan), *Kōtanahaḷḷi* (Nan), *Ganganūru* (CRN), *Channappanapura* (CRN), *Chīranahaḷḷi* (Mys), *Jāganakōṭe* (Heg), *Jompanahaḷḷi* (Heg), *Dāsanūru* (Nan), *Dugganahaḷḷi* (Nan), *Dēvanūru* (Nan), *Nanjanāyakanahaḷḷi* (Heg), *Narachanahaḷḷi* (KRN), *Nāṭanahaḷḷi* (KRN), *Parvatanapura* (Guṇ), *Puṭṭanapura* (CRN), *Basavanapura* (CRN), *Manchanahaḷḷi* (KRN), *Manuganahaḷḷi* (Huṇ), *Mādanahaḷḷi* (Nan), *Mudukanapura* (TNP), *Mūkanahaḷḷi* (Huṇ), *Hunasunūru* (Nan), *Hōtanahaḷḷi* (Nan).

ii) *-r-*

Ayyarabīḍu (PP), *Kakkarahaḷḷi* (Nan), *Kāḍavaḍḍaraguḍi* (Huṇ), *Vaḍḍarahaḷḷi* (Huṇ), *Heḷavaramaṭha* (Nan).

iii) *-d-*

Avarekāyiguḍḍada Kāvalu (PP), *Gariguḍḍada Kāvalu* (Nan), *Chapparadahaḷḷi* (PP), *Rāmanathapuradahuṇḍi* (TNP).

iv) *-ina-*

Arasinakere (Mys), *Kanchinakere* (KRN), *Guruvinapura* (Nan), *Bēvinahaḷḷi* (CRN), *Maḍuvinabīḍu* (CRN), *Mavinahaḷḷi* (Mys), *Saṇabinakoppa* (PP).

Arasinakere (Mys), *Kanchinakere* (KRN), *Guruvinapura* (Nan), *Būvuiahaḷḷi* (CRN), *Maḍuvinabīḍu* (CRN), *Mavinahaḷḷi* (Mys), *Saṇabinakoppa* (PP).

v) *-a-*

Kallahaḷḷi (Man), *Kūḍalapura* (Nan), *Nēraḷakuppe* (Huṇ), *Bidaragūḍu* (Nan), *Mūḍalapura* (CRN), *Hullahaḷḷi* (Nan).

vi) Noun specifics are used also without any suffix in the adjectival or relational sense.

Araḷikumari (PP), *Kaggalipura* (CRN), *Kurahaṭṭi* (TNP), *Kūḍahaḷḷi* (CRN), *Kumbāraguṇḍi* (CRN), *Kumbārahaḷḷi* (Nan), *Kurihuṇḍi* (Nan),

Kētahaḷḷi (CRN), *Kongahaḷḷi* (Nan), *Kōṭekere* (Guṇ), *Kōḍihaḷḷi* (Guṇ), *Jakkahaḷḷi* (Koḷ), *Jaṭṭihuṇḍi* (Mys), *Jālahaḷḷi* (Nan), *Jinnahaḷḷi* (Heg), *Nanjahaḷḷi* (CRN), *Nēnekaṭṭe* (Guṇ), *Būdahaḷḷi* (TNP), *Manchahaḷḷi* (Heg), *Mallahaḷḷi* (Heg, Mys, Nan), *Mūkahaḷḷi* (Guṇ), *Vaḍḍagere* (Guṇ).

29. A compound consists of more than one part or word or component. Whenever two or more words coalesce to form a single compound word, morphophonemic changes occur and these changes relate only to specifics. These changes include loss of one or two phonemes. It is also possible that assimilation of the last and first phonemes of specifics and generics respectively takes place.

i) *Inidu + māvu = Immāvu* (Nan), *Kar + guṇḍi = Kagguṇḍi* (PP), *Kar + kere = Kaggere* (KRN), *Kiridu + ūru = Kittūru* (PP), *Kiridu + kunda = Kirgunda* (Nan), *Kempu (?) + kāki = Kenganki* (CRN), *Bīramma + haḷḷi = Bīrambaḷḷi* (Heg), *Būdamma + haḷḷi = Būdambaḷḷi* (CRN), *Beḷ + matti = Bemmatti* (PP), *Maha + kōḍu = Mākōḍu* (PP), *Hiridu* + (> heṙ) - *guṇḍi = Hegguṇḍi* (CRN), *Hiridu* (Hēr) + *bāḷu = Hebbāḷu* (KRN).

ii) Kannada is a borrowing language. Hence words are freely taken from any language that comes into contact with it. Since Skt. came into contact with Kannada during its formative period, many words of Skt. origin percolated into Kan. vocabulary. Though Skt. words are freely used in Kan. writings, the combination of both Skt. and Kan. words are not generally permitted, since they jar on the ear. Still incongruous compounds (arisamasas) are in use. While constituting such compounds however, care has been taken to see that there is no unpleasant disharmony between the Skt. and the Kan. words that go to make compounds. Examples of incongruous compounds consisting VNS are given below.

Ankahaḷḷi (Guṇ), *Arēpāḷya* (Koḷ), *Arēpura* (Guṇ), *Arjunahaḷḷi* (KRN), *Ādibeṭṭahaḷḷi* (TNP), *Kaggalipura* (CRN), *Kaṭṭepura* (CRN), *Karṇakuppe* (Huṇ), *Karpūrahaḷḷi* (KRN), *Kaḷḷipura* (Guṇ), *Kāmahaḷḷi* (Nan), *Kebbepura* (CRN), *Kemmaṇṇupura* (Mys), *Gangāvāḍi* (CRN), *Gūḷipura* (CRN), *Gōhaḷḷi* (Huṇ), *Chandrabīḍu* (Mys), *Chikkalakshmīpura* (TNP), *Tammaḍipura* (TNP), *Dēvarasahaḷḷi* (Nan), *Dēvarāyaseṭṭipura* (Nan), *Dēvaḷḷi* (CRN), *Doddalakshmīpura* (TNP), *Dhanagere* (Koḷ), *Nanjāpura* (TNP), *Nanjarājapura* (CRN),

Nanjēdēvanapura (CRN), *Narasīpura* (Nan), *Panchavaḷḷi* (PP), *Piriyāpaṭṇa* (PP), *Basavāpura* (CRN), *Bastipura* (CRN), *Benkipura* (Huṇ), *Bharatavāḍi* (Huṇ), *Bhūgatahaḷḷi* (Mys), *Bhairapura* (TNP), *Bhōgavāḷuvaḍeyanapura* (Nan), *Masaṇapura* (CRN), *Mahadēśwarabeṭṭa* (Koḷ), *Mādāpura* (TNP), *Mādhavagere* (Mys), *Vājamaṇgala* (Mys), *Sankahaḷḷi* (Heg), *Sambaravaḷḷi* (KRN), *Sindhuvaḷḷi* (Mys), *Sēnāpatihaḷḷi* (TNP), *Sōmavārapēṭe* (CRN), *Sōmahaḷḷi* (Guṇ), *Hanchipura* (Heg), *Haḷepura* (Nan), *Hārupura* (Heg, Nan), *Huṇḍīpura* (Guṇ), *Huraḷīpura* (Heg), *Hullēpura* (CRN), *Hosapura* (Guṇ, Nan).

It may be noted here that one at least of the components of the compound should be Skt. and the rest, Kan.

iii) Mixtures of Kannada and Arabic words may be considered as consistuting incongruous compounds. The number of such components is not large.

Ameerahosahaḷḷi (Guṇ), *Arabigere* (Koḷ), *Mārthahaḷḷi* (Koḷ), *Hussainapura* (Huṇ).

iv) *Kesirāja* accepts compounds containing the corrupted forms of other languages and Kannada since they glue together harmoniously.[14]

Agata (Agatsya) Gowḍanahaḷḷi (Guṇ), *Ittiga (Istikā) halli* (PP), *Aichana (Aditya) haḷḷi* (KRN), *Aitanahaḷḷi (Ādityana) haḷḷi* (PP), *Kaṇṇā (vishṇa) gāla* (Guṇ), *Kamara (Kammāra) haḷḷi* (Guṇ), *Koḍa (Koḍa < Kuṭajaka) Sōge* (Guṇ), *Komārana (Kumāra) haḷḷi* (Mys), *Gaḷige (Ghaṭikā) kere* (KRN), *Gumbha (Kumbha)_halli* (Mys), *Goravana (Guru) haḷḷi* (TNP), *Chāma (Shyāma) haḷḷi* (Mys), *Chāmalā (Shyāmatā) pura* (KRN), *Chowḍa (Chamuṇḍa) haḷḷi* (Mys), *Jakka (Yaksha) haḷḷi* (Guṇ), *Jan (Yajna) nūru* (CRN), *Javana (Yama) haḷḷi* (Mys), *Janta (Yantra) gaḷḷi* (Mys), *Jōgana (Yōga) haḷḷi* (Mys), *Sirumata (Srīmatā) pura* (PP), *Terakaṇāmbi (Trikadamba) pura* (Guṇ), *Dugga (Durga) haḷḷi* (Mys), *Narasa (Narasimha) mangala* (CRN), *Nāraṇa (Nārāyaṇa) pura* (Guṇ), *Basavana (Vrishabha) haḷḷi* (PP), *Basavarāja (Vrishabharaja) pura* (KRN), *Benagana (Vināyaka) haḷḷi* (KRN), *Belavatta (Bilvapatra)* (Mys), *Bommana (Brahma) haḷḷi* (CRN), *Vastilingana (Vasatilinga) pura* (Guṇ), *Seṭṭi (Srēshti) haḷḷi* (TNP), *Sappayyana (Sarpa) pura* (CRN),

14. **Śabdamaṇidarpaṇa**, p. 347, Sutra (314).

Singana (Simha) pura (CRN), *Suttūru (Śrotriyūru)* (Nan), *Sūra (Sūrya) haḷḷi* (Nan).

Note: **Āspatrekāvalu** (Huṇ), though it contains a word of English origin cannot be called an incongruous compound since **Āspatre** is the corrupted form of Hospital.

v. Generally VNS with Skt. words taking both the positions in a compound are not found in large numbers. Most of the VNS are formed of Kannada words only. Examples of VNS with Skt. words are given below.

Ankapura (Heg), *Agastyapura* (TNP), *Kallināthapura* (Mys), *Kārya* (Nan), *Kriṣṇā* (Huṇ), *Kriṣṇarājapura* (Heg), *Kētupura* (TNP), *Kailasapura* (PP), *Kōmalāpura* (PP), *Gargēśwari* (TNP), *Gōpālapura* (Mys), *Chāmarājanagara* (CRN), *Jayapura* (Mys), *Tāṇḍavapura* (Nan), *Dēvarājapura* (CRN), *Dēvalāpura* (CRN), *Dēśipura* (Guṇ), *Dharmapura* (Huṇ), *Nandipura* (PP), *Nandināthapura* (Heg), *Nāgaraghaṭṭa* (PP), *Nāgavāla* (Mys), *Nārāyaṇapura* (KRN), *Paramāpura* (Guṇ), *Paśupati* (KRN), *Pura* (Heg), *Mangala* (CRN), *Mallarājapura* (Heg), *Mallināthapura* (Huṇ), *Mālāpura* (Guṇ), *Ranganāthapura* (TNP), *Rangasamudra* (TNP), *Rāghavāpura* (Guṇ), *Rājāpura* (PP), *Rāmasamudra* (CRN), *Rāmāpura* (Koḷ), *Lanke* (Heg), *Lingāpura* (PP), *Lingāmbudhi* (Mys), *Lalithādripura* (Mys), *Lakshmaṇāpura* (Heg), *Lakshmipura* (Koḷ, PP), *Varuṇa* (Mys), *Vallāmbudhi* (KRN), *Vijayāpura* (Guṇ), *Vijayaśrīpura* (Mys), *Venkaṭāpura* (KRN), *Sreerangapura* (CRN), *Sreerāmapura* (KRN), *Śāntipura* (Heg), *Śivapura* (Guṇ, CRN), *Satyāgāla* (PP), *Sanyāsipura* (KRN), *Sāligrāma* (KRN), *Siddalingapura* (Mys), *Siddāpura* (Heg), *Sōmanāthapura* (TNP), *Sōmasamudra* (CRN)_ *Sōmēśwarapura* (Mys), *Hampāpura* (KRN, Koḷ, Nan), *Hariyālapura* (Heg).

30. Elision of phoneme in a compound: It happens in two ways: i) when the last syllable of the first component and the first syllable of the second component are similar, the phoneme of the first component elides; ii) Due to economy of effort, one phoneme of a double consonant gets elided.

i *Kannāyakanahaḷḷi (Kanna + nāyakanahali)* (TNP), *Chikkāḍanahaḷḷi (Chikka + Kāḍanahaḷḷi)* (Huṇ), *Chikyātanahaḷḷi (Chikka*

+ kyātanahaḷḷi) (Huṇ), *Chilkunda (Chiluka + kunda)*[15] (Huṇ), *Chennanjana Oḍeyanapura (Chenna + nanjana Oḍeyanapura)* (Koḷ).

ii. *Kaṇayanahuṇḍi*[16] (Heg), *Kamarahaḷḷi* (Guṇ), *Guḍamāranahaḷḷi* (Mys), *Chikaṇāpura*[16] (Guṇ), *Jakahaḷḷi* (Heg), *Timakāpura* (PP), *Nāgaṇapura* (Nan), *Basavaṭige* (nan), *Bematti* (PP), *Mutagūru* (PP), *Vaḍagere* (Yel). *ṇ, m, ḍ, k, k, m, ṇ, ṭ, m, t, ḍ,* respectively of these VNS are lost

MISCELLANEOUS

Some special features of VNS, noticed in this area of study are recorded here. it is true that these features though rare are found in almost all the districts.

1. Renaming of Village names

The renaming of villages has been in vogue from time immemorial and in all countries. A village may be renamed in order to honour a god, a great personality, a royal dignitary, a military leader, a religious reformer, a political chief, an artist, a patriot etc., to commemorate an important event and to satisfy the aspirations of a community living in the particular village.

Original Name	Changed Name
Arikoṭhāra (CRN)	*Chāmarājanagara*
Karikālamādahaḷḷi (Guṇ)	*Chennananjarāyapura*
Kaliyūru (TNP)	*Anantakīrtimahānagara*
Kiṭṭūru (Heg)	*Krisṇāpura*
Gaḷigekere (KRN)	*Rāmapura* *(in the name of the Rāmamma)*
Gommaṭahaḷḷi (Guṇ)	*Rāghavāpura*
Tarikallu (Huṇ)	*Kaṇṭhīravasamudra*
Togaravāḍi (Huṇ)	*Dharmāpura*
Bannūru (TNP)	*Śrīrāmapura*

15. Actually three phonemes are elided here.
16. Two phonemes each of these VNS are elided: ṇ & y, k and n.

Beṭṭṭahaḷḷi (TNP)	*Dēvarājapura*
Mālangi (TNP)	*Jananāthapura agrahāra*
Hullāṇa (Gen)	*Kamalāpura*

Except *Chāmarājanagara,* no other changed names are in vogue now. Only when a name is changed in consequence of the urge from the people, the changed name is likely to survive. There is a story (it is a fact too) about the retention of the name, *Chāmarājanagara.* The then-Maharaja of Mysore decided that the memory of his father should be perpetuated by renaming *Arikoṭhāra* as *Chāmarājanagara* and building a temple also in his name. Even after renaming the village in pursuance of a royal decree, people were not using the new name on account of their old habit. It became imperative for the officers to popularise the new name. Sentinels were stationed in each of the tollgates. people entering and exiting the town used to be stopped and interrogated as whereto or wherefrom they were going. Only when they uttered the correct name they were permitted to enter in or go out of the town.

Some of the VNS such as the present *Rāmanagara* (Bangalore district) whose immediate earlier name was Close-pet after a British Commissioner, gains quick currency as soon as it is changed into an Indian name. When a PN is changed into a name consisting of Skt. word or words, it is liable to be forgotten very soon.

2. Village names after females

Village names after females are very small in number while compared with VNS after males. A comparative study of these names leads to the conclusion that in the process of naming the villages, the society proved itself as a male-dominated one. Among the female names, names of goddesses also are included.

i. VNS after Goddesses

Gowrikere (Huṇ), *Chāmalāpura* (Heg, Nan, KRN), *Chikkalakshmīpura* (TNP), *Dēvalāpura* (CRN, Heg), *Doḍḍalakshmīpura* (TNP), *Bommalāpura* (Heg, Guṇ), *Masaṇikuppe* (Heg), *Mārihosahaḷḷi* (Guṇ), *Lakshmīpura* (Koḷ), *Śāmalāpura* (Heg).

ii. VNS after Womenfolk

Akkadēvarahaḷḷi (Heg), *Akkūru* (TNP), *Ajjipura* (Koḷ), *Ammanapura* (CRN), *Kanchamaḷḷi* (Heg), *Kōmalāpura* (PP), *Gaṭṭitigipura* (Heg), *Gowdīkere* (Huṇ), *Chandakavāḍi* (CRN), *Channipuradamōḷe* (CRN), *Bhinnambaḷḷi* (Nan), *Chennamgere* (KRN), *Javanikuppe* (PP), *Tippalāpura* (Huṇ), *Timakāpura* (PP), *Timmarājipura* (Koḷ), *Tirumalāpura* (PP), *Dēvīrammanahaḷḷi* (Nan), *Nāgalagere* (TNP), *Lakkikuppe* (KRN), *Lakkipura* (Guṇ), *Lakkūru* (Guṇ), *Hariyālapura* (Heg).

It may be possible that some of the names in the first category, for example, Gowrikere and *Lakshmīpura,* may refer to human beings, and a few in the second category, for example, *Nāgalagere* may have been derived from names of goddesses. It is also likely that *Lakkikuppe* and *Lakkipura* in the second category may have got their names from a plant like *Lakkigiḍa* in Kannada (which has its equivalent in Latin as Vitex negundo or Trifolia lin). Since sufficient information is not available to prove which is which, the present categorisation could stand for the present.

Most of the names in Kannada have natural gender. *Gangā* or *Gange* is always feminine, whereas *Bīra* and *Kyāta* are masculine. These means are used in the opposite genders also: Ganga can be used in masculine gender; *Bīra* becomes *Bīri,* and *Kyāta* becomes *Kyātamma* in feminine gender. The names of villages which have peculiarities is gender are noted below:

Kyātamānahaḷḷi (Mys), *Ganganakuppe* (PP), *Bīrihuṇḍi* (Mys).

3. Structure of Village names

i. VNS generally have two or more components. There are a few names which have only one component. Such a component is mostly specific.

Agara (Yel), *Āvarti* (PP), *Igli* (Nan), *Iṭna* (Heg), *Uganeya* (Nan), *Kaggala* (KRN), *Kaḷale* (Nan), *Kārya* (Nan), *Kārle* (Guṇ), *Kuppe* (KRN), *Kupya* (TNP), *Kuḷya* (Heg), *Kūdigi* (Heg), *Keḍaga* (KRN), *Kesare* (Mys), *Koppa* (PP), *Kohāl* (Heg), *Chillu* (TNP), *Chincili* (TNP), *Chenga* (KRN), *Chowli* (PP), *Talaḷe* (Guṇ), *Tandre* (KRN), *Taṇḍasi* (Heg), *Tumbuḷa* (TNP), *Dūra* (Mys), *Nagarle* (Nan), *Niṭre* (Guṇ), *Nisana* (Heg), *Nēraḷe* (Nan), *Pāḷya* (Koḷ), *Pura* (Heg), *Baḍaga* (Heg),

Marase (Mys), *Baragi* (Huṇ, Heg), *Bāgali* (CRN), *Bārse* (PP), *Beḷale* (Nan), *Bhērya* (KRN), *Magge* (Heg), *Majjine* (Heg), *Maḷāra* (Heg), *Maḷali* (Heg, KRN), *Mangala* (Koḷ, Guṇ, CRN), *Mālangi* (TNP, PP), *Minniya* (Koḷ), *Mirle* (KRN), *Motta* (Heg), *Lanke* (Heg), *Varuna* (Mys), *Vāranchi* (Huṇ), *Sakkare* (KRN), *Savve* (Heg), *Sāgaḍe* (CRN), *Sāgya* (KRN, Heg), *Sōsale* (TNP), *Harave* (CRN), *Harale* (Koḷ), *Hanchya* (Mys), *Hemmige* (TNP), *Hāḍya* (KRN, Nan), *Hāḷalu* (Mys), *Hura* (Nan), *Hūgiya* (Koḷ), *Hairige* (Heg), *Homma* (CRN), *Miṇya* (Koḷ).

It is not unlikely that some of these names may have been the combination of two components originally and may have worn out or diminished in course of time. The worn-out parts are not easily traceable. Agara is the corrupted form of *Agrahāra*. *Mālangi* may be the worn-out form of *Mahālinga*. *Niḍidu + are* may be the original form of *Niṭre*. Further study will bring forth the truth.

ii. VNS with two components. Specifics and generics, is the rule.

iii. VNS with three components are not rare.

Ara + gowḍana + haḷḷi (Mys), *Aṭṭu + guḷi + pura* (CRN), *Kaṭṭa + vāḍi + pura* (Nan), *Kaṭṭe + manugana + haḷḷi* (Heg), *Kari + muddana + haḷḷi* (Huṇ), *Kade + Manugana + haḷḷi* (Huṇ), *Kāḷe + manugana + haḷḷi* (PP), *Koṇan + ūru + pura* (Nan), *Kōḍi + Chāmana + haḷḷi* (Heg), *Chikka + indu + vāḍi* (Koḷ), *Chikka + kāḍana + haḷḷi* (Huṇ), *Kōṇana + hase + haḷḷi* (Huṇ), *Gangādhara + basavana + haḷḷi* (PP), *Garike + kaṭṭe + Kāvalu* (Heg), *Chikka + kāḍana + haḷḷi* (Huṇ), *Chikka + kere + yūru* (Heg), *Chikka + bīchana + haḷḷi* (Huṇ), *Chiṭṭi + kyātana + haḷḷi* (Huṇ), *Jōdi + harihara + pura* (Nan), *Dāri + bēvu + ūru* (Guṇ), *Pinni + kyātana + haḷḷi* (Huṇ), *Basti + Māda + haḷḷi* (Huṇ), *Māde + gowḍana + huṇḍi* (TNP), *Mara + bhugatana + pura* (Heg), *Marṭi + kyātana + haḷḷi* (Mys), *Mutturāyana + hosa + haḷḷi* (Huṇ), *Meṇasi + kyātana + haḷḷi* (TNP), *Vaḍli + manugana + haḷḷi* (Huṇ), *Vasti + lingana + pura* (Guṇ), *Vārānchi + guru + pura* (Huṇ), *Hulle + hos + ūru* (KRN), *Hegga + vāḍi + pura* (CRN), *Hon + nūru + kuppe* (Heg).

It is doubtful whether some of the names cited above could be taken as three-component-names: Eg. *Aragowḍanahaḷḷi*, *Kāḷemanuganahaḷḷi*, *Karimuddanahaḷḷi*, *Chikkakāḍanahaḷḷi*, *Mādegowḍanahuṇḍi*. In these examples, all the specifics constitute only one component. Each of these names, *Aragowḍa, Karimudda, Mādegowḍa* etc., form only one unit. In the name *Aragowḍa,* the two elements, *Ara* and *Gowḍa* cannot be separated. Hence, it is considered that such of these names form only one component.

It may be noted that in some of these names, two generics are found, *Kaṭṭayādipura, Heggavādipura, Honnūrukuppe.* Probably these villages without the last generics must have existed originally. At the time of christening a newly established village, the old name with the addition of a new generic must have been thought of.

iv. VNS with four components are rather rare. VNS with more than four components are not usually available in this area. This is, of course, a common feature of VNS of Karnataka.

Kandā + gāla + hosa + haḷḷi (Guṇ), *Kudi + nīru + muddana + haḷḷi* (Huṇ), *Kura + haṭṭi + hos + ūru* (Koḷ), *Guḍi + Bhadrana + hosa + haḷḷi* (PP), *Gowḍi + mācha + nāyakana + haḷḷi* (Heg), *Doḍḍa + hej + jūru + kere + kāval* (Huṇ), *Maguvina + haḷḷi + mela + Kāmana + haḷḷi* (Guṇ), *Kal + lūru + Nāgana + haḷḷi + Kāval* (Mys).

Since *kuḍiniru* is an attribute of *Mudda,* it cannot be separated from the basic name. The same rule applies to *Gowḍi māchanāyaka* also. Hence, these two names may be considered as double component units. According to this explanation, *Guḍibhadranahosahaḷḷi* is a triple component unit. Except the last one, the rest may be considered as quadruple units. *Maguvinahaḷḷimēla Kāmanahaḷḷi* is an exception where there are five components.

But one thing is certain; that the VNS with more than two components are secondary or duplicate ones which have their originals elsewhere.

4. Sanskritisation/Anglicisation

Sanskritisation or Anglicisation of VNS is a phenomenon which may be noticed occasionally in and outside Karnataka. Eg. *Bēlūru* is sanskritised as *Vēlāpuri, Srīrangapaṭṭaṇa* is pronounced as *Seringapaṭam.* But it has not been possible to come across such a phenomenon in the area of this study, except the Anglicised pronunciation of the VNS like Maisuru, that too rarely.

PART–II

SEMANTIC STUDY

A

Abbaḷati (PP) Kan + Kan; N + Suf + N; Abba(e) + ḷ + ati < haṭṭi ? Mother's home; PN.

Abbūru (KRN, pp, Huṇ); Kan + Kan; N + N; Abbe + ūr; Mother's village; PN.

Achaṭṭipura (CRN); ? + Skt; N + N; Achaṭṭi + pura ?

Aḍaganahaḷḷi (KRN); -di- (Huṇ); Kan + Kan; N + Suf + N; Aḍiga + (n)a + haḷḷi; Cook's village; PN. ~ Aḍahaḷḷi (Heg).

Aḍagūru (KRN, Huṇ); Kan + Kan; V adj + N; Aḍagu + ūru; Hiding habitat; GPN.

Aḍakanahaḷḷi (Nan); Kan + Kan; N + Suf + N; Aḍaka + (n)a + haḷḷi; PN.

Agara (Yaḷ) < Aghrāra < Agrahāra; Skt.; (Huṇ 32/1669; Koḷ 30/1321); SX/RN; A village gifted to Brahmans; ~ Agara + Dēva + (r)a + haḷḷi (Yaḷ) Brahmans' village of gods.

Agasanahuṇḍi (Heg); Kan + Kan; N + Suf + N; Agasa + (n)a + huṇḍi; Washerman's hamlet; EN.

Agasthyapura (TNP); Skt + Skt; N + N; Agastya + pura; A village after a sage by name Agasthya; RN.

Agathagowḍanahaḷḷi (Guṇ); Kan < Skt + Kan; N + Suf + N; Agatha < agasthya + gowḍa + (n)a + haḷḷi; PN.

Agaṭhthūru (Heg); Kan < Skt + Kan; N + I + N; Agath < Agasthya ? + th + ūru; PN.

Ajjipura (Koḷ 70-12th); Kan + Skt; N + N; Ajji + pura; grandmother's village; PN.

Akala (Nan); Kan < Skt + Kan; N + N; Aka < Akka < Arka + āla; Catoropis gigantes + Ficus Indica Roxb; vide DIPN.

Akkūru (TNP 16-1749); Kan + Kan; N + N; Akk(a) + ūru; Elder sister's village ~ Akkadēva + (n)a + haḷḷi; PN.

Ankahaḷḷi (Guṇ, Nan); Skt + Kan; N + N; Anka + haḷḷi; A warrior's village; PN ~ Ankanahaḷḷi (KRN 117-1741, pp, TNP, Heg. Huṇ); Ankanaseṭṭipura (CRN); Anka + (n)a + seṭṭi + pura; Ankapura (Heg)

Angaṭahaḷḷi (Huṇ); ? + Kan; N + N; Angaṭa + haḷḷi; ?

Aṭṭuguḷipura (CRN); Kan + Kan + Skt.; V + N + N; Aḍ(ṭṭ)u + guḷi + pura; Aḍu - to cook, kuḷi - to cook. The two words together mean collective outdoor cooking; MN ~ Aṭṭuguḷiyapura (CRN 242-1656).

Aṇṇarāyanapura (Huṇ); Kan + Kan < Skt + Skt; N + Suf + N; Aṇṇa + rāya < rāja + (n)a + pura; Brother King; PN.

Aṇṇūru (Guṇ, Heg 10/115); Kan + Kan; N + N; Aṇṇ(a) + ūru; elder brother's village; PN ~ Aṇiyūru (Guṇ 150/1521); Aṇṇeyūru (Guṇ 156/1521).

Attahaḷḷi (TNP); Kan + Kan; N + N; Atta(i) + haḷḷi; Name after the red wooded fig tree, Ficus recemona; FLN ~ Attiyakuppe (Hun 12/1172); Attigōḍu; (PP).

Anagaṭṭi (Heg); Kan + Kan; N + N; Ana < Āne (?) + gaṭṭi < haṭṭi (?); elephant Pen; FAN.

Anagaḷḷi (Mys); Kan + Kan; N + N; Ana < Āna (?) < g(k)aḷḷi; a village where big milkhedge, Euphorbia tirukaḷḷi grows; FLN.

Antarasante (Heg); Skt + Kan < Skt; Adj + N; Antara + sante; An interior village where fairs are held; CN.

Amachavāḍi (CRN 260-1368, Mys); Kan + Skt + Kan; N + N; Amacha < Amātya + vāḍi; A hamlet after a minister vide DIPN; ~ Amchavāḍi (CRN 253-1273, 252-1380).

Ambalāre (PP) Ambala + are (?)

Ambaḷe (Yal 208-673, Nan); SX; Kan; N; An open hall; MN ~ Ambala (Yaḷ 17-11th), Ambalai (210-1244), Ammeḷe (15-1283).

Ameerhosahaḷḷi (Guṇ); Arab + Kan + Kan; N + Adj + N; Ameer + hosa + haḷḷi; a new village after Ameer; HN.

Ammanapura (CRN); Kan + Skt; N + Suf + N; Amma + (n)a + pura; Grand mother's village; PN; Amma = Father (OK).

Arabigere (koḷ); Arab + Kan; N + N; Arabi + g(k)ere; A village founded by an Arab; EN.

Aragowḍanahaḷḷi (Mys); Kan + Kan + Kan; N + Suf + N + N; Ara + gowḍa + (n)a + haḷḷi; PN; Ara = dharma. ~ Arakere (KRN); N + N; A village after a tank constructed for charity.

Arakalavāḍi (CRN 301/1555); Kan + Kan + Kan; N + N + N; Ara(e) + kala + vāḍi; GPN; A village where there is a quarry.

Araḷikaṭṭe (CRN); Kan + Kan; N + N; Araḷi + kaṭṭe; A village after a tank raised around a peepul tree; FLN. ~ Araḷikumari (PP); A village estabilshed after clearing the forest where peepul trees grew.

Arasinakere (Mys); Kan + Kan; N + Suf + N; Aras(u) + in(a) + kere; A village founded by a king; HN.

Aravaṭṭige Koppal (TNP); Kan + Kan; N + N + N; Ara < Aṟa + vaṭṭige + koppal; A hamlet where a charity shed existed; RN.

Arēnahaḷḷi (PP); Kan < Skt + Kan; N + Suf + N; Are < Āreya < Ārya + (n)a + haḷḷi; A village after an ārya, a cultured man; PN. ~ Āreyanahaḷḷi (71/1586).

Arepāḷya (Koḷ); Kan + Kan; N + N; Are < aṟe + pāḷya; A village after a rock; GPN. ~ Arepura (Guṇ 61/1048).

Ariyūr (Nan 377/1502); Kan + Kan; V + N; Ari + y(ū)r; A village known for thrashing corn (?) vide DIPN.

Arjunahaḷḷi (KRN); Skt + Kan; N +; Arjuna + ; A mythological name, being the third brother of Pāṇḍavas or the tree terminalia arjuna; RN.

Avalkandahaḷḷi (Yaḷ); Kan + Kan + Kan; Vad + N + ; Aval + Kanda + ; pounded or beaten bulbous root (?).

Avarekāyiguḍḍada Kāval (PP); Kan + Kan + Kan + Kan; N + N + N + Suf + ; Avarē + kāyi + guḍḍa + (d)a = ; a hillock where a species of pulse, phaseolus radiatus grows; FLN.

Ayyājayanahuṇḍi (Mys); Kan + Kan + Kan; N + N + Suf + ; Ayya + Aj(j)ay(y)a + (n)a + (a doublet); Grandfather; PN.

Aḷaganchi (Heg, Nan); Kan + Kan (?); ad + N; Aḷa < Haḷa (?) + k(g)anchi; Old Kanchi < Conjeevaram or sour orange (?); FLN.

Aḷagumūle (Koḷ); Kan + Kan; N +

Aḷalahaḷḷi (Koḷ); Kan + Kan; N + ; Aḷala + ; Terminalia chebula; FLN. ~ Aḷalūru (PP).

Ādibeṭṭahaḷḷi (TNP); Skt + Kan + Kan; N + N + N; Ādi + beṭṭa + haḷḷi; A village near the original hiḷl; GPN.

Ālahaḷḷi (Koḷ 11-1514); Kan + Kan; N + N; Āla + haḷḷi; A village after a banyan tree; FLN. ~ Ālagōḍu (TNP); Kōḍu = branch; Ālambāḍi Kāval (KRN); Ālambāḍi (Koḷ 45-17th); Ālam(ma) + b(v)āḍi; PN. Ālambūru (Nan); Ālanahaḷḷi (Heg 13-1670, Mys, pp); PN. Ālatthūr (Guṇ); Ālkere agrahāra (Yaḷ); Ālakere; 168-1519; Ālūru (CRN, 186-1058, 108-1165).

Āanandūru (Mys 14/13th, 112/1797); Skt + Kan; N + N; Ānand(a) + ūru; pleasure village; MN.

Ānapura (Koḷ); Kan + Skt; N + ; Ana + ; elephant's town (?); FAN.

Āṇḍipāḷya (Koḷ); Tam + Kan; N + ; Āṇḍi + pāḷya; After religious mendicant of the Śaivas; RN.

Ānechowkūru (PP); Kan + Kan + Kan; N + N + N; Āne +chowk(a) + ūru; A village named after elephant's resort; FAN. ~ Ānemāḷa (Heg); Ānivāḷu (PP); N + N; Āni + v(b)ālu.

Āspatrekāval (Huṇ); Kan < Eng + Kan; N + ; Āspatre < hospital + ; MN.

Āswāḷu (Hun, pp); Kan + Kan; N + N; Asu + v(b)āḷu (?) ~ Asumbāḷu (Huṇ 24/1162).

Āvarti (PP); SX; Skt; Repetition, Return ?

Āyarabīḍu (PP); Kan + Kan; N + Suf + ; Āya < ayya + (r)a + ; After a jangama; RN. ~ Āyarahaḷḷi (Huṇ, Mys, KRN 117/1741).

B

Bakkarehaḷḷada Kāvalu (KRN); Kan + Kan + Kan; N + N + Suf + N; Bakkare + haḷḷa + (d)a + ; A village by the side of a rivulet, strewn with pieces of pot, GPN.

Bankaḷḷi (Nan); Kan < Skt + Kan; N + N; Banka < Vakra + haḷḷi; a corner village (?); NN. ~ Bankavāḍi (Heg 99/1504).

Baḍagalapura (CRN); Kan + Skt; N + Suf + ; Baḍaga + l(a) + ; Northern village; NN.

Baṇḍahaḷḷi (KRN); Kan < Skt + Kan; Adj + ; Baṇḍa < Bhāṇḍa + (Skt?); rich village; MN.

Baṇḍigere (CRN 263/1316); Kan + Kan; N + N; Baṇḍi + g(k)ere; A village named after a tank near which carts were manufactured or stationed; CN. ~ Baṇḍipāḷya (Mys); Baṇḍipura (Guṇ).

Badanaguppe (CRN, Heg 145/1573); Kan + Kan; N + N; Badana + g(k)uppe; Brinjal village; FLN. ~ Badanavāḷu (Nan); Badanivāḷa (Nan 273/1488).

Bandigowḍanahaḷḷi (CRN, 26/1368); Kan + Kan + Kan; N + N + Suf + ; Bandi + gowḍa + (n)at + ; PN.

Bannahaḷḷi (TNP); Kan + Kan; N + N; Banna < Banni + ; Prosopis Spicigera Lin; FLN. ~ Bannaḷḷi (TNP 15/1612); Bannihaḷḷi (TNP 16/1749); Bannavāḍi (Heg); Bannikuppe (Huṇ 20/17th, KRN); Bannisārige (Yaḷ); Bannitāḷapura (Guṇ); Bannūr (TNP 73/1367); Banniyūru (TNP 47/9th, 60/1421); Vanniyūr (TNP 68/11th); Vahnipura (TNP 48/9th).

Baraḍanapura (Mys); Kan + Skt; N + ; Baraḍa + (n)a + ; An empty person (?); PN.

Baragi (Heg, Guṇ); SX; Kan; < Baragu; A kind of grain, paspalum frumentaceum; FLN.

Barase (PP); SX; Kan; A name applied to several small species of euphorbia (?).

Balachavāḍi (Guṇ 136/1513); Kan < Skt + Kan; Balacha + ; A village named after a powerful man; PN.

Ballahaḷḷi (Guṇ 71/1537, Mys); Kan + Kan; N + ; a village after a knowledgeable person; PN. ~ Ballēnahaḷḷi (Huṇ); N + Suf + ; Ballēna < Ballayyana.

Basalāpura (PP); Kan + Skt; N + ; The plant basella cordifolia lim; FLN.

Basavanahaḷḷi (TNP, Mys); Kan < Skt + Kan; N + Suf + ; Basava < Vrishabha + (n)a + ; a village after a bull or PN. ~ Basavana ēṇi (PP); Basavanakōṭe (Heg 71/15th); Basavanahaḷḷi (PP); Basavapaṭṇa (KRN); Basavanapura (TNP 174/1542, Nan, CRN); Basavapura (Guṇ 115/1543, CRN); Basavaṭṭi (CRN 126/791); Basavaṭṭige (Nan).

Basavarājapura (KRN); Kan < Skt + Skt; N + N + ; Basava + rāja + ; PN. A saint of the 12th cen. RN.

Bastimādahaḷḷi (Huṇ); Kan < Skt + Kan < Skt + Kan; N + N + ; Basti < Vasati + māda < Mahadēva + ; A village after Māda who hails from a place where Jains live; PN. ~ Bastimādaḷḷi (Huṇ 32/1669); Bastipura (CRN, Koḷ 91/7th).

Baṭaguppa (Koḷ); Kan < Skt + Kan; N + N; Baṭa < Bhaṭa (Skt ?) + g(k)uppa; After a brave warrior/A free land granted by a ruler to a learned Brāhmaṇa (?); MN.

Baṭiganahaḷḷi (KRN 87/1606); Kan + Kan; N + Suf + ; Baṭiga + (n)a + ; PN (?).

Baḷḷūru (KRN); Kan + Kan; N + N; Baḷḷu + ūru; A village named after a jackal; FAN.

Bāchagowḍanahaḷḷi (Huṇ); Kan + Kan + Kan; N + N + Suf + ; PN; A village after a man who deals with adzes; PN. ~ Bāchahaḷḷi (KRN, Guṇ 184/1598); Bāchanahaḷḷi (Guṇ); Bāchihaḷḷi (Guṇ 183/1598).

Bāḍuga (Heg); SX; Kan < Skt; < Vāṭikā (Skt ?).

Bāgali (CRN); SX; Kan < Bāgil ?; A gate.

Bāgūru (TNP, Nan); Kan + Kan; N + N; Bāg(e) + ūru; The tree acacia; FLN. ~ Bāgevūru (TNP 96/1497).

Bāṇagavāḍi (TNP); Skt + Kan; N + ; Bāṇaga + ; A preparer of fireworks; MN. ~ Bāṇahaḷḷi (CRN).

Bāvalāḷu (PP); Kan + Kan; N + N; Bāvala + ā(hā)ḷu; A place where bats are in plenty (?); FAN.

Beḍaguḷi (CRN); Kan + Kan; N + N; Beḍa(gu) + guḷi; The beautiful low-lying area (?); GPN. Vide DIPN.

Beddalapura (Heg); Kan + Kan; N + N; Beddala + pura; Dry land; GPN.

Bekkere (PP 43/1619); Kan + Kan; N + N; Be(ḷ)k + kere; White tank; GPN.

Bekya (PP); SX; Kan ?

Benkipura (Hun); Kan + Skt; N + N; Benki + pura; Fire village; GPN.

Belavatta (Mys); Kan < Skt + Kan < Skt; N + N; Bela < Bilva + vatta + patra (Skt); Wood apple, Aegle marmelos; FLN. ~ Bellavatta (Mys 116/1517).

Beḷachalavāḍi (Guṇ); Kan + Kan; N + N; Beḷachala + vāḍi; A hamlet known for raising agricultural crops; GPN; Vide DIPN. ~ Beḷachavāḍi (Guṇ 45/10th); Byāḷachalavāḍi (Guṇ 61/1126).

Beḷaganahaḷḷi (Heg); Kan + Kan; N + Suf + N; Beḷaga + (n)a + haḷḷi; A white man's village; PN.

Beḷagunda (Nan); Kan + Kan; Adj + N; Beḷ + a + g(k)unda; A village near a white mountain; GPN. ~ Biḷagunda (PP); Biḷikere (Hun 21/1843); Biḷigere (Nan, Huṇ); Biḷigiriranganabeṭṭa (Yaḷ 196/1667, 198/1190); Beḷavāḍi (Nan 159/1504, Guṇ, Mys).

Beḷale (Nan. 161/1632); SX; A small spinous tree, wood apple; FLN.

Beḷattūru (Huṇ, pp, Heg, Koḷ 85/1678); Kan + Kan; Adj + Suf + ; Beḷ + att + ;. Village surrounded by white earth; GPN. ~ Viḷattūr (Koḷ 86/12th).

Bemmatti (PP); Kan + Kan; N + N; Beḷ + matti; White teak of the genus Terminalia; FLN.

Beṇagallu (PP); Kan + Kan; N + N; Beṇa < Beḷ + g(k)allu; White stone; a stone as white as butter; GPN.

Beṇḍagaḷḷi (Nan, Guṇ); Kan + Kan; N + N; Beṇḍa(e) + g(h)aḷḷi; Hibiscus esculentus Lin; FLN.

Beṇḍaravāḍi (CRN, Guṇ); Kan + Kan; N + N; Beṇḍar + a + vāḍi; Hunters' hamlet (?); EN; Vide DIPN.

Beṇṇegere (Heg); Kan + Kan; N + N; Beṇṇe + g(k)ere; A village where butter is available; CN.

Benaganahaḷḷi (KRN, Mys 215/1175); Kan < Skt + Kan; N + Suf + ; Benaga < Vināyaka (Skt) + (ṅ)a + ; A village after Vināyaka, the son of Siva; RN. ~ Benakanahaḷḷi (TNP 121/16th); Binakanahalli (TNP).

Beraṭahaḷḷi (Guṇ 109/13th, 111/1188); Kan + Kan; V + N; Beraṭa < beraṇtu + haḷḷi; A village founded after digging (?); GPN.

Beṭṭadabīḍu (Heg, Guṇ 147/1448); Kan + Kan; N + Suf + ; Beṭṭa + (d)a + ; An abode or village on or near a mountain; GPN. ~ Beṭṭadapura (CRN, pp 10/1600, 59/1607); Beṭṭadatunga (pp 105/ 15th, 107/1300, 110/1586); Beṭṭadūru (Huṇ); Beṭṭahaḷḷi (TNP 8/ 1513, Heg 48/1255, CRN, KRN, Guṇ 133/1311, 130/16th); Beṭṭadahaḷḷi (TNP 16/1749); Vīṭṭan (Tam) > beṭṭada + paḷḷi (TNP 84/1179); Beṭṭadamādahaḷḷi (Guṇ); Beṭṭadāvare [Mountain lotus] huṇḍi (Heg).

Bēgūru (Guṇ, Heg, PP); Kan + Kan; N + N; Bēg(v)(u) + ūru; A village full of Margosa trees; FLN. ~ Dāribēgūru (Guṇ) [dāri = road]; Hirebēgūru (CRN 348/1372) [old margosa village]; Bēhūru (Guṇ 44/1663); Vēgūru (TNP 148/17th); Bēvinahaḷḷi (KRN); Bēvinatāḷapura (CRN); Bēvinapaḷḷi (TNP 95/1497).

Bēḍarapura (CRN 5/1818); Kan < Skt + Skt; N + Suf + ; Bēḍa < Vyādha + (r)a + ; A village of huntsmen; EN. ~ Bēḍarahaḷḷi (PP); Byāḍarahaḷḷi (KRN).

Bērambāḍi (Guṇ 216/1562, 219/10th, 20/1090); Kan + Kan; N + Suf + N; Bēr + am + b(p)āḍi; A place where herbal roots grow (?); FLN.

Bēvinahaḷḷi (KRN); Vide Bēgūr.

Biḍagalu (Heg); Kan + Kan; N + N; Biḍa (i/u) + g(k)al(l)u; A lone or loose stone; GPN.

Bidarahaḷḷi (Heg); Kan + Kan; N + Suf + ; Bidar + a + ; A village where bamboo grows; FLN. ~ Bidaragūḍu (Nan).

Biḷagunda (PP); Vide Beḷagunda.

Billahaḷḷi (PP); Kan < Skt + Kan; N + ; billa < bhilla (?) + ; A village of huntsmen; EN. ~ Billaḷḷi (Heg); Billanahosahaḷḷi (Huṇ).

Biḷugali (Nan); Kan + Kan; Adj + N; biḷu + g(k)al(l)i(u); A village where white stone is available; GPN. ~ Byāḍarabiḷugali (Nan 26/15th. 27/1594); Rājanabeḷagali (pp 91/1407).

Bisalavāḍi (CRN); Kan + Kan; N + Suf + N; Bisa(i)l + a + vāḍi; A village where sunshine is in plenty; NN.

Bīchanahaḷḷi (Heg 150/1499, KRN); Kan + Kan; N + Suf + ; B(P)īcha + (n)a + ; A short man; PN. ~ Chikka [small] bīchanahaḷḷi (Huṇ); Doḍḍa [big] bīchanahaḷḷi (Huṇ).

Bīḍanahaḷḷi (TNP, pp); Kan + Kan; N + Suf + ; Bīḍ(u)a + (n)a + ; A village after a campaigner; PN.

Bījaganahaḷḷi (Huṇ); Skt + Kan; N + Suf + ; Bījaga + (n)a + ; A village after a man who produces seeds; PN.

Bīranahaḷḷi (Heg, Huṇ, KRN 117/1741); Kan < Skt + Kan; N + Suf +; bīra < vīra (Skt) + (n)a + ; A valorous man; PN. ~ Bīrathammanahaḷḷi (Huṇ); PN; Bīrawāla (Heg 122/1079).

Bokkahaḷḷi (Nan); Kan + Kan; N + ; Bokka + ; A village of flat land, GPN. ~ Bokkepura (CRN).

Bogganapura (CRN); Kan < Skt + Skt; N + Suf + ; Bogga < Bhōga [plenty, rich] (?) / < bagga < vyāghra (Skt) [tiger] + ; FAN. ~ Boggapalli (Nan 13/19th).

Bommalāpura (Heg, Guṇ, Huṇ 43/1013, Nan 174/1318, 175/9th); Kan < Skt + Skt; N + Fem.Ind. + ; Bomma < brahma (Skt) + la + ; Wife of Brahma, Saraswathi; FPN.

Bommanahaḷḷi (CRN, Guṇ 135/1492, TNP, Mys 194/1506); Kan < Skt + Kan; N + Suf + ; Bomma < Brahma (Skt) [creator]; PN. ~ Bommanāyakanahaḷḷi (TNP) PN; bommēnahaḷḷi (Mys, KRN 117/1741, CRN 243/1648).

Boppanahaḷḷi (Heg); Kan + Kan; N + Suf + ; boppa [Father] + (n)a +; PN.

Bōganahaḷḷi (pp 71/1586); Kan < Skt + Kan; N + Suf + ; Bōga < bhōga + (n)a + ; A village after a happy or ruling man; PN. ~ Bōgāpura (CRN).

Bōḷanahaḷḷi (Huṇ); Kan + Kan; N + Suf + ; Boḷa [A man with a bald head] + (n)a; PN.

Būchahaḷḷi (Huṇ); Kan + Kan; N + ; Būcha + ; A village where mildew occurs; NN.

Būdabāḷu (Koḷ); Kan < Skt + Kan; N + ; būda + < bhūti/Budha; Ash field/the plant Mercury; GPN. ~ Būdahaḷḷi (Koḷ); Būdambaḷḷi (CRN), Būdithiṭṭu (CRN), Būdanūru (Heg).

Bylaguppe (Guṇ); Kan + Kan; N + N; Byla < bayalu + g(k)uppe; A village in an open plain; GPN. ~ Bylakuppe (PP), Bylāpura (KRN), Bylāru (Nan), Bylūru (Koḷ).

Byranatta (Koḷ); Kan < Skt + Tam; N + N; Byra < bhyrava + natta A town after Bhyrava, A form of Śiva; RN. ~ Byrāpura (Heg, TNP 16/1749, 30/1392); Bayiravapura (TNP 30/15th).

Byāṭahaḷḷi (Mys); Kan + Kan; N + ; Byāṭa < bēṭe + ; A village whose residents are known for hunting; EN.

Bhadrayyanahaḷḷi (Koḷ 73/1105); Skt + Kan; N + Suf + ; Bhadrayya + (n)a + ; [Strong and prosperous man]; PN.

Bharatavāḍi (Huṇ); Skt + Kan; N + N; Bharata + vāḍi; Village after an epic person, Bharata; RN.

Bhērya (KRN 87/1606); SX; < bhēri [A kettle-drum]; / < byāri < vyāpāri (Skt ?) [a muslim tradesman]; EN.

Bhīmanabīḍu (Guṇ); Skt + Kan; N + Suf + ; Bhīma + (n)a + ; A village after Bhīma, a Mahābhārata hero; RN. ~ Bhīmanahaḷḷi (Heg).

Bhōgādi (Mys); Skt + Kan ?; N + N; Bhōga + ādi; [Any winding curve, an army in column] ? ~ Bhōgavāḷu Voḍeyanapura (Nan).

Bhugatahaḷḷi (Mys, TNP) Kan < Skt + Kan; N + N; Bhugata < Bhukta + ; The act of eating, food; MN.

Bhujaganapura (CRN); Skt + Skt; N + Suf + ; Bhujaga + (n)a + ; A village after a person who bears the name of serpent god; PN.

Bhuvanahaḷḷi (pp 42/12th, KRN); Skt + Kan; N + ; Bhuvana + ; A forest village (?)/A village which represents the world; MN. ~ Būvanahaḷḷi (KRN 117/1741).

Bhūtanahaḷḷi (PP); Skt + Kan; N + Suf + ; Bhūta + (n)a + A creature, a demon, an element; PN.

C

Chakkūru (Heg, pp); Kan < Skt + Kan; N + N; Chakk(a) < Chakra + ūru; A village where wheels are manufactured (?); CN.

Challahaḷḷi (Huṇ); Kan + Kan; N + ; Challa + ; A village where fun and amusements are found; MN.

Channaguṇḍi (Heg); Kan + Kan; N + ; Channa + ; Beautiful, red; PN. ~ Channakallu Kāval (PP); Channalinganahaḷḷi (Koḷ), Channamallipura (Guṇ), Channamallupura (Guṇ 61/1126); Channapaṭṇa (Nan); Chnnappanapura (CRN 246/1613), Chennanje Vaḍeyanapura (TNP), Channasōge (Huṇ).

Channamgere (KRN); Kan + Kan; N + N; Channa + am(ma) + g (k)ere; FPN.

Chandagālu (KRN); Kan + Kan; N + N; Chanda + g(k)ālu; Beautiful village; GPN. ~ Chandahaḷḷi (TNP 18/1726), Chandavāḍi (TNP 210/15th).

Chandakavāḍi (CRN 214/1698); Kan + Kan; N + ; Chandak(k)a + ; FPN.

Chandrabīḍu (Mys); Skt + Kan; N + ; Chandra + ; Village named after the moon NN.

Changa (KRN 47/1741); SX; Kan; That which is red; leaping.

Changadarahaḷḷi (KRN); Kan + Kan; Adj + N + ; Chan + g(k)adara +; Fine spindle.

Changaḍi (Koḷ); Kan + Kan; N + N; Changa + aḍi < vāḍi; (?); Name of a ruling family; HN.

Changowḍanahaḷḷi (Heg); Kan + Kan < Skt + Kan; N + N + Suf + ; Chan(na) + gowḍa + (n)a + ; PN.

Chapparadahaḷḷi (PP); Kan + Kan; N + Suf + ; Chappara + (d)a + ; Pandal; MN

Charapura (PP); Kan < ? + Skt; N + ; Chara < Chāra + ; A village where fodder for cattle is available.

Chaṭṭanahaḷḷi (Mys); Kan + Kan; N + N; Chaṭṭa + (n)a + haḷḷi; A village established by a disciple.

Chāmalāpura (Heg 17/1669, KRN, Nan); Kan < Skt + Skt; N + Fen.Ind; Chāma + lā < Śyama + lā + ; Dark coloured lady; FPN,

Chāmanahaḷḷi (Heg, TNP); Kan < Skt + Kan; N + Suf + ; Chāma < Śyāma + (n)a; Dark coloured man; PN.

Chāmarājanagara (CRN 5/1828); Kan < Skt + Skt + Skt; N + N +; Chāma + rāja + ; PN. ~ Chāmarāyana Kōṭe (PP); Original name; Arakoṭhāra (10/1281, 293/1532) ~ Arekoṭhāra (315/1551), Arikuṭhāra (60/1518), Arikoṭāra (294/1767).

Chāmuṇḍibeṭṭa (Mys 135/1127, 136/1620, 148/1827); Skt + Kan; N +; Chāmuṇḍi + ; RN.

Chāṭipura (CRN); Kan + Skt; N + ; Chāṭi + ; A whip made of cord or leather/barter (?); MN.

Chibukahaḷḷi (KRN); Skt + Kan; N + ; Chibuka + ; Chīn (?);

Chidaravaḷḷi (TNP 100/13th, 99/1420, 103/1498); Kan < Skt + Kan; V + N; Chidara < Chidra (?)/Chedaru + v(h)aḷḷi; A slit, a fissure, to disperse, scatter (?).

Chikka, an adjective, meaning little, small or young. Generally, whenever a person migrates from his original village and founds a new village, he calls it a small village. For example, Bīchanahaḷḷi becomes Chikkabīchanahalli. There is a good number of villages named in this fashion only. A selected few names which are found in inscriptions are given below:

Chikaṇāpura (Guṇ); Chikaṇā < Chikkaṇṇa; Chikkanapura (81/1482); ~ Chikkaṇṇanahaḷḷi (81/1482); Chikkabyranakuppe (Heg); PN. Chikkādiganahaḷḷi (Huṇ); PN. Chikkahomma (Nan 298/1526); Chikkakānya (Mys) (?)/Chikkānya (196/1064)/Chikānya (198/10th); Chikkakavalande (Nan); Kan + Skt + Skt; Adj + N + N; Chikka + Kaval < Kapila + ande < Nandi/Chikkakavalande (306/1292); Chikkakavalandi (306/1292); Kiriya Kavalandi (301/10th); Chikkamaḷali (PP)/Chikkamaḷale (134/16th); Chikkanahaḷḷi (Mys); PN. Chikkanandi (Heg)/Nan 380/17th; Chikkanāyakanahaḷḷi (KRN); PN. Chikkāṭi (Gun)/Nan 318/1761; Chikkavoḍḍaraguḍi (KRN); ~ Chikkavaḍḍaraguḍi (117/1741); Chikkayyanachatra (Nan); PN. Chikkelūru (Koḷ); Adj + N + N; Chikka + ele + ūru; small leaf.

Chillahaḷḷi (Heg); Kan + Kan; Adj + ; Chilla + ; A small village; MN.

Chilukavāḍi (Koḷ 11/1514); Tel + Kan; N + ; Chiluka + V(P)āḍi; Parrot; FAN. ~ Chilkunda (Huṇ)/Chiluka + kunda.

Chimili (TNP); SX; Kan (?); A parrot; the sound of a parrot (?).

Chinchahaḷḷi (Koḷ); Kan + ; N + ; A village which has a well/tamarind tree or fruit (?).

Chinnambaḷḷi (Nan); Kan + Kan; N + N; Chinna(ma) + b(h)aḷḷi; A village after a gold-like lady; FPN.

Chiṭṭēnahaḷḷi (PP); Kan + Kan; Adj + Suf + ; Chiṭṭa < Chiṭṭayya + (n)a; After a small or short man; PN. ~ Chiṭṭanakuppe (32/1669).

Chirakanahaḷḷi (Guṇ 150/1521); Kan + Kan; N + Suf + ; Chiraka < Chiṟu + (n)a + ; After a small man; PN.

Chiṭṭikyātanahaḷḷi (Huṇ); Kan + Kan < Skt + Kan; Adj + N + Suf +; Chiṭṭi + Kyāta + (n)a + ; After a small Folk god; RN.

Chīranahaḷḷi (Huṇ); Kan + Kan; N + Suf + ; Chīra + (n)a + ; After a a man wearing rag or cloth; [The dress of a Buddhist priest].

Choṭnahaḷḷi (Heg); Kan + Kan; N + Suf + ; Choṭ < Choṭṭa/Chōṭa (?) + (n)a + ; A Crooked or small person.

Chōḷēnahaḷḷi (Mys, KRN 46/1761); Kan < Tam + Kan; N + Suf + ; Chōḷe < Chōḷayya + (n)a + ; A man from the coast of Coromandel; PN.

Chōranahaḷḷi (Mys); Skt + Kan; N + Suf + ; Chōra + (n)a + ; After a thief; PN.

Chowḍanahaḷḷi (Heg, CRN, Mys); Kan < Skt + Kan; N + ; Chowḍa < Chāvuṇḍa; Chāmuṇḍa; RN. ~ Chowḍēnahaḷḷi (PP).

Chowhaḷḷi (TNP); Kan < Skt + Kan; Adj + ; Chow < Chatuh + ; A village with a square or a village where many roads meet; GPN. ~ Chowkahaḷḷi (KRN) Chowkūru (PP).

Chowti (PP); Vide Chowhaḷḷi.

Chunchanahaḷḷi (Nan); Kan + Kan; N + Suf + ; Chuncha + (n)a + ; After a person with red or brown colour; PN. ~ Chunchanakaṭṭe (KRN 96/18th, 100/18th).

D

Daḍadahaḷḷi (KRN, Mys, TNP 79/1667, 16/1749); Kan < Skt + Kan; N + Suf; Daḍa < taṭa + (d)a + ; A village on the river bank; GPN. ~ Daḍadakallahaḷḷi (Mys).

Dammanahaḷḷi (KRN); Kan < Skt + Kan; N + Suf + ; Damma < Dharma + n(a) + ; A man devoted to pious act; PN.

Daṇāyakanapura (TNP); Kan < Skt + Skt; N + Suf + ; Daṇāyaka < Daṇḍanāyaka + (n)a + ;/Doṇenāyaka + (n)a + ; A general (?); A person in charge of a natural receptacle of water between two rocks; PN.

Daṇḍikere (Mys); Kan < Skt + Kan/Kan + Kan; N + ; Daṇḍ(u) + / Daṇde + ; A tank where army is stationed/a nearby tank; MN.

Daṇṭahaḷḷi (Koḷ); Kan + Kan; N + ; Daṇṭa(u) + ; A village where a kind of green vegetable grows; FLN.

Dāripura (Mys); Kan + Skt; N + ; Dāri + ; A village on the road; GPN.

Dāsanapura (Heg, Huṇ 32/1669, Koḷ 20/1842); Kan < Skt + Skt; N + Suf + ; Dāsa + (n)a + ; A village after a devotee; PN ~ Dāsanūru (Nan 302/1512, 290/1278, CRN 302/1536; 29/1744, Hun 32/1669).

Daṭṭagaḷḷi (Mys); Kan + Kan; Adj + N; Daṭṭa + g(h)aḷḷi; Crowded or dense village; MN.

Degganahaḷḷi (KRN 106/1259); Kan + Kan; N + Suf + ; Degga + (n)a + ; A village after a big or robust man (?).

Dēbūru (Nan 133/1818); Kan < Skt + Kan; N + ; dēb < dēv + ; After a God; RN.

Dēmahaḷḷi (CRN); Kan < Skt + Kan; N + ; Dēma < dēva + ; A village after a god; RN. ~ Dēmaḷḷi (119/1512).

Dēpāpura (Guṇ); Kan < Skt + Kan; N + ; Dēpa < dēva (?) After a god; RN. ~ Dēpēgowḍanapura (Nan) PN; Dēpura (PP).

Dēśavaḷḷi (CRN); Skt + Kan; N + N; Dēśa + v(h)aḷḷi; A village with merchant guilds/a noted or excellent place. ~ Dēśapura (25/1665); Dēśipura (CRN 33/1668, Guṇ).

Dēvagaḷḷi (Mys 204/1274); Skt + Kan; N + ; Dēva + g(h)aḷḷi; In the name of god or a person or a king. ~ Dēvanahaḷḷi (204/1294); Dēvanūru (Mys, Nan 277/1517, 278/1808, 338/1530) Dēvarahaḷḷi (Guṇ, Huṇ); K-Dēvarahaḷḷi (Yaḷ 168/1519); Dēvarājapura (CRN); Dēvarasanahaḷḷi (Nan); Dēvarāyaseṭṭipura (Nan).

Dēvalāpura (CRN 313/17th, 314/1218; Heg, Guṇ; Huṇ 32/1669; Mys 193/1184); Skt + Kan; N + Fem.Ind + ; Dēva + lā + ; Goddess or FPN. Dēvala also means an attendant (?); ~ Dyāvalāpura (Mys, KRN 46/1761).

Dēvīrammanahaḷḷi (Nan); Skt + Kan < Skt + Kan; N + N + Suf + ; Dēv(i) + īramma < Vīramma + (n)a + ; FPN.

Dhanagaḷḷi (Mys); Skt/Kan + Kan; N + N; Dhana/dana + g(h)aḷḷi; Wealth, Cattle; MN. ~ Dhanagere (Koḷ).

Dharmāpura (Huṇ 24/1162); Skt + Skt; N + N; Dharmā + pura; Tagaravāḍi and Manneyabūvanahaḷḷi converted into an agrahāra and named Dharmāpura - A village known for pious act; RN. ~ Dammāpura (25/1115).

Diṇḍagāḍu (PP); Kan + Kan; N + N; Diṇḍa + g(k)āḍu; The tree Anogeissus lati folia; FLN.

Dinnahaḷḷi (Koḷ); Kan + Kan; N + ; Dinna < diṇṇe + ; A village on a rising ground; GPN.

Doḍḍa means large, big. Explanations given under 'Chikka' applies to this word also:- byaḷāḷu (PP) ~ Belahāḷu (121/1545); Bellahāḷu (122/1344) -hejjūru (Huṇ); -Kānya (Mys); -Kavalande (Nan) ~ Periyakavalandai (268/15th); Hiriyakavilande (311/1437); -malagōḍu (TNP); -mōḷe (CRN); -kūtanūru (Guṇ 224/1405).

Doḷḷipura (CRN); Kan + Skt; Adj/N + ; Doḷḷi (?) / < ḍōlu + ; A hollow village/A village after a large drum (?).

Dorekere (PP); Kan + Kan; N + N; Dore + kere; Named after a king; PN.

Ḍōranahaḷḷi (KRN); Kan + Kan; N + Suf + ; Ḍōra + (n)a + ; After a person who colours leather; PN.

Duddagere (Mys); Kan + Kan; N + N; Dudda + g(k)ere; The inner pulpy mass of a cucumber; A village where cucumbers are grown; FLN ~ Duddahaḷḷi (KRN).

Duggahaḷḷi (Nan); Kan < Skt + Kan; N + ; dugga < Durga + ; A village difficult of access, a fort. ~ Duggahaṭṭi (Yaḷ); Dugihaṭṭi (12/1511).

Dundāsanapura (guṇ); Kan + Skt + Skt; Adj + N + Suf + ; Dun < dundu + dāsa + (n)a + ; A mendicant or a devotee given to prodigality; PN.

Duyyamkandahaḷḷi (Yaḷ); N + N + ; Duyyam (?) + kanda + ?

Dūra (Mys) SX; Skt; A distant village.

Dytanakerekāvalu (Huṇ); Kan < Skt + Kan; N + Suf + N + ; Dyta < Daitya + (n)a + kere; After a demon; PN.

G

Gaḍiguḍḍadakāvalu (Nan); Kan + Kan + Kan; N + N + Suf + ; Gaḍi + guḍḍa + (d)a + ; A hillock which forms the border of a village.

Gaḷaganakere (PP); Kan + Kan; N + Suf + ; Gaḷaga < gaḷapa (?) + (n)a + ; A loquacious man. It may even mean a person whose shape is similar to bamboo basket; PN.

Gaḷigekere (KRN 10/890, 104/1577, 107/1741); Kan < Skt + Kan; N + ; Gaḷige < ghaṭika + ; A period of time; [< galage = storage]; MN.

Gaṇaganūru (CRN 105/12th, 107/1387); Skt + Kan; N + Suf + N; Gaṇaga < gaṇaka + (n)a + ūru; After an astrologer; PN. ~ Gaṇiganūru (Yaḷ 179/1564).

Gandhanahaḷḷi (KRN); Skt + Kan; N + Suf + ; Gandha + (n)a + ; After a seller of perfumes or medical drugs; MN.

Gangaḍahaḷḷi (Heg); Kan + Kan; N + ; Gangaḍa < gangaḷa; A place of manufacture of metal plates for eating; MN. ~ Gangaḍahosahaḷḷi (Heg).

Ganganadoḍḍi (Koḷ); Skt + Kan; N + Suf + ; Ganga + (n)a + ; [Perhaps connected with the river Ganga]; PN. ~ Ganganakuppe (PP); Gangavāḍi (CRN).

Gangādharabasavanahaḷḷi (PP); Skt + Kan < Skt + Kan; N + N + Suf + ; Gangādhara + basava + (n)a + ; After Śiva-bull; RN. ~ Gangādharana Kaṭṭe (Koḷ).

Garaganahaḷḷi (Guṇ); Kan < Skt + Kan; N + Suf + ; Garaga < gārgya (?) + (n)a + ; Name of a sage; RN Garuganahaḷḷi (40/1320, 26/1506).

Gargēśwari (TNP); Kan < Skt + Skt; N + N; Garaga < gārgya + īśwari; The wife of the sage Gārgya (?); RN.

Gariguḍḍa (PP); Kan + Kan; N + N; Gari + guḍḍa; After a hill where grass grows; FLN.

Garike Kaṭṭe Kāvalu (Heg); Kan + Kan + Kan; N + N + ; Garike + kaṭṭe + ; After a tank where grass grows; FLN. ~ Gaṟikegāla (Nan 215/1082).

Gaṭṭavāḍi (Naṇ); Kan < Skt + Kan; N + N; Gaṭṭa < ghaṭṭa + V(P)āḍi; A village on the ghaut, a mountain range; GPN. ~ Gaṭṭavāḍipura (Nan).

Gaṭṭigatipura (Heg); Kan + Skt; N + ; Gaṭṭiga(i)ti + ; After a strong, valiant woman; FPN.

Gāgēnahaḷḷi (Huṇ); Kan + Kan; N + Suf + ; Gāgē < gāgayya + (n)a + ; [gaggayya = rough man ?]; PN.

Gāḷipura (CRN 294/1767); Kan + Skt; N + ; Gāḷi + ; A windy (town); NN.

Gāṇiganakoppalu (TNP); Kan + Kan; N + Suf + ; Gāṇiga + (n)a + ; After an oil-miller. ~ Gāṇiganūru (Yaḷ 172/13th, 179/1594).

Gāvaḍagere (Huṇ 6/1633); Kan < Skt + Kan; N + ; Gāvaḍa > gowḍa < grāmāvriddha + ; After a village headman; PN.

Gāyanahaḷḷi (KRN); Skt + Kan; N + ; Gāyana + ; A Village famous for the art of singing; MN. ~ Gāyanapali (77/1377).

Gejjeganahaḷḷi (Nan 208/1586); Kan + Kan; N + Suf + ; Gejjega + (n)a + ; A person who wears tiny bells [gejjuga = a prickly climbing shrub ?]; PN. ~ Gejjagahaṭṭi (212/489); Gejjeyyana Vaḍḍara Kāval (Huṇ).

Gerasanahaḷḷi (Huṇ); Kan + Kan; N + Suf + ; Gerasa + (n)a + ; After a person who manufactures baskets, winnows (?); PN.

Geredaḍa (KRN); Kan + Kan < Skt; N + N; Gere + daḍa < taṭa; A village on a bank which is like a streak. ~ Gēradaḍa (87/1606).

Giragūru (PP); Kan + Kan; N + N; Girag(a) < girugaṭe ? + ūru; A village where a wind driven wheel is installed (?); MN.

Gīkahaḷḷi (Nan); Kan + Kan; N + ; Gīka(u) + ; a kind of grass from which mats are made; FLN.

Gobbaḷikāvalu (PP); Kan + Kan; N + ; gobbaḷi + ; A village where Acacia arabica wild grows.

Goddanapura (Nan); Kan + Skt; N + Suf + ; Godda + (n)a + ; A village where a kind of black ant is found; [ficus asperrima roxb]; FAN.

Gollanabīḍu (Heg); Kan + Kan; N + Suf + ; Golla + (n)a + ; Cowherd's camp; EN. ~ Gollarahosahaḷḷi (PP).

Goṇatagāla (Nan); Kan < Skt + Kan; N + N; Goṇata < Guṇavanta + g(k)āla; After a man of character; PN. ~ Guṇavantagāla (273/1488).

Goraguṇḍi (KRN); Kan < Skt + Kan; N + ; Gora < gorava < Guru +; a place where Śaiva beggars live. ~ Gorahaḷḷi (PP); Gōrahaḷḷi (PP 21/16th); Goravanahaḷḷi (TNP).

Goreyūru (Koḷ); Kan + Kan; N + Suf + N; Gore + Y + ūru; A village with mire, wet soil; GPN.

Gōhaḷḷi (Huṇ, Mys); Skt + Kan; N + ; Gō + ; Cattle village; FAN.

Gōḷūru (Heg 148/16th, Nan); Kan + Kan; N + ; Gōḷ(i) + ; A village famous for Fig tree; FLN.

Gōnahaḷḷi (Nan); Kan + Kan; N + ; Gōna(u) + ; After the tree careya arborea Roxb; A shrubby creeper like Ugani; FLN.

Gōpālapura (Mys 104/1667); Skt + Skt; N + ; After the epic figure Krishṇa; RN.

Gōvindanahaḷḷi (Huṇ); Skt + Kan; N + Suf + N; Gōvinda + (n)a + ; Mythological name; RN. ~ Gōvindavādi (CRN).

Gowḍahaḷḷi (Yaḷ 1/1654); Kan < Skt + Kan; N + ; Gowḍa < Grāmavriddha; After a village headman; PN. Gowḍenahaḷḷi (KRN).

Gowḍikere (Huṇ); Kan < Skt + Kan; N + N; Gowḍi + kere; A village after the wife of a village headman; FPN. ~ Gowḍimāchanāyakanahaḷḷi (Heg).

Guḍumanahaḷḷi (Heg 35/1518); Kan + Kan; N + Suf + ; Guḍuma + (n)a + ; Corpulent, bulky fellow; PN. [< guḍuvana = a big pot].

Guḍḍēnahaḷḷi (PP); Kan + Kan; N + Suf + ; Guḍḍē < guḍḍayya + (n)a + ; After a hill-man; PN.

Guḍibhadranahosahaḷḷi (PP); Kan + Skt + Kan + Kan; N + N + Suf + Adj + N; Guḍi + bhadra + (n)a + hosa + haḷḷi; A new village in the name of Bhadra attached to a temple; PN. ~ Guḍiseṭṭihaḷḷi (Huṇ).

Guḍumādanahaḷḷi (Mys); Kan + Kan < Skt + Kan; N + N + Suf + ; guḍu < guḍasalu + māda < Mahadēva + (n)a +; After Māda who lives in a thatched hut; PN.

Gujjēgowḍanapura (Myṣ); Kan + Kan < Skt + Skt; Adj + N + Suf +; gujjē(a) + gowḍa + (n)a + ; After a short man; PN.

Guḷḷēdahaḷḷi (PP); Kan + Kan; N + Suf + ; Guḷḷe < guḷeya + (d)a + ; A settlement of migrated people; MN.

Gumbaḷḷi (Yaḷ); Kan < Skt + Kan; N + N; gumb(a) < Kumbha + (h)aḷḷi; A village where pots are made; CN. ~ Gumbahaḷḷi (186/10th, 187/1512, 195/1189); Gumbihaḷi (199/1510).

Gummanahaḷḷi (KRN); Kan + Kan; N + Suf + ; gumma + (n)a + ; After a devil-like person; PN. ~ Gummanūru (77/1377).

Guṇḍattūru (Heg); Kan + Kan; Adj + Suf + ; Guṇḍu + at + ; After a round stone; round form; GPN.

Guṇḍēgāla (Koḷ); Kan + Kan; N + + N; guṇḍē < guṇḍayya + g(k)āla; After a deep man, a dandy; PN.

Guṇḍlapēṭe (Guṇ 80/1751); Kan + Kan; N + Suf + ; Guṇḍ(u) + (l)a + ; After a round stone/deep water; GPN.

Gungrālachatra (Mys); Kan + Skt; N + Suf + ; Gungr(u) < gunguru + āla + ; After mosquitos ?; FAN.

Gurūru (Mys 194/1576); Skt + Kan; N + N; Guru + ūru; After any venerable person, a teacher; PN. ~ Guravūru (188/1191); Guruvinapura (Guṇ 100/1665).

Gūḷipura (CRN); Kan + Skt; N + ; Gūḷi + ; After a stud bull; FAN.

H

Habaṭūru (PP); Kan + Kan; N + N; Habaṭ(a) < Habbu ? + ūru; Extended village ? MN.

Habbanakuppe (Huṇ); Kan < Skt ? + Kan; N + Suf + ; Habba < Parva _ (n)a + ; A village after a person who conducts festivals; MN.

Haḍajana (Mys); SX; Kan; < haḍade; An annual allowance of grain or money to carpenters, barbers etc. A village where such people live HN. ~ Haḍadana (185/1384).

Hadināru (Nan 208/1593); Kan + Kan; N + N; Had < pat (din) + āru The Headquarters of sixteen villages; HN.

Hgaranahaḷḷi (Huṇ); Kan + Kan; N + Suf + ; Hagara + (n)a +; After an unimportant man; PN.

Haginavāḷu (Nan 384/17th; Guṇ 175/1488); Kan + Kan; N + N; Hagina + v(b)āḷu; After a gum plant; FLN.

Hakkalapura (Guṇ); Kan + Skt; N + ; Hakkala (u) + ; This is a kind of grant which permits donees to gather gleanings of corn; MN.

Halagannahaḷḷi (PP); Skt + Kan; N + Suf + ; Halaga + (n)a; After a person, well versed in beating tabor; a person who wields plough; PN. ~ Haḷaganahaḷḷi (19/1338, 20/1611).

Halasūru (pp, Heg); Kan + Kan; N + ; Halasu + ; A village famous for jack fruit; FLN.

Halavāra (TNP); SX; Kan; A village of many people; MN.

Hallare (Nan 373/17th); Kan + Kan; Hal + are; The village having for its landmark tooth like bolder; (DIPN)/GPN.

Haḷe precedes a name and indicates that the village is old. Haḷebīḍu (Huṇ) = old camp; Haḷe magge (Heg); Haḷepēṭekaṇṭhāpura (PP); Haḷeyūru (Heg, KRN 16/1623, pp); Haḷepura (Nan 32/1222).

Haḷḷadakoppalu (Huṇ); Kan + Kan; N + Suf + ; Haḷḷa + (d)a +; A village situated on a flat land, a valley, a declivity; GPN. ~ Haḷḷadapura (Guṇ 85/1550); Haḷḷadamādahaḷḷi (Gun 82/10th, 83/11th).

Hammige (PP); SX; Kan; A rope, a band (?).

Hampāpura (Heg, Koḷ, Nan, KRN 113/1033, 112/1422, 104/1577, 117/1741); Kan ? + Skt/Kan < Skt + Skt; N + ; Hampa < Padmapa (?) + ; After Hampa; PN. [Equal share or division].

Hanahaḷḷi (CRN); Kan + Kan; N + N; Hana < Pane; A village where palmyra trees grow; FLN. ~ Hanagōḍu (Huṇ); Hanasōge (KRN).

Hanchīpura (Heg, Guṇ 1/1439, Nan 124/1663); Kan + Skt; N + ; Hanchi + ; A general name of Cyperus; FLN. ~ Hanchitāḷapura (CRN); Hanchya (Mys, Huṇ); Hanchiya (Mys 118/1496).

Handanahaḷḷi (Huṇ); Kan + Kan; N + Suf; Handa + (n)a + ; After a person who is not a coward; PN. [Hande = a coward].

Haṇḍarakaḷḷi (CRN); Kan + Kan + Kan; N + N + N; Haṇḍar (?) + ak < cakka + a(h)alli (?); FPN. Haṇḍarakkanahaḷḷi (182/1240); Haṇḍarakanahaḷḷi (228/1289).

Handhuvinahaḷḷi (Nan); Kan + Kan; N + Suf + ; Handhu (?) + (vin)a + ; (?); PN.

Handiguḍḍa Kāvalu (PP); Kan + Kan + Kan; N + N + N; Handi + guḍḍa + Kāvalu; A pighill; Fan. [Varāha giri = Sanskritised name].

Haṇḍitavaḷḷi (PP 129/16th); Kan < Skt + Kan; N + N; Haṇḍita < paṇdita + v(h)aḷḷi; A village after a scholar; PN.

Hangaḷa (Guṇ); SX; Kan < Skt; Hangaḷa < Pañchakula [< Pankila = muddy soil]; A village inhabited by five artisan classes (DIPN). ~ Panguḷa 198/1275, 202/1656; Hanguḷa 158/15th; Hangula 149/ 1417; Hangaḷahosahaḷḷi (Guṇ); Hangaḷapura (Guṇ).

Hangarepura (CRN 1/1605); Kan + Skt; Hangare [hangaru] + ; An evergreen shrub dodonaca Viscosa Lin. ~ Hangarabōyanahaḷḷi (KRN 107/1643).

Haniyambaḷḷi (TNP); Kan + Kan; N + N ; Haniyam(m)b(h)aḷḷi; A village after a mature lady; FPN.

Hanumanāḷu (TNP); Skt + Kan; N + Suf + N; Hanuma + (n)a + (h)āḷu; After the monkey god; RN.~ Hanumanahaḷḷi (KRN); Hanumanapura (CRN, Nan).

Hanūru (Koḷ 82/1522); Kan + Kan; N + N; Han(i) + ūru; A place where rain falls in drizzle; NN.

Haradanahaḷḷi (CRN 259/14th, 263/1316, 260/1368, 265/1425; Huṇ, KRN, Nan); Kan + Kan + Kan; N + Suf +; Harada + (n)a + ; After a trader; CN. ~ Haradanapaḷi (KRN 27/1377); Haradūru (pp 56/17th, 57/1661). [Another name Vāṇijyapuri (Skt) Gaz].

Haraḷe (Koḷ); SX; Kan; A village where the castor oil plant is cultivated; FLN. ~ Haraḷakōṭe (Huṇ 169/1531); Haraḷahaḷḷi (pp. Huṇ); Haraḷu Kōṭe (CRN 224/1523).

Harambaḷḷi (KRN); Kan + Kan; N + N; Haram < hāruv(m) ? + b(h)aḷḷi; A Brahman's village (?); EN.

Haratale (Nan 387/11th); Skt + Kan; N + N + ; Hara + tale; Śiva's head (?); RN. [heḍatale (?) = the back of the head]. Harattale (Guṇ 61/1126 ?).

Harave (CRN 389/1486, 396/1493, 397/1622; Huṇ 1/13th, 2/1315); SX; Kan; An extension; GPN. [Amaranthus oleraceus wild] ~ Haravemallarājapaṭṇa (PP).

Harilāpura (PP); Skt + Skt; N + ; Harilā < hariyāla + ; FPN. ~ Haḍlāpura (Col).

Harinahaḷḷi (pp 136/16th); Kan < Skt + Kan; N + ; Harina < hariyanna (?) + ; After a person, by name Harina; PN. [hariṇa = deer ?].

Hasugūli (Guṇ); Kan < Skt + Kan; N + VN; Hasu < Paśu + g(k)uli; One who kills cows (?); PN. [A sort of prickly night shade]. ~ Hasukuli (26/1506); Hasuguli (28/1546); Hasukali (31/1217, 40/1320).

Hasuvaṭṭi (TNP); Kan < Skt + Kan; N + N; Hasu + V(P)aṭṭi; After a cattle house; FAN. ~ Hasuvina Kāval (PP).

Hatwāḷu (Nan, Heg); Kan + Kan; N + N; hat(ti) + w(b)āḷu; A village where cotton fields flourish; FLN. ~ Hattivāḷa (389/1582); Hattavāḷu (390/1818); Hattivāḷu (Guṇ 389/1502).

Hāḍya (KRN, TNP 16/1749, Nan); SX; Kan; Hādiya < hāḍi < pāḍi; a settlement. ~ Hāḍiya (Guṇ 40/1320); [renamed as Rāghavāpura].

Hārohaḷḷi (Huṇ, Mys 119/13th); Kan + Kan; N + ; Hāro < hāruva + ; A Brahman's village. ~ Haruvahaḷḷi (105/1535; KRN 107/1643); Hārūpura (Heg, Nan 212/1639).

Hebbalaguppe (Huṇ, Heg 61/1088, 62/1346); Kan + Kan; N + N; Hebbala + g(k)uppe; A place where a big army is stationed; GPN. [Hebbāḷa(u) + guppe; See Hebbāḷu].

Hebbasūru (CRN 73/1574); Kan + Kan; N + N; Hebba + sūru; A big slopy roof [< Chhūri (Skt) a knife]; MN. ~ Hebasūru (27/1377); Hebsūru (KRN).

Hebbāḷu (KRN, Mys 115/18th); Kan + Kan; Adj + N; Heb < hiri + bāḷu; A village where great livelihood obtains; GPN. ~ Hebbaḷalu (KRN 88/1543).

Hebya (Nan 179/15th) SX; Kan; A big village; MN.

Heḍatale (Nan); Kan + Kan; Adj + N; Heḍa + tale; The back of the head; a hired village; MN. ~ Yaḍatale (Guṇ 10/16th); Eḍatale (340/1292).

Heḍeyāla (Nan, Guṇ 120/1489, 40/1514); Kan + Kan; N + N; Heḍe + (y)āla; A village which has a Hoodlike banyan tree nearby; FLN.

Heggaḍahaḷḷi (Heg 118/1829, Guṇ, Nan); Kan + Kan; N + ; Heggaḍa < per + gaḍe +; After a village headman; PN. ~ Heggaḍahaḷḷi (Heg 64/15th, 46/15th); Heggadadēvanakōṭe (Heg), Heggaḍāpura (Heg).

Heg < peg < per (adj) which precedes a village name means large, big.

Heggandūru (Huṇ 36/1186); Hegganūru (Heg); Heggatūru (PP); Heggoṭhāra (CRN 387/1527, 386/16th,'5/1828) = A big granary, a house, a big fort; Heggūru (TNP); Heggavāḍi (CRN 84/1410, Heg 117/137, Guṇ 149/1417). Pergavāḍi (CRN 85/1242); Pergaipāḍi (86/13th); Heggavāḍipura (CRN); Heggōḍi < Heggavāḍi (Guṇ 168/1417).

Hejjige (Nan); SX; Kan; Adj + Suf; Hej + ige; A large one; MN.

Hejjoḍlu (Huṇ); Kan + Kan; Adj + N; Hej + j(s)oḍlu ~ soḍaru; A village where big lamps are made; CN. ~ Kirasoḍlu (Huṇ).

Hemmanahaḷḷi (Mys 214/1186, 216/1195); Kan + Kan; N + Suf; Hemma < hem + (n)a + ; After a big or great man; PN. ~ Hemmahaḷḷi (215/1175).

Hemmaragāla (Nan 329/1292); Kan + Kan + Kan; Adj + N + N; Hem + mara + g(k)āla; A big tree/deer - a village where either of the two exists; FLA/FAN.

Hemmige (Huṇ, TNP); SX; Kan; Adj + Suf; Hem + (m)ige; A big village; MN. ~ Hemmugė (TNP 248/1526, 249/1530) [Renamed as Harihararājēndrapura, TNP 256/1397].

Heṇṇegere Kāval (Heg); Kan + Kan + Kan; N + N + N; Heṇṇe + g(k)ere + kāval; Is it eṇṇe (oil) gere kāval ? or a tank after a woman ?

Hiṇḍaguḍlu (Huṇ); Kan + Kan; N + N; Hiṇḍa(u) + guḍlu < gudisilu; A collecion of sheds; MN.

Hinakal (Mys 107/18th); Kan + Kan; Adj + N; Hin(a) + kal; A village behind a stone; the hinder part of a stone; GPN.

Hire/Hīre (adj) which precedes a village name means large, big, old.

Hirekāti (Guṇ); (Kāṭi : a bison, a huntsman, the name of a golla, a cowherd); Hiremaḷali (PP) [Renamed Achyutēndrapura 105/1535]; Hirihaḷḷi (Heg 55/1533); Hiriyūru (TNP 126/1309, 127/1354).

Hiṭṇahaḷḷi (PP);. Kan + Kan; N + ; Hiṭna < hiṭṭana + ; A person who deals with flour; CN. ~ Hiṭnahebbāgilu (PP); Hiṭṭuvalli (TNP).

Hoḍike Kaṭṭe Kāvalu (Huṇ); Kan + Kan + Kan; N + N + ; Hoḍike + kaṭṭe + ; a tank where elephant grass grows; FLN.

Hoḷalavāḍi (Nan 183/15th, 396/1514); Kan + Kan; N + N; Hoḷala < poḷal + vāḍi; A town village; doublet; MN. ~ Horaḷavāḍi (Gaz).

Hoḷehuṇdi (Heg); Kan + Kan; N + ; Hoḷe + ; A village near a river; GPN. ~ Hoḷesālu (TNP).

Homma (CRN 148/1380); SX; Kan; That which flourishes [Gold ?]; MN. ~ Poḷma (CRN 147/?); Piriyahoḷma (CRN 294/977) [Another name: Akaḷanka chaturvēdimangalam].

Hommaragaḷḷi (Heg); Kan + Kan + Kan; N + N + N; Ho(n)m + mara < mare + g(h)aḷḷi; A village where golden deer are found; FAN. ~ Hommarahaḷḷi (Heg 12/1253).

Hoṇakahaḷḷi (Guṇ); Kan + Kan; N + ; Hoṇaka < Poṇarke + ; A village known for fighting; [Hoṇaka = Honnakka]; HN.

Hoṇḍarabāḷu (Koḷ 90/1549, CRN 231/1512, 232/1540); Kan + Kan; N + N; Hoṇḍara + bāḷu; Is it a caste name ?; EN. ~ Hānarabāḷu (CRN 231/1512); Honnarabāḷu (231/1512).

Hongalavāḍi (CRN 239/1578); Kan + Kan + Kan; N + N + Suf + N; Hon + g(k)al + a + vāḍi; After a gold stone. ~ Hongavāḍi (21/1545).

Honganūru (CRN 155/10th, 158/11th, 159/1525, 160/1517, 162/1517, 168/11th, 120/1648); Kan + Kan; N + Suf + N; Honga + (n)a + ūru; PN. ~ Hongavaḷḷi (Guṇ).

Hongaṭe (Mys); Kan + Kan < Skt; N + N; could it be: hon + gaṭṭe or hon + kōṭe ? MN.

Honnahaḷḷi (CRN 260/1368); Kan + Kan; N + ; Honna < hon + ; PN. ~ Honnēnahaḷḷi (Huṇ, KRN 117/1741); Honneyanahaḷḷi (Huṇ 37/ 1303, 71/1586); Honnūru (Yaḷ 13/9th, 14/10th, 15/1283); Honnūru Kuppe (Heg); Honnagowḍanahaḷḷi (Guṇ 17/1476, 213/1537); Honnegowḍanahaḷḷi (CRN, Guṇ).

Horaḷahaḷḷi (TNP); Kan + Kan; N + N; Horaḷa + haḷḷi; After a family called, Horaḷa; EN.

Horeyāla (Guṇ 53/1596, 59/975); Kan + Kan; N + N; Hore + y(ā)la; A banyan in the vicinity, neighbourhood; FLN. ~ Mariyāla (CRN); Koḍiyāla (KRN) = umbrella-like banyan.

Hosa is generative adjective which means new when it precedes a village name. Hosa agrahāra (KRN 116/1741); Hosahaḷḷi (TNP 90/ 326; pp 71/1586; KRN 107/1643, CRN, Mys, Heg); Posahoḷalu (Heg 135/1107); Hosahuṇḍi (Mys); Hosakōṭe (Mys 104/1667, Heg. Huṇ, KRN, TNP, Nan); Hosapura (TNP 289/1519, CRN, Nan, Guṇ); Hosavīḍu (Nan).

Hulikura (Heg); Kan + Kan < Skt; N + N; Huli + kura < khura (Skt); A village after the tiger's hoof; FAN.

Huḷimāvu (Nan); Kan + Kan; Adj + N; Huḷi + māvu; A village where sour mango is grown; FLN. ~ Immāvu (Nan); Sweet mango.

Hullahaḷḷi (Nan 137/1371); Kan + Kan; N + ; Hulla(u) + ; Grassy village [Triṇapura (Skt) Guṇ 113/1638].

Hullemāḷa (Heg); Kan + Kan; N + ; Hulle + ; Deer field; FAN. ~ Hullēnahaḷḷi (Huṇ); Hullepura (CRN); hulleḥaḷḷi (Heg 89/1493); Hullāḷu < Hulleyāḷu (Huṇ, CRN, Guṇ, Koḷ); Hullāṇa (Guṇ 159/ 1413, 125/16th).

Huluganahaḷḷi (Huṇ); Kan + Kan; N + Suf; Huluga < huliga + (n)a; After a tigerly man; PN. ~ Huliganamaraḍi (Guṇ) [Vyaghrāchala; Gaz].

Hunagaḷḷi (Heg); Kan + Kan; N + N; Hunaga < puṇuga + haḷḷi; After a civet; FAN/PN. ~ Hunuganahaḷḷi (TNP, Heg).

Huṇasanāḷu (Nan 375/1569); Kan + Kan; N + Suf + N; Huṇasa + (n)a + (b)āḷu; A man who grows tamarind tree; FLN/PN. Huṇisenāḷu (Nan 327/1164); Huṇiseneḷalu (Nan 172/17th); Huṇasanahaḷḷi (Heg); Huṇisehaḷḷi (Heg 67/1497); Huṇasinapura (Guṇ); Huṇasavāḍi (PP); huṇasūru (Heg, TNP 16/1749); Huṇusegāla (Huṇ); Huṇasekuppa (Heg); Huṇasekoplu (PP); Huṇasagahaḷḷi (TNP).

Huṇḍipura (Guṇ 61/1126 ?); Kan + Skt; N + N; Huṇḍi + pura; A hamlet town; GPN. (Doublet).

Hura (Nan 135/1399, Heg 75/1559, 43/1527, 119/1531); SX; Kan < Skt; Hura < pura; A town. ~ Hūradahaḷḷi (Guṇ 93/1553, Gaz).

Husakūru (Nan 385/870 ?); Kan + Kan; N + N; Husaku < usuku (?) + ūru; A sandy town; GPN. ~ Husagūru (262/969).

Hussainapura (Huṇ); Arab + Skt; N + Suf + ; Hussain + a + ; After a Muslim by name Hussain; PN.

Huttūru (Guṇ, Koḷ); Kan + Kan; N + N; Hutt(a) + ūru; A village of white ant hills; GPN.

Huyilāḷu (Mys); Kan + Kan; N + N; Huyil < puyyil + (b)āḷu; A battle field; HN [Crying, beating].

Hūṭagaḷḷi (Mys); Kan + Kan; N + N; Hūṭa + g(h)aḷḷi; A united village; GPN.

Hyrige (Heg, Huṇ); Kan + Kan; N + N; Hyr < payir + ige < gey; a village of green fields; FLN.

Hyākanūru (TNP, Gaz); Kan + Kan; N + Suf + ; Hyāka < hyga < havīka (?) + (n)a + ; [Hyāka < paika, Haḷepaika]; A village where hyaka caste people live; EN.

I

Ibjāla (Nan 157/1504); Kan + Kan; Adj + N; Ib + jāla; two thorny babool trees (?); FLN. [Ibha + jāla = Elephant snare; FAN; DIPN].

Inḍavāḷu (TNP); Skt + Kan; N + N; Inḍa < Indu + v(b)āḷu; Named after the moon; NN. ~ Indavāḍi (Koḷ 30/1321).

Igli (Nan); SX; Kan; < Iggāli; Two wheeler; MN. ~ Iggāli (204/10th); Iggili (212/1639).

Ilwāla (Mys); < Ilwala (?); A mythological name; RN.

Ikkaḍahaḷḷi (Koḷ); Kan + Kan + Kan; Adj + N + N; Ik < Ir + kaḍa + haḷḷi; A village having two sides or parts or rows; MN.

Irasavāḍi (CRN 153/1516, 152/16th); Kan + Kan; N + N; Irasa(u) + vāḍi; A village where iron aixles are manufactured; CN.

Iruvidhi (Heg); Kan + Skt; Adj + N; Iru + vidhi < vīdhi; A village with two streets (?); MN.

Iṭṇa (Heg); SX; Kan; Iṭṇa < Iṭṭaṇa < Iṭṭaḷa; A village of abundance, shelter; MN.

Iṭṭigahaḷḷi (PP); Kan < Skt + Kan; N + ; Iṭṭiga < Ishṭikā (Skt) + ;. A village where bricks are made; CN.

Īranakere (Mys); Kan < Skt + Kan; N + Suf + ; Īra < Vīra + (n)a + ; PN.

Īśwaragowḍanahaḷḷi (Nan); Skt + Kan < Skt + Kan; N + N + Suf + N; Īśwara + gowḍa + (n)a + Haḷḷi; PN.

Îchanahaḷḷi (KRN, pp); Kan < Skt + Kan; N + Suf; Îcha < Āditya (Skt) + (n)a + ; After a Sun man; PN. ~ Îchuru (PP).

Înūru mārigudi jangalu (Heg); Kan + Skt + Kan + Kan < Eng; Adj + N + N + N; Înūru + māri + guḍi + jangalu; Forest named after five hundred temples of Durga; RN.

Îtanahaḷḷi (pp 103/1535); Kan < Skt + Kan; N + Suf + ; Îta < Āditya + (n)a + ; After a Sun-man.

Îyyanapura (CRN); Kan + Skt; N + Suf + ; Îyya < ayya + (n)a + ; A village after a jangama; PN. [Ayyanapura -Gaz].

J

Jakkahaḷḷi (Gun, Heg, Koḷ 88/1544); Kan < Skt + Kan; N + ; Jakka < yaksha/chakra; a village after certain demigods who are with Kubēra [wheel, cart]; RN/PN.

Jannūru (CRN); Kan < Skt + Kan; N + ; Jan(na) < yajna + ; A village where men revel in sacrifice RN/PN.

Jantagaḷḷi (Mys); Kan < Skt + Kan; N + N; Janta < danta + g(h)aḷḷi; A village where elephants' tusks are available; FAN. [jante : a rafter].

Jaṭṭihuṇḍi (Mys); Kan < Tel + Kan; N + ; Jaṭṭi + ; A village of professional wrestlers; EN.

Javanikuppe (PP); Kan < Skt + Kan; N + ; Javani < Javana < davana + ; A village where the plant ariemisia indica and its flowers are grown [May be proper name also]; FLA/FPN.

Jayapura (Mys); Skt + Skt; N + N; Jaya + ; It is to commemorate victory; HN.

Jābagere (Huṇ) ?

Jāganakōṭe (Heg 145/1573); Kan < Skt + Kan; N + Suf + ; Jāga < yāga/tyāga + (n)a + ; After a man who has made sacrifice; PN.

Jālahaḷḷi (Nan 378/1378); Skt + Kan; N + ; Jāla + ; A village where fishing nets are available; CN.

Jāṭagāṭipura (Heg); Kan < Skt + Skt; N + N; Jāṭagāṭi < Jaṭṭigiti (?)/ Jāḍagitti + ; After a woman of wrestler or the jāḍara (weaver's) community; FPN/EN.

Jinakanahaḷḷi (Koḷ); Kan + Kan; N + Suf + ; Jinaka < Jīna + (n)a +; A village where a miser lives; PN. [Jina + Akka + (n)a + haḷḷi ?].

Jinnahaḷḷi (Heg 24/17th, 25/13th); Kan < Skt + Kan; N + ; Jinna < Jina + ; Jains' settlement.

Jiyyāra (Heg); Skt + Kan < Skt; N + N; Jīya + āra < āgāra; Master's dwelling place; PN.

Jīnahaḷḷi (Huṇ); Kan + Kan; N + ; Jīna + ; A village of a niggardy, miserly man; PN. [vide Jinakanahaḷḷi].

Jompanahaḷḷi (Heg); Kan + Kan; N + Suf + ; Jompa + (n)a + ; [Cluster]; After a man who prepares flower clusters; PN.

Jōḍihariharapura (Nan); Mhr + Skt + Skt + Skt; N + N + N + ; Jōḍi + hari + hara + ; Hariharapura which has been granted in favour of heriditary officers. ~ Jōḍi meḷḷa haḷḷi (Yaḷ).

Jōganahaḷḷi (pp 36/16th, 37/1130, 38/1614); Kan < Skt + Kan; N + Suf + ; Jōga < Yōga + (n)a + ; After a meditaror; PN. [Mendicant].

Jyōtigowḍanapura (CRN 199/1479, 201/1339); Skt + Kan < Skt + Skt; N + N + Suf + ; Jyōti + gowḍa + (n)a + ; A village estabilshed by a lightlike man; PN.

K

Kabbahaḷḷi (Guṇ); Kan + Kan; N +; Kabba(u) + ; A village where sugar cane is grown; FLN. ~ Kabbaḷi (91/1610); Kambaḷi (92/9th).

Kachuvīnahaḷḷi (Huṇ); Kan + Kan; Adj + Suf + N; Kach(ch)u < Karchu < Kaḷchu + (Vīn)a + haḷḷi; A village near where water in which raw rice has been washed, flows (?); MN.

Kaḍabūru (Guṇ, Nan); Kan + Kan; N + ; Kaḍab(u) + ūru; A village famous for a kind of cake boiled in steam; MN.

Kaḍajaṭṭi (Nan); Kan + Kan; N + N; Kaḍaja + (h)aṭṭi; A village full of wasps (?); FAN.

Kaḍakoḷa (Mys); Kan + Kan; Adj + N; Kaḍa + koḷa; Last tank near which the village is situated; GPN. ~ Kaḍegadde (Heg); Kaḍemanuganahaḷḷi (Huṇ).

Kaggaḷa (KRN, Guṇ 127/15th); Kan + Kan; Adj + N; Kar/Kag + kaḷa; A village of black or hard floor or field. ~ Kaggere (KRN); Kagguṇḍi (PP); GPN.

Kaggalibōre Kāvalu (KRN); Kan + Kan + Kan; N + N + ; Kaggali + bōre + ; A raised ground where the tree mimosa sundra Roxb grows; FLN. ~ Kaggalūru (Nan 381/16th); Kaggalīpura (CRN. Mys 99/1694, KRN 117/1741).

Kakkarahaṭṭi (Nan 281/13th); Kan + Kan; N + Suf + N; Kakka + (r)a + haṭṭi; A village of this caste; EN.

Kaligowḍanahaḷḷi (Guṇ); Kan + Kan < Skt + Kan; N + N + Suf + ; Kali + gowḍa + (n)a + ; A village founded by a warrior, hero; PN. ~ Kaliyūru (TNP).

Kalkere (PP); Kan + Kan; N + ; Kal + ; A village where tank has been built with stone; GPN. ~ Kalkunda (Nan 254/1017); Kalukunda (246/1527); Kalkuṇike (Huṇ); Kallahaḷḷi (Guṇ, KRN, Huṇ 38/12th, 40/1276, Mys 1/1821, Nan); Kallambāḷu = Kallamma + bāḷu (Heg 76/16th, 74/1211, 73/1738); Kallūrunāganahaḷḷi (Mys 109/11th).

Kallināthapura (Mys); Kan + Skt + Skt; N + N + ; Kalli < Kali + nātha + ; After the God, Kallinatha; RN.

Kalmahaḷḷi (Nan); Kan < Skt + Kan; N + ; Kalma < Kāḷamma (?) + ; FPN (?).

Kaḷabūchanahaḷḷi (Huṇ); Kan + Kan + Kan; N + N + Suf + ; Kaḷa < Kaḷḷa (?) + būcha + (n)a + ; Thiefish worm (?); PN.

Kaḷale (Nan 359/13th, 25/18th); SX; Kan; A village where tender bamboo shoots are available [butter milk]; FLN. ~ Kaḷile (Huṇ) [Vēṇupuri, Gaz]; Kaḷalavāḍi (Mys).

Kaḷasūru (Heg); Kan < Skt + Kan; N + N; ·Kaḷas(a) < Kalaśa + ūru; A prominent village; MN. [A vase, a dome].

Kaḷastavāḍi (Mys); Kan < Skt + Kan; N + Suf + N; Kaḷasta < Kaḷasada (?) + V(P)āḍi; [A vase, dome].

Kaḷḷipura (CRN, Guṇ, TNP); Kan + Skt; N + ; Kaḷḷi + ; A village where milk hedge grows in plenty; FLN.

Kamarahaḷḷi (Guṇ); Kan < Skt + Kan; N+ ; Kamara < Kammāra + ; A village of blacksmiths; EN. ~ Kamaravāḍi (CRN); Kamaravaḷḷi (Mys); Kammāravaḷḷi (263/1685).

Kambipura (PP); Kan + Skt; N + ; Kambi + ; A village where iron banḍs/clubs are made; MN. [A thick bamboo].

Kampalāpura (PP 117/9th, 118/1174, 119/1687); Kan + Skt; N + ; Kampalā < Kampaṇa + ; The headquarters of a district; GPN.

Kandāgāla (Guṇ, Heg, Nan); Kan < Skt + Kan; N + N; Kanḍā < Skānda + g(k)āla; After Lord subrahmanya; RN. ~ Kandēgāla

(PP); Kandadagāla (Heg 160/1520) [Skandagiri - Gaz]; Kandāgāla hosahaḷḷi (Guṇ).

Kandalike (Heg); SX; Kan; N + Suf; Kandal(a) + ike; A village where new shoots (?) are found; FLN.

Kaṇagāla (Huṇ); Kan + Kan; N + N; Kaṇa + gāla; A battle field; HN [A thrashing floor] [Could it be derived from Kaṇagile ? = fragrant oleander].

Kanakanahaḷḷi (Heg); Skt + Kan; N + Suf + ; Kanaka + (n)a + ; A village named after a golden man; PN.

Kaṇēnūru (Nan 141/1337); Kan + Kan; N + Suf + N; Kaṇe < Kaṇeya + (n)a + ūru; After a bowman, archer; PN. ~ Kaṇeyūru (146/1337).

Kaṇiyanapura (Guṇ); Kan + Skt; N + Suf + ; Kaṇiya + (n)a + ; A sooth sayer; PN. ~ Kaṇivūru (149/1417); Kaṇiyanaguṇḍi (Heg).

Kanuganahaḷḷi (KRN); Kan + Kan; N + Suf; Kanuga + (n)a + ; A dreamer's village (?); PN.

Kannahaḷḷi (TNP); Kan + Skt + Kan; N + ; Kanna < Krishṇa + ; PN. ~ Kannāyakanahaḷḷi (TNP); Kannamangala (Yaḷ 71/13th); Kaṇṇāgāla (Guṇ 228/1315); Kannēgāla (Guṇ); Kaṇṇavagāla (CRN 173/14th).

Kaṇṇūru (Koḷ); Kan < Skt + Kan; N + ; Kaṇṇ(a) < Krishṇa + ; PN. [Eye]. ~ Kaṇṇānūru (56/1408; CRN 274/1485).

Kanchanahaḷḷi (TNP, Heg); Kan < Skt + Kan; N + Suf + ; Kancha(u) < Kānsya + (n)a + ; After a man who deals with brass metal. ~ Kanchugāra Koppalu (KRN); Kanchinakere (Koḷ).

Kaṇḍeyyanapāḷya (Koḷ); Kan + Kan; N + Suf + ; Kaṇḍeyya + (n)a +; After a swordsman. ~ Kaṇḍegowḍanahaḷḷi (Heg).

Kappaḍihanta (KRN); Kan + Suf + Kan; N + ; Kappaḍi < Karpaṭa +; A village where a religious mendicant in patched clothes live; RN.

Kappasōge (Nan); Kan + Kan; Adj + N; Kappa(u) + sōge; A village where black palmleaves are found; FLN.

Karaḍihaḷḷa (CRN); Kan + Kan; N + ; Karaḍi +; A gorge haunted by bearers; FAN.

Karakālamādahaḷḷi (Guṇ); Kan + Kan + Kan < Skt + Kan; Adj + N + N + N; Kara(i) + kāla + māda < Mahadēśwara + ; After a black legged māda; PN. [May refer to the Chola king Karikāla] [Named Chennananjarāyapura by Chennananjarāja Oḍeya].

Karakānahaḷḷi (Mys); Kan + Kan; N + Suf + ; Karaka + (n)a + ; After a black man [Hailstone (Skt) ?]; PN.

Karangūru (Huṇ); Kan + Kan; N + N; Karang(u) < Karaku + ūru; A village where charcoal is available; MN.

Karigaḷa (Heg); Kan + Skt; Adj + N; Kari + gaḷa < gāla; Black neck (?). ~ Karigaḷḷi (Nan 250/9th); Karimuddanahaḷḷi (Huṇ); Karinanjanapura (CRN).

Karlapura (Nan); Kan + Skt; N + ; Karla < Kaṟalu + ; a village where brackish or saline soil is found; GPN.

Karṇakuppe (Huṇ); Skt + Kan; N + N; Karṇa + kuppe; After one of the heroes of Mahābhāratā; MN.

Karōhaṭṭi (TNP); Kan + Kan; Vadj + ; Karō < Kareyuva + ; A pen or a village where milch cows are gathered [May be a pen for calves].

Karpūravaḷḷi (KRN); Skt + Skt; N + N; Karpūra + vaḷḷi < valli; A village where thick leaved lavendar is grown; FLN.

Kartāḷu (KRN); Skt + Kan; N + N; Karta < Kartṛ + āḷu < bāḷu; A village belonging to the master; PN. ~ Karattāḷu (69/1767, 70/12th cen). [Kar + tāḷu : black palmyra (?)]

Kasuvinahaḷḷi (Nan); Kan + Kan; N + Suf; Kasuv(u) + (in)a + ; A village with fertile soil/a grass with fragrant soil; GPN.

Kaṭṇavāḍi (CRN); Kan + Kan; N + ; Kaṭṇa < kāṭaṇṇa + ; After a forester, a huntsman; EN. [Kaṭṇa = a building]. ~ Kaṭṭaṇavāḍi (310/1237 ?, Yaḷ 65/1737); Kaṭnāḷu (KRN); Kāṭanāḷu (115/15th); Kāṭavāḷu (Heg); Kāṭanahaḷḷi (KRN 15/15th); Kāṭūru (Nan 164/1231); Kāṭṭūru (Nan 156/1198, Heg 16/1670).

Kaṭṭavāḍi (Yaḷ); Kan + Kan; N + ; Kaṭṭa(e) + ; A village which has a tank, embankment; GPN. ~ Kaṭṭeyāla (Nan 212/639); Kaṭṭevāḍi (CRN 5/1878); Kaṭṭepura (Heg); Kaṭṭemanuganahaḷḷi (Heg 5/9th, 4/1264); Kaṭṭehuṇḍi (Heg); Kaṭṭehuṇasūru (Heg).

Kavudavāḍi (Yaḷ - Gaz); Kan + Kan; N + ; Kavuda (i ?) + ; A village where quilted rage are used for bed or covering (?); MN.

Kayyambaḷḷi (TNP); Kan + Kan; N + N; Kayyam < Kayyamma + b(-h)aḷḷi; After a woman who churns; PN.

Kāḍahaḷḷi (CRN, TNP 15/1622); Kan + Kan; N + ; Kāḍa + ; After that name [Forest man]; PN. ~ Kāḍanahaḷḷi (Mys); Kāḍasūru (Heg); Kāḍavaḍḍaraguḍi (Hun).

Kāgalavāḍi (CRN 159/1425, 177/1570); Kan + Kan; N + ; Kāgala +; crow (?) FAN. [< Kāgaḍi = a cradle suspended from the roof (?)].

Kāhaḷḷi (Nan 212/1639); Kan + Kan; VN + ; Kā + Kāpa + ; Guard-like village; HN [a forest]. ~ Kāpahaḷḷi (248/1514).

Kākanakōṭe (Heg); Mal + Kan; N + Suf + ; Kāka + (n)a + ; After a man from Malabar area; PN. ~ Kākanahaḷḷi (KRN).

Kāḷanahuṇḍi (CRN 403/17th); Kan < Skt + Kan; N + Suf + ; Kāḷa < Kāla + (n)a + ; After a black man [Yama]; PN. ~ Kāḷēnahaḷḷi (KRN); Kāḷetimmanahaḷḷi (PP).

Kāmagowḍanahaḷḷi (Huṇ); Skt + Kan < Skt + Kan; N + N + Suf + ; Kāma + gowḍa + (n)a + ; After a person who has adopted the name of the God of love; PN. ~ Kāmanahaḷḷi (PP, Nan 317/1762); Kāmēnahaḷḷi (KRN); Kāmagere (Koḷ 62/1354, 57/1366); Kāmahaḷḷi (Nan).

Kānikere (CRN); Kan + Kan; N + Ṣuf + ; Kān + i + ; A village near the forest tank; GPN. ~ Kānūru (PP).

Kāragahaḷḷi (TNP); Kan + Kan; N + ; Kāraga < Kāruga (?) + ; After a blackman [< Kāraka = torment, torture ?].

Kārāpura (Heg); Kan + Skt; N + N; Kār(ā) + ; Cloudy, rainy village; NN.

Kārehuṇḍi (Heg); Kan + Kan; N + ; Kāre + ; A village where spinous shrub webera tetandra wild grows; FLN. ~ Kārepura (Nan); Kāravura (169/1114).

Kārle (Guṇ); SX; Kan; N + Suf; Kār + le; A cloudy rainy place (?).

Kārya (Nan); SX; Kan/Skt; Vide Kārehuṇḍi above; ~ Kāreya (282/968, 283/12th); Working place (?)

Kebbēpura (Heg, CRN, Guṇ); Kan + Skt; N + N; Keb < Kem + bay + ; A village with red soil field; GPN.

Kelasūru (Guṇ); Kan + Kan; N + N; Kelasa + ūru; A village with different occupations [Kelasi = a barber]; MN. ~ Kellasūru (28/1029); Kelasūrupura (Guṇ).

Kellūru (PP, Yaḷ 71/13th); Kan + Kan; N + N; Kell(a) + ūru; A village noted for fibre; MN. Kellamballi = Kellamm(a) + baḷḷi ? (CRN); Kellahaḷḷi (CRN); Kellupura (Nan).

Keḷaganahaḷḷi (PP); Kan + Kan; Adj + Suf + ; Keḷagu + (an)a + ; A village at the lower side, downwards [Keḷava = An old man ?].

Kembal (Nan); Kan + Kan; Adj + N; Kem + b(p)al; A village the soil of which is like red tooth; GPN. [Kem + bāḷ = red field].

Kempanahaḷḷi (Huṇ); Kan + Kan; N + Suf + ; Kempa + (n)a + ; After a red man; PN. ~ Kempanapura (TNP, CRN 143/1169, 145/991, 146/1018).

Kenchalagūḍu (Mys); Kan + Kan; N + Fem.Ind + ; Kencha + la + ; After a red woman; PN. ~ Kenchanagōḍu (203/18th); Kenchanahaḷḷi (KRN, Heg 149/379).

Kengāki (CRN 317/18th ?); Kan + Kan; Adj + N; Ken + g(k)āki; A village where red common spinous shrub grows; FLN. ~ Kengaḍūru (Koḷ 11/1514).

Kerehaḷḷi (CRN 351/1275); Kan + Kan; N + ; Kere + ; A village by the tank; GPN. ~ Kereyūru (Huṇ).

Kesare (Mys); SX; Kan; A village situated on a miry soil; GPN. ~ Kesarekere (PP 50/17th).

Kestūru (KRN, CRN, Yaḷ 21/16th, 23/1319); Kan + Kan; N + N; Kesara + turu; Any miry place where thorny shrub grows (?);

GPN. ~ Kesraturu (Koḷ 85/1678); Kesavattūru (11/1654); Kesavatūru (7/1512).

Kēḍaga (KRN 77/1377 ?); SX; Kan; One who ruins or is ruined (?); PN.

Kērgaḷḷi (Mys); Kan + Kan; N + N; Kēr + g(h)aḷḷi; A village which looks like a wall (?); MN.

Kētahaḷḷi (CRN, Heg, TNP); Kan + Kan; N + ; Kēta + ; After a low, vile, wicked god of that name; PN. ~ Kētihaḷḷi (CRN 379/1668, 380/1531); Kētupura (TNP); Kētanahaḷḷi (Heg 14/1332); [Kētagowḍa of Tagaḍūru converted the old settlement of 'Valike' into an agrahāra and named it Kētanahaḷḷi in 1322, Gaz]; Kyātanahaḷḷi (Heg); Kyātamāranahaḷḷi (Mys); Meṇasinākyātanahaḷḷi (TNP); Ketanahaḷḷi (Heg 48/1255).

Kilagere (CRN, Guṇ 308/1425); Kan + Kan; N + ; Kila + ; lower tank ? ~ Kelligere (Guṇ 306/1318).

Kiḷalīpura (CRN); Kan < Skt + Skt; N + ; Kiḷalīi < Kīlār < Kṣhīrāgāra (?) + ; A village with a milk dairy; CN. [Kīlāla = a blazing flame ?].

Kiragasūru (CRN, TNP 16/1749); Kan + Kan + Kan; Adj + Adj + N; Kira + ga(ho)s(a) + ūru; Small new village; HN. ~ Kiṟigusūru (TNP 35/15th); Kiridā(gā)sūru (34/1564); Kiṟugusūru (TNP 68/10th); Kiruvusūru (142/12th).

Kiru denotes smallness or young age and it generally precedes the village name. Kirugunda (Nan 191/1170); Kirajāji (Huṇ); Kirālu (Mys); Kiranelli (PP); Kirisoḍlu (Huṇ); Kirangūru (PP, Huṇ 35/1091).

Kittūru (PP 142/12th, 144/1008, 143/12th; Heg 123/1079, 126/1672); Kan + Kan; Adj + N; Kiri(du) + ūru; Small village [< Kīrtipura] [Another name Ananta Kīrti mahānagara (Heg 123/1079)].

Kīḷanapura (Mys); Kan + Kan; N + Suf; Kīḷa + (n)a + ; After a small man; PN.

Kailāsapura (PP): Skt + Skt; N + ; Kailāsa + ; A heavenly abode; RN.

Koḍagahaḷḷi (TNP); Kan + Kan; VN + ; Koḍaga(e) + ; A gifted village; RN.

Koḍasōge (Guṇ); SX; Skt; < Kuṭajaka; The village where small tree cluytia colina Roxb grows; FLN. ~ Koḍesīge (Heg); Koṭasōge (136/1516); Koṭṭasōge (149/1417).

Kokkanahaḷḷi (CRN); Kan + Kan; N + Suf; Kokka < Konga (?) + (n)a + ; The village of an outcaste; PN.

Kollēgowḍanahaḷḷi (Heg); Kan + Kan < Skt + Kan; N + Suf + ; Kollē + gowḍa + (n)a + ; After a pole dancer, a rope dancer; PN.

Koḷavige (Huṇ); SX; Kan; N + Suf; Koḷavi + ge; A villge where a blow pipe/A bamboo tube is made; CN.

Koḷatūru (TNP); Kan + Kan; N + N; Koḷat(a) < Koḷata + ūru; a new village; MN. ~ Koḷattūru (TNP 104/1260) [Another name Pratāpahariharapura TNP 17/1749).

Koḷḷēgāla (Koḷ 2/11th, 4/13th); Kan + Kan; N + ; Koḷḷē(a) + ; A deep place/gorge; GPN. [Pillage, plunder]; ~ Koḷgegāla (1/1569); Koḷāgāla (Yaḷ 145/1703, Nan 316/1761); Koḷḷāgāla (TNP 16/1749; CRN 291/1744, Nan 3/1761); Kollāgāra (CRN 291/1744); Koḷḷāgāra (Yaḷ 71/13th); Kōḷigāla (Nan 32/1053, 34/1063); Kōḷagāla (Heg 33/1053).

Komārabīḍu (Mys 210/1223, 211/1167); Kan < Skt + Kan; N + ; Komāra < Kumāra + ; After Skānda, son of Śiva; RN. ~ Komārnapura (Yaḷ); Kumārabīḍu (Mys 207/1121, 209/1414).

Kongahaḷḷi (Nan, Koḷ 87/12th); Kan ? + Kan; N + ; Konga + ; After an inhabitant of Kongu nāḍu; EN. ~ Kongarahaḷḷi (Koḷ); Kongaḷḷi Kāval (Nan).

Koppa (PP); SX; Kan; A small village on a raiṣed land; GPN. ~ Koppalu Kāḷahuṇḍi (TNP).

Korlahosahaḷḷi (PP); Kan + Kan + Kan; N + Adj + ; Korla < Korale + hosa + ; After a kind of millet; FLN.

Koṭaganahaḷḷi (CRN 258/1523); Kan + Kan; N + Suf + ; Koṭaga < Koṭṭiga + (n)a + ; After a man who lives in a shed; PN.

Kottalavāḍi (CRN 310/1303); Kan + Kan; N + ; Kottala + ; A village with bulwark, a bastion; HN.

Kottēgāla (Huṇ, Heg, TNP); Kan + Kan; N + N; Kottē < Krotta < Koḷata + gāla; A new village; MN. ~ Kottāgāla (Nan 395/1514; Heg 12/1670); Kottagāla (Heg 12/810); Kottavaḷḷi (PP 71/1586); Kottamangala (Heg 15/9th); Kottanūru (Koḷ, Guṇ 49/14th, 48/18th).

Koṭṭige Kāval (Huṇ); Kan + Kan; N + ; Koṭṭige + ; A village exclusively meant for open; a barn; MN.

Kōchanahaḷḷi (Mys); Kan + Kan; N + Suf + ; Kōcha + (n)a + ; After a perverse, foolish fellow; PN.

Kōḍahaḷḷi (Guṇ); Kan + Kan; N + ; Kōḍa < Kōḍu + ; A village on the top of a hillock; GPN. [Kōḍi = An outlet of a tank].

Kōḍihaḷḷi (Guṇ 134/1521; PP 71/1586); Kan + Kan; N + ; Kōḍi + ; A village situated near the outlet of a tank; GPN. ~ Kōḍi Chāmanahaḷḷi (Heg); Kōḍimōḷe (CRN); Kōḍiugane (CRN).

Kōhaḷa (Heg); SX; Kan ?; [Kōhala = Any intoxicating drink, a musical instrument; Kohala = a water lily]. ~ Kohaṇa (19/15th).

Kōgilavāḍi (PP); Kan < Skt + Kan; N + ; Kōgila(e) < Kōkila + ; A village after a cuckoo; FAN. ~ Kōgilūru (KRN); Kōgiyūru (41/10th).

Kōḷūru (KRN); Kan + Kan; N + N; Kōḷ(i) + ūru; After a fowl; FAN. [Kōḷ = havoc, plunder ?]. ~ Kōḷiyūru (43/12th).

Kōmalāpura (PP 47/11th, 46/17th); Skt + Skt; N + ; Kōmalā + ; After a delicate beautiful woman; FPN.

Kōṇagahaḷḷi (TNP); Kan + Kan; N + Suf + ; Kōṇa + ga(?) + ; After a male buffalo ?; FAN.

Kōṇanahosahaḷḷi (Huṇ); Kan + Kan; N + Suf + N + Adj + ; Kōṇa + (n)a + hosa + haḷḷi; After a male buffalo; FAN. ~ Kōṇanūru (Nan); Kōṇūru (Nan 152/1312); Kōṇanūrupura (Nan); Koṇasūru (PP); Kōṇegowḍanahuṇḍi (Heg).

Kowlanahaḷḷi (PP); Skt + Kan; N + Suf + ; Kowla + (n)a + ; After the worshipper of active power or Kāḷi; PN. [Kōla = devil dance, a boar] ?

Kuḍakūru (PP 92/997); Kan + Kan; N + N; Kuḍa(i)k(e) + ūru; A village where small earthen pots are made; EN. [Kuḍu = uneven or hilly land ?]. ~ Kuḍuvūru (93/16th).

Kuḍinīrumuddanahaḷḷi (Huṇ 32/1669); Kan + Kan + Kan + Kan; V Adj + N + N + Suf + ; Kuḍi + nīru + mudda + (n)a + ; Muddanahaḷḷi where drinking water is available; PN.

Kuḍugi (Heg); SX; Kan; That which is bent. [Simple iron scrapper (?)].

Kudēru (CRN 72/1578); Kan + Kan; N + N; Kud(ir) + (h)ēru; A village where there is a granary; MN; DIPN [Boiling]. ~ Kudihēru (104/1413); Kudiheru (73/1409).

Kukkarahaḷḷi (Mys); Kan + Kan; N + ; Kukka + (r)a + ; A village where the particular community lives; EN.

Kukkūru (TNP); Kan + Kan; N + ; Kukku + ; A village where herons or cranes are found in large numbers; FAN.

Kulagāṇa (CRN 322/1216); SX; Kan; < Kollaṇa; Play, performance ?; [Kula + gaṇa = a set of Jains]. ~ Kolagāṇa (Gaz); Kollana (CRN 343/1173); Kollaṇa (341/12th).

Kullūru (CRN, Huṇ); Kan + Kan; N + ; Kullu < Kuḷḷu < Kuruḷ; After cakes ofdried cowdung; MN. [The whole, open, expanded].

Kuḷya (Heg); SX; Kan; < Kuḷḷu < Kuruḷ; After cakes of dried cowdung (?); MN.

Kumachahaḷḷi (CRN); Kan + Kan; N + N; Kumach < Gumacha < Gubbachchi; After a sparrow ?; FAN.

Kumbārahaḷḷi (Mys); Kan < Skt + Kan; N + ; Kumbāra < Kumbhakāra + ; After pot makers; EN. ~ Kumbrahaḷḷi (Nan).

Kuṇagaḷḷi (Koḷ); Kan + Kan; N + N; Kuṇa < Kuṇiha + g(h)aḷḷi; A village famous for dancing; MN. [Kuṇuku = a play, a sport]; ~ Kuṇangil (CRN 187/1207); Kuṇagahaḷḷi (Guṇ); Kuṇagihaḷḷi (214/1380).

Kuṇigalu (Heg); Kan + Kan; N + N; Kuṇi + g(k)allu; After a stone with a hole; GPN. [Dancing stone ?].

Kundakere (Guṇ); Skt + Kan; N + ; Kunda + ; A village in the vicinity of a hill; GPN. [A kind of jasmine]. ~ Kundūru (Heg 81/1218, 83/

1180); Kundutūru (112/9-10th, 114/1087, 117/1137); Kundanahaḷḷi (PP).

Kunnapaṭṇa (Heg); Kan < Skt + Kan; N + ; Kunna < Krishṇa; [A man with severed hands]; PN.

Kuntanahaḷḷi (TNP); Kan + Kan; N + Suf + ; Kunta + (n)a + ; After the user of a lancer; PN. [A village where one sat ?]. ~ Kuntūru (Koḷ 11/1154, 9/1544); Kundattūru (10/10th).

Kuppahaḷḷi (KRN); Kan + Kan; N + ; Kuppa + ; A village on a raised ground; GPN. ~ Kuppūru (Mys 224/1173); Kuppalūru (Mys); Kuppe (KRN); Kuppēgāla (Mys); Kuppēkoḷagaṭṭa (Huṇ); Kuppchanta (KRN).

Kupparavaḷḷi (Nan); Kan + Kan; VN + N; Kuppara + (b)aḷḷi; After a jumping creeper; FAN. [A village which is reached by jumping].

Kupya (TNP); SX; Kan; A base metal. [A bottle-like vessel]; HN.

Kurahaṭṭi (Nan); Kan + Kan; N + ; Kura(i) + ; Sheepfold; FAN. ~ Kurahaṭṭi hosūru (Koḷ); Kuṟipaṭṭi (CRN 126/791); Kuṟahaṭṭi (Nan 328/1662); Kurihuṇḍi (Nan).

Kurnigāla (Heg, Gaz) ?

Kurubahaḷḷi (KRN); Kan + Kan; N + ; Kuruba + ; A shepherd's hamlet; EN. ~ Kurubārahaḷḷi (Mys 225/1497); Kurubūru (TNP); Kuṟibūru (16/1749, 287/1343); Kurubarahosahaḷḷi (Huṇ).

Kuṭṭavāḍi (Huṇ 32/1669); Kan + Kan; N + ; Kuṭṭa < Koṭṭa + ; A cow pen or a granary; MN.

Kūḍanahaḷḷi (Mys); Kan + Kan; N + Suf + ; Kūḍa + (n)a + ; After a man in company; PN.

Kūḍlāpura (Nan 322/1148); Kan + Skt; N + ; Kūḍlā < Kūḍalā + ; A town at the confluence of rivers. ~ Kūḍalāpura (324/11th); Kūḍalūru (Koḷ 55/1398); Kūḍlūru (CRN, TNP, Huṇ).

Kūgalūru (Nan 370/11th); Kan + Kan; VN + N; Kūgal + ūru; A village at a calling distance [Kūgal = A stone which makes sound when beaten].

Kūtanahaḷḷi (Mys); Kan + Kan; N + Suf + ; Kūta < Kōta + (n)a + ; After a low caste tribe; PN. ~ Kūtanapura (CRN 300/1511); Kūtanūru (Guṇ).

Kūrgahaḷḷi (Mys); Kan + Kan + Kan; VN + N + N; Kūr + g(k)al + haḷḷi; After a sitting stone; GPN. [Kūrige = a sowing machine]. ~ Kūrgallu (PP); Kūragallu (28/1339, 31/1532, 32/1453).

L

Lakkasōge (Heg); Kan < Skt + Kan; N + N; Lakka < Lakṣha + sōge; A village noted for lakhs of peacocks; FAN.

Lakkikuppe (KRN); Kan + Kan; N + : Kan < Skt + Kan; Lakki + ; After the shrub or small tree Vitex negando Lin. FLN. [Lakki < Lakshmi] ~ Lakkūru (Guṇ 112/1665); Lakkīpura (Guṇ).

Lakshmaṇāpura (Nan, Heg, Guṇ 149/1417, 112/1665); Skt + Skt; N + N; After Lakshmaṇa; RN.

Lakshmīpura (KṘN, Koḷ, PP, Mys); Skt + Skt; N + N; Lakshmī + pura; After the goddess Lakshmi; RN. ~ Lakumīpura (Guṇ 149/1417).

Lalitādripura (Mys); Skt + Skt + Skt; N + N + N; Lalitā + (a)dri + pura; A beautiful mountain town; GPN.

Lanke (Heg); SX; Skt; After the name of a female evil spirit; FPN.

Lāḷankere (Huṇ); Kan + Kan; N + Suf + ; Lāḷa + (n)a + ; After a kind of reed or a horseshoe or one who shoes horses; PN. ~ Lāḷandēvanahaḷḷi (KRN).

Lingāmbudhi (Mys 205/1828); Skt + Skt; N + N; Linga + ambudhi; A village in the vicinity of the tank named after the god, 'Siva; RN. ~ Linganapura (Koḷ, CRN); Lingāpura (PP); Lingēnahaḷḷi (Heg).

Lokkere (Guṇ); Kan + Kan; N + N; Lok < Lakki + kere; Vide Lakkikuppe; FLN. ~ Lokkaḷḷi (Huṇ 32/1669); Lokkanahaḷḷi (Koḷ).

M

Machare (Heg); Kan + Kan; N + N; Mach < Machchu + are; A village after the stone meant for sharpening knives; MN.

Macchūru (Heg); Kan + Kan; VN +; Macchu + ; A lovable village; MN. [Maccha < Matsya = Fish].

Maḍahaḷḷi (Nan); Kan + Kan; N + ; Maḍa + ; The village which has a small channel near by; MN. [Maḍa < Maṭha = a hermitage]. Maḍavāḍi (TNP).

Madaragaḷḷi (Mys); Kan + Kan; N + Suf + N; Mada < Māda + (r)a + g(h)aḷḷi; A cobbler's village; EN.

Maḍuvinabīḍu (CRN); Kan + Kan; N + Suf + ; Maḍu + (Vin)a + ; The village which has deep water nearby; MN. ~ Maḍuvinahaḷḷi (Nan).

Maddūru (Guṇ 77/1476, Mys, Yaḷ, Nan 262/969); Kan + Kan; N + N; Madd(u) < Mardu < Marundu + ūru; The village where medicinal plants are grown; FLN. ~ Marudūru (Huṇ); Marddūru (Heg 90/ Ganga Śrīpurusha).

Madhuvanahaḷḷi (KRN, Koḷ); Skt + Kan; N + Suf + ; Madhu + (van)a + ; [Spring, honey]; After a person; PN.

Magge (Ḣeg 142/998, 143/1419); SX; Kan; A bud ?

Maguvinahaḷḷi mēla Kāmanahaḷḷi (Guṇ); Kan + Kan + Kan + Skt + Kan; N + Suf + N + Particle + N + Suf + N; Magu + (vin)a + haḷḷi + mēla + Kāma + (n)a + ; Magu = child; mēla = upper part; kāma = god of love; Kāmanahaḷḷi which is beyond Maguvinahaḷḷi; PN.

Mahadēśwara beṭṭa (Koḷ 77/17th); Skt + Kan; N + ; Mahadēśwara +; After a saint's name; RN.

Malaganakere (PP); Kan + Kan; N + Suf + ; Malaga + (n)a + ; PN. [Malega = a wanderer in the mountains ?].

Malārapāḷya (Yaḷ 169/150, 170/1647); Kan < Skt + Kan; N + ; Malāra < Mālā-hāra + ; A string of glass bracelets; After a seller of such bracelets; MN. ~ Mallāra (Heg); Mallārapāḷya (Yaḷ).

Maleyūru (CRN 335/1422, 365/1355, 361/1814; Heg 86/1531; TNP); Kan + Kan; N + N; Male + (y)ūru; A village near a hill; GPN. ~ Malekundi (Nan).

Mallahaḷḷi (Heg, Mys, Nan, KRN); Skt + Kan; N + N; Malla + Haḷḷi; After a wrestler; PN. ~ Mallayyanapura (CRN 299/1532).

Mallarājapura (Heg); Skt + Skt + Skt; N + N + ; Malla + rāja + ; After the king of a race of strong people; PN.

Mallēdēvanahaḷḷi (CRN); Kan + Skt + Kan; N + N + Suf + ; Malle < Male < Malla + dēva + (n)a + ; After the god of the hill, Śiva; RN. ~ Maladēvanahaḷḷi (227/1333); Maledēvanahaḷḷi (260/1368).

Mallināthapura (Huṇ, PP 8/1398, 89/1403); Skt + Skt; Mallinātha + pura; After the name of a Jaina Tīrthankara; RN.

Mallūpura (CRN, Nan); Skt + Skt; N + ; Mallū + ; Same as Malla; PN. Mallupura (Nan 113/1513).

Maluganahaḷḷi (KRN); Kan + Kan; N + Suf + ; Maluga + (n)a + ; Same as Malagana kere (?); PN.

Maḷalagadde (Heg); Kan + Kan; N + Suf + ; Maḷal < Maṇ + a + ; The village with sandy fields; GPN. ~ Maḷalavāḍi (Huṇ 6/1633, 7/1829; Mys 99/1674); Maṇalevāḍi (135/1127); Maṇalūru (Nan 164/1231); Maralūru (Nan); Maṇalūru (164/1231); Maḷallūru (Guṇ 61/11th).

Maḷali (KRN, Heg); SX; Kan; After a kind of fish; MN. ~ Maṇali (Heg 123/1079; KRN 9/1136, 10/12th, 11/1813, Nan 354/1278); Hiremaḷali (PP); Hiryamaḷali (132/1425).

Maḷavaḷḷi (Guṇ 61/1126, 26/1506); Kan + Kan; N + N; Maḷa < Malar + v(h)aḷḷi; A villagewhere flowers are grown; FLN. [Malava = a hill tribe ?].

Mañchabōyanahaḷḷi (Huṇ); Kan + Kan + Kan; N + N + Suf + ; Mancha + bōya +(n)a + ; After an excellent, handsome palanquin bearer; PN. ~ Mañchadēvanahaḷḷi (PP); Mañchagowḍanahaḷḷi (Heg); Mañchaguṇḍipura (CRN); Mañchahaḷḷi (Guṇ, Heg 38/16th); Mañchanahaḷḷi (KRN); Mañchēdēvanahaḷḷi (PP); Mañchēnahaḷḷi (KRN 117/1741).

Maṇagaḷḷi (Guṇ, Koḷ); Kan + Kan; N + N; Maṇa < Maṇaga + a(h)ḷḷi; After the son of the soil; PN. [Maṇiyagāra = a man who holds a local office ?]. ~ Maṇaganahaḷḷi (CRN).

Maṇḍakaḷḷi (Mys); Kan + Kan; N + N; Maṇḍaka < Maṇḍakki + haḷḷi; a village where roasted rice is prepared; MN. [Maṇḍa + kaḷḷi = Milkhedge].

Maṇḍanahaḷḷi (Mys); Skt + Kan; N + ; Maṇḍana + ; a village where the art of decoration is available (?); MN.

Maṇḍiganahaḷḷi (KRN); Kan + Kan; N + Suf + ; Maṇḍiga + (n)a + ; After a person who knows the preparation of Maṇḍige, a kind of dish (?); PN.

Mangaḷa (CRN, Guṇ, Koḷ); SX; Skt; An auspicious village; a village assigned to Brahmans ~ Mangaḷūru (Nan).

Manuganahaḷḷi (KRN, Huṇ, PP, Heg 65/15th); Skt + Kan; N + Suf +; Manuga + (n)a + ; After the father of the human race (?); PN.

Maraḍipura (TNP 131/19th); Kan + Skt; N + ; Maraḍi < Moraḍi + ; A village with a stony rough surface; GPN. ~ Moraḍiyapura (TNP 132/1528); Maraḍiyūru (PP).

Maradūru (PP, Huṇ 71/1586); Kan + Kan; N + N; Marad(u) < Mardu < Marundu + ūru; Any drug; Vide Maddūru; FLN.

Maravūru (Huṇ 4/11th, 13/16th, 15/1106); Kan + Kan; N + N; Mara + (v)ūru; A village full of trees; FLN. ~ Marūru (Huṇ).

Maraśe (Mys); SX; Kan; Hidden, concealed [Maraśe < Maruv(p)ase = a hidden layer]. ~ Maruvaśe (188/1191); Mariyase (186/9th, 189/17th); MN.

Mariyāla (CRN 66/1870); Kan + Kan; N + N; Mari + (y)āla; a small banyan tree; FLN.

Masagāpura (CRN 65/1719); Kan + Skt; N + ; Masagā + ; The village noted for whetters; MN. [Dusky colour, mildew ?]. ~ Masahaḷḷi (Guṇ 23/1546; Heg 113/1527).

Masaṇāpura (CRN); Kan < Skt + Skt; N + ; Masaṇā < Smaśāna + ; A village with a cemetry; MN. ~ Masaṇakuppe (Heg).

Maṭakere (Huṇ); Kan < Skt + Kan; N + ; Maṭa < Maṭha + ; A village with a hermitage/a school; MN. ~ Maṭakeri (Heg 35/1518, 43/1581); Maṭhakere (36/1497); Maḍakere (36/1497).

Māchabōyanahaḷḷi (Huṇ); Vide Manchabōyanahaḷḷi [Mācha = Mañcha]; PN. ~ Māchanāyakanahaḷḷi (Heg); Māchadēvanahaḷḷi (PP); Māchanahaḷḷi (KRN 117/1741).

Mādahaḷḷi (Mys, Guṇ, KRN, TNP 15/1622); Kan < Skt + Kan; N + ; Māda < Mahadēva + ; PN. ~ Mādahaḷḷi Kāvalu (Huṇ); Mādāpaṭṇa

(Guṇ); Mādhapaṭṭaṇa (Guṇ 150/1521); Mādāpura (TNP, Heg, CRN, Nan); Mādanahaḷḷi (Nan); Mādanapaḷḷi (338/1513); Mādagaḷḷi (Mys); Mādavāḍi (TNP); Mādavāḍe (81/1089); Mādēgowḍanahuṇḍi (TNP).

Mādalavāḍi (CRN); Kan < Skt + Kan; N + ; Mādala < Mātulanga +; A village where Citrus medica Lin grow; FLN.

Mādhavagere (Mys); Skt + Kan; N + ; Mādhava + ; Viṣhṇu, Kriṣhṇa; PN. ~ Mādhavapaṭṭaṇa (136/1513).

Māḍrahaḷḷi (Guṇ, TNP); Kan + Kan; N + ; Mādra < Mādara (?) + ; a village of cobblers; EN. ~ Mādigahaḷḷi (TNP).

Māgaḷi (PP); SX; Kan; The village where the herb, Coleus barbatus Benth grows [Māgaṇi = a division of a taluk or district]; FLN.

Māguḍilu (Heg); Kan < Skt + Kan; Adj + N; Mā < Mahā + guḍilu < guḍisalu; A village which consists of sheds; MN.

Maidanahaḷḷi (Huṇ); Kan + Kan; N + ; Maidana < Mayduna; A village founded by a sister's husband or a husband's brother; PN.

Mailambūru (Huṇ); Kan < Skt + Kan; N + N; Maila < Mayura + amba + ; After mother peacock; FAN.

Mākanahaḷḷi (PP); Kan + Kan; N + Suf + ; Māka < Mūka/Mārka ? + (n)a + ; PN. ~ Mākanapura (Nan).

Mākōḍu (PP 147/12th, 148/1165); Kan + Kan; N + N; Ma < Māvu + kōḍu; After the branch of mango tree; FLN.

Māḷanāyakanahaḷḷi (KRN); Kan < Skt + Skt + Kan; N + N + Suf + ; Māḷa < Mahaḷa < Mahālaya + nāyaka + (n)a + ; Annual ritual intended for ancestors. A person who performs this [A plain, ground]; PN.

Mālangi (PP, TNP, Koḷ 12/1514); SX; Kan; Mānangi; A small well, [< Mahālingi]. ~ Hosamālangi (Koḷ) [In Chola records, its form is Māyilangai; Renamed as Jagannāthapura agrahāra]; MN.

Māḷāpura (Guṇ); Kan < Skt + ; N + ; Māḷā < Māḷa < Mahaḷa < Mahālaya + ; After annual ritual intended for ancestors [Mālā = a place where garlands are made]; MN.

Māmbaḷḷi (Koḷ 147/1301, 57/1360); Kan + Kan; N + N; Māvu + b(h)aḷḷi; A place where mangoes flourish; FLA. ~ Māmpaḷḷi (Yaḷ 111/1290, 147/1301, 157/1246). ~ Māvinahaḷḷi (Mys, TNP).

Māṇikyapura (Mys 213/1685); Skt + Skt; N + N; A place where gems are available; CN.

Māragowḍanahaḷḷi (Huṇ, KRN, TNP, Mys 213/1685); Skt + Kan < Skt + Kan; N + N + Suf + ; Māra + gowḍa + (n)a + ; PN. [Māra = a love god]. ~ Māragoṇḍanahaḷḷi (KRN 117/1741); Māranahaḷḷi (Huṇ); Māranapura (TNP); Māraśeṭṭihaḷḷi (Mys).

Mārbaḷḷi (Mys); Kan + Kan; V + N; Mār < Māṟu + b(h)aḷḷi; A place of sale; CN.

Mārchahaḷḷi (Heg, KRN); Skt + Kan; N + N; Mārcha < Māriṣha/Mārīcha ? + haḷḷi; After an honourable man/a rākshasa; PN. ~ Mārarchahaḷḷi (KRN 107/1643).

Mārṭahaḷḷi (KOḷ); Kan < Eng + Kan; N + ; Mārṭa < Mārtha + ; PN.

Mārtikyātanahaḷḷi (Mys); Kan + Kan + Kan; N + N + Suf + ; Mārti < Moraḍi + Kyāta + (n)a + haḷḷi; The village founded by him; PN.

Māyanāyakanapura (Guṇ); Skt + Skt + Skt; N + N + Suf + ; Māya + nāyaka + (n)a + ; After a person or leader possessing powers of illusion. [A conjuror, a juggler ?]; PN. ~ Māyigowḍanahaḷḷi (KRN); PN.

Māvanūru (Mys, TNP); Kan + Kan; N + Suf + N; Māva + (n)a + ūru; A village founded by mother's brother/wife's or husband's father; PN. ~ Māvattūru (KRN).

Mellahaḷḷi (PP); Kan + Kan; N + ; A beautiful nice village; MN.

Meṇasinakyātanahaḷḷi (TNP); Kan + Kan + Kan; N + Suf + N + ; Meṇasu < Meḷasu + (in)a + kyāta + (n)a + ; [Meṇasu = pepper, chilli]; PN.

Mēgaḷāpura (Mys); Kan + Skt; Dir. Par + Suf + ; Mēgu + aḷā + ; The village on the upper side; GPN. ~ Mēlmāḷa (CRN); Mēlumāḷa (216/1593); Mēlūru (CRN 236/1492, KRN 82/17th, PP 71/1586, 139/1615); Mēgaḍahaḷḷi (TNP 16/1749).

Mēṭagaḷḷi (Mys); Kan + Kan; N + N; Mēṭa(i) + g(h)aḷḷi; Excellence; A big man; A post in the middle of a threshing floor. ~ Mētikuppe (Heg).

Miṇya (Koḷ); SX; Kan; A village that glitters; MN.

Mirle (KRN); Kan + Kan; VN + Suf; Miru + le; a place which shines; MN. Mirile (88/1543, 89/1299); Mirlle (92/15th); Mirile (94/17th); Mirale (95/17th); Miraḷe (100/18th).

Motta (Nan 151/14th, 152/1312); SX; Kan; A collection of villages; MN.

Mōḍaḷḷi (Koḷ); N + N; Kan + Kan; Mōḍa + a(ha)ḷḷi; A cloudy village; NN. ~ Mōḍahaḷḷi (53/1535); Mōḍihaḷḷi (62/1354).

Muḍiguṇḍa (Koḷ 55/1398, 62/1354); Kan + Kan; N + VN; Muḍi + guṇḍa < goṇḍa; The place where the crown or hair was taken; MN. ~ Muḍigoṇḍaśōḷapuram (98/1189); Muḍiguppe (87/1606).

Muḍukutorebeṭṭa (TNP); Kan + Kan + Kan; VN + N + ; Muḍuku + tore + ; A village near the bend of the river; GPN.

Muṇḍiganahaḷḷi (KRN); Kan + Kan; N + Suf; Muṇḍiga + (n)a + ; A village of barbers/a kind of paddy; EN/FLN.

Muṇḍūru (KRN 77/1677, 78/1677); Kan + Kan; N + ; Muṇḍ(a) + ; A village of barbers [The name of a Rākshasa].

Munjanahaḷḷi (KRN); Skt + Kan; N + Suf + ; Munja + (n)a + ; A sort of grass used to make rope etc.; a person who deals with it; PN.

Muddēnahaḷḷi (PP); Kan + Kan; N + Suf + ; Muddē < Muddayya + (n)a + ; After a charming man; PN.

Mudukanapura (TNP); Kan + Skt; N + Suf + ; Muduka + (n)a + ; A town initiated by an old man; MN. ~ Muḍukanapura (103/1498).

Mukkaḍahaḷḷi (CRN); Kan + Kan + Kan; Nu + Adj + N + ; Mu < Mūru + (k)kaḍa + ; A village with three borders. Kaḍa also means a river; GPN.

Mukōḍihaḷḷi (CRN 1376/1316); Kan + Kan + Kan; Nu + N + ; Mu < Mūru + kōḍi + ; A village situated in between three outlets; GPN.

Muḷḷūru (Koḷ 16/17th, Nan 377/1502, Mys); Kan + Kan; N + JC + ; Muḷ + ḷ + ; A village noted for thorns. Muḷūru (Guṇ 120/1489. Nan 395/1514).

Muttalavāḍi (TNP); Kan + Kan; N + ; Muttala + ; After the bastard teak, Butea frondosa Roxb; FLN.

Mutagūru (PP); Kan + Kan; N + N; Mutag(a) < Muttaga + ūru; A village known for Palasa trees; (Butea frondosa Roxb); FLN.

Muttatti (TNP 39/9th); Kan + Kan; N + N; Mutt + atti; A village where old ficus (racemosa Lin) is found; FLN.

Muttige (CRN); SX; Kan; A seige or a blockade. Muttage (104/1413); Mutige 5/1828).

Muruḍagaḷḷi (Mys); Kan + Kan; N + N; Muruḍa(u) + g(h)aḷḷi; A village surrounded by rugged, uneven land; GPN.

Mūḍagūru (Guṇ 61/1126); Kan + Kan; ND + Suf + ; Mūḍa + (g)a +; Eastern village; GPN. ~ Mūḍanakōḍu (CRN 321/1542); Mūḍlāpura (CRN, Huṇ); Mūḍalakuppe (KRN); Mūḍlukoppalu (107/1643).

Mūgūru (TNP 260/16th, 261/1277); Kan + Kan; N + N; Mūg < mog + ūru; A village which gives shelter; MN. ~ Mogūru (276/1261, 278/1279, 284/14th); Mōgūru (261/1277, 270/16th).

Mūkaḷḷi (CRN); Kan + Kan; N + N; Mūka + (a)ḷḷi; The village of a dumb man; Name of a dānava; MN. ~ Mūkahaḷi (72/1578, Guṇ 149/1417); Mūkahaḷḷi (Guṇ); Mūkanahaḷḷi (Huṇ 16/1124).

Mūlepeṭlu (KRN 107/1643); Kan + Kan; N + N; Mūle + peṭlu; The plant sida mauritiana Herit which is in a corner; FLN.

Mysūru (Mys 1/1821); Kan < Skt + Kan; N + N; Mys < Mahisha + ūru; After a buffalo; FAN. ~ Maisūru (27/1499); Mahisūru (5/1843, 74/1839); Mahiṣāpura (13/18th); Mysunāḍu (185/1384).

N

Naḍehādi (Heg, Gaz); Kan + Kan; N + N; Naḍe + hādi; A villge on a path very clear for walking; MN.

Nagarle (Nan); SX; Skt; Nagar(a) + le > āla > ālaya; A city settlement; MN. ~ Nagarala (239/10th); Nageraḷa (240/10th).

Nagartahaḷḷi (Mys); Skt + Kan; N + ; Nagartha + ; The village of merchant class; CN.

Nallūru (CRN, Heg 119/1531, Huṇ 24/1162, 32/1669); Kan + Kan; Adj + ; Nal(l) + ; A delightful, blessed village; MN.

Nandagaḷḷi (Mys); Skt + Kan; N + N; Nanda + g(h)aḷḷi; After the name of a cowherd, the foster father of Krishna; RN.

Nandiguṇḍa (Nan 201/1021); Skt + Kan; N + N; Nandi + guṇḍa < Koṇḍa; A village after the bullockhill; GPN. ~ Nandiguṇḍapura (Nan); Nandipura (TNP); Nandināthapura (Heg).

Nanjahaḷḷi (CRN); Kan + Kan; N + ; Nanja < Nanjuṇḍa + ; after the god who digests poison, Śiva; PN. ~ Nanjanagūḍu (Nan); Nanjanāthapura (Heg); Nanjanāyakanahaḷḷi (Heg); Nanjāpura (TNP); Nanjarājapura (CRN 175/16th); Nanjēdēvanapura (CRN 400/1865; 401/1531).

Nannigahaḷḷi (200/17th); Kan + Kan; N + ; Nanniga + ; After a man who speaks truth; PN.

Narachanahaḷḷi (KRN); Kan + Kan; N + Suf + ; Naracha + (n)a + ; After an emaciated person; PN. [< Nārācha = an arrow or a pen ?].

Naragyātanahaḷḷi (TNP); Skt + Kan + Kan; N + N + Suf + ; Nara + g(k)yāta < kēta + (n)a + ; After a musceled low wicked god; PN.

Narasamangala (CRN 295/1337); Skt + Skt; N + N; Narasa < Narasimha + mangala; After the god man-lion; PN. ~ Narasimhamangala (299/13th); Narasāmbudhi (Nan 253/16th); Narasīpura (Heg, Nan 116/1655).

Navilūru (Nan 208/1586, PP, CRN 9/1281, 239/1578); Kan + Kan; N + ; Navil + ; a village famous for peacocks; FAN. ~ Nāvaluru (Nan 111/1575).

Nāchanahaḷḷi (Mys 164/19th); Kan + Kan; N + Suf + ; nācha + (n)a + ; After a person who gets embarassed easily; PN.

Nāḍanahaḷḷi (Mys); Kan + Kan; N + Suf + ; Nāḍa + (n)a + ; After the chief of a country; PN. ~ Nāḍappanahaḷḷi (KRN, Huṇ 32/1669).

Nāgalakere (TNP); Skt + Kan; N + Fem.Ind. +; Nāga + la + ; A village after a snake lady; PN.

Nāganahaḷḷi (CRN, Heg, Huṇ, Mys, PP 71/1586); Skt + Kan; N + Suf + ; Nāga + (n)a + ; A village after a proper name which means an elephant, a serpent or a great man; PN. ~ Nāganapura (Nan); Nāgaraghaṭṭa (PP 129/16th); = pertaining to Nāga race; Nāgawāla (Mys); Nāgawaḷḷi (CRN); Nāgivaḷḷi (274/1485); Nāgavalli (206/16th).

Nāraḷāpura (PP); Kan < Skt + Skt; Nāraḷā < Nārikēla? + ; After cocoanut trees. FLN.

Nāraṇāpura (Guṇ); Kan < Skt + Skt; N + ; Nāraṇā < Nārāyaṇa + ; After the god Nārāyaṇa; RN. ~ Nārayaṇāpura (KRN).

Nāṭanahaḷḷi (KRN); Kan + Kan; N + Suf + ; Nāṭa + (n)a + ; After the chief of a country; PN.

Nāykanahuṇḍi (Heg); Kan < Skt + Kan; N + Suf + ; Nāyka < Nāyaka + (n)a + ; After a leader/a chief/a master.

Nellitāḷapura (Nan); Kan + Kan + Skt; N + N + Suf + ; Nelli + tāḷ + a + ; The village famous for trees phylanthus emblica Lin; FLN.

Nemmanahaḷḷi (Heg); Kan + Kan; N + Suf + ; Nemma + (n)a + ; After a person who can be relied upon for support; PN.

Neṭṭakallahuṇḍi (Heg, Guṇ 149/1417); Kan + Kan + Kan; V Adj + N + Suf + ; Neṭṭa + kal(l) + a + ; A village where a stone is fixed firmly in the ground; GPN.

Nēgattūru (Huṇ) ?; Kan + Kan; N + Suf + N; Nēg < Nēgil/Nēyge + att + -ūru ?; A village known for ploughs or weaving (?); MN.

Nēṇekaṭṭe (Guṇ); Kan + Kan; N + N; Nēṇe + kaṭṭe; A village where there is a platform for making ropes ? MN.

Nēraḷe (Nan, PP); SX; Kan; A village known for Eugenia jambolana Lam; FLN. ~ Nirali (Heg 158/1663, KRN 158/1663); Nērile (Guṇ 135/1492, 335/1495); Nirli (Nan 341/1766); Nēraḷūru (KRN 111/12th); Nēraḷakuppe (Huṇ, PP); Doḍḍanērile (PP 8/1612).

Nijaganahaḷḷi (KRN); Skt + Kan; N + Suf + ; Nijaga + (n)a + ; After a truthful man; PN.

Nilasōge (TNP 16/1749); Skt + Kan; Adj + N; Nila < Nīla + sōge; A village famous for blue feathered peacocks; FAN.

Nilavāḍi (PP); Kan + Kan; V Adj + N ; Nila + vāḍi; A settlement; an abode; MN. [Nīla + vāḍi; PN ?]. ~ Nelavāḍi (90/1613).

Nīlavāgilu (Huṇ, Heg); Kan + Kan; N + N; Nila + vāgilu; A village where side posts of doors are made; MN. ~ Nilavāgili (Heg 160/1520).

Nilangāla (PP); Skt + Kan; N + Suf + N; Nila < Nīla + n + g(k)āla; a village built by Nīla (?); PN.

Nisana (Heg); SX; Kan < Skt; [Niśāni = An ensign, a flag ?]. MN.

Niṭre (Guṇ); Kan + Kan; Niṭ < Niḍidu + (a)re; A village where arock looks prominent; GPN. ~ Niṭere (28/1029); Niṭṭare (320/972, 62/1009); Niṭṭarai (61/1126).

Nuggahaḷḷi (Mys); Kan + Kan; N + ; Nugga(e) + ; A village where Moringa pterigos-perma gaert (drumstick) grows; FLN.

Nūraḷikuppe (Heg); Kan + Kan; N + ; Nūraḷi < Nurjugal (?) + ; A village of gravel land; GPN.

P

Paḍagūru (Guṇ); Kan + Kan; ND + ; Paḍag(u) + ; Western village; GPN. ~ Paḍukōṭe (Heg); Paḍuvala agrahāra (Nan); Paḍuvala marahaḷḷi (Nan); Paḍalu marahaḷḷi (300/1672).

Panchavaḷḷi (PP); Skt + Kan; N Adj + ; Panch + ; A group of five villages; MN.

Panjanahaḷḷi (Guṇ 97/16th); Kan + Kan; N + Suf + ; Panja < Panje + (n)a + After a weak, helpless person; PN. [A torch bearer ?].

Paramāpura (Guṇ); Skt + Skt; Adj + ; Paramā + ; Excellent town; MN.

Parvatanapura (Guṇ); Skt + Skt + ; N + Suf + ; Parvata + (n)a + ; After a man named after a hill; PN.

Pasayyanapura (Guṇ); Kan < Skt; N + Suf + ; Pasayya < Pasāyta + (n)a + ; A village after a master ofrobes; PN.

Paśupati (KRN); Skt + Skt; N + N; Paśu + pati; Village named after Śiva; RN

Paṭṭehuṇḍi (TNP); Skt + Kan; N + ; Paṭṭe + ; The village known for woven silk; silk garments; CN.

Pāḷya (Koḷ); SX; Kan; A camp, a settlement, a hamlet; HN. ~ Pāḷyam (41/1163); Pāḷeya (45/16th).

Pārekoppalu (Huṇ); Kan + Kan; N + ; Pāre + ; A hamlet where a rock looks prominent; GPN.

Penjahaḷḷi (Heg); Kan + Kan; N + ; Penja < Pachcha (?) + ; A foolish or a mad man ? [< Penche = a peacock ?]; PN.

Pillahaḷḷi (TNP, Mys); Kan + Kan; N + ; Pilla + ; After the God, Bhairava [a child]; RN. [Piḷḷa].

Piriyāpaṭṇa (PP 1/1590); Kan + Kan; Adj + N; Piriyā + paṭna; A big town; MN. [After Changāḷva Piriyarājadēva; ancient name Singanapaṭṭaṇa].

Ponnachi (Koḷ); Kan + Kan; N + N; Pon + achi < achchi; Gold like mother; a village after her; FPN.

Puṇajūru (CRN 241/982, 240/1429); Kan + Kan; N + N; Puṇaj(i) + ūru; A village which has dustlike dry soil; GPN. ~ Puṇujūru (274/1485).

Pura (Heg, Guṇ 150/1521, Nan 17/1517, 262/1639); SX; Skt; A town. ~ Purada kaṭṭe (Heg).

Puṭṭanapura (CRN); Kan + Skt; N + Suf + ; Puṭṭa + (n)a + ; After a small or young man; PN. ~ Puṭṭēgowḍanahuṇḍi (Mys 184/9th ?).

Puttanapura (Guṇ 120/1640); Kan + Skt; N + Suf + ; Putta + (n)a +; An anthill, a person who emerges from it. [Putta < Putra ?]; GPN. ~ Pūtanapura (157/17th, CRN 217/1545).

Pūnāḍahaḷḷi (PP); Kan + Kan + Kan; N + N + Suf + ; Pū + nāḍ + a + ; A village where flowers are grown in plenty; FLN.

R

Ragalekuppe (Heg); Kan < Mhr + Kan; N + Suf + ; Ragala < ragad + a + ; A village of abundance (?); MN.

Ranganāthapura (TNP); Skt + Skt; N + ; Ranganātha + ; The name of God; RN. ~ Rangasamudra (TNP).

Rangayyana Koppalu (Huṇ); Kan < Skt + Kan + Kan; N + Suf + ; Rang(a) + ayya + (n)a + ; Personal name ofter the God Ranga; PN.

Raṭṭanahaḷḷi (Mys); Kan < Skt + Kan; N + Suf + ; Raṭṭa < Rāshṭraka (?) + (n)a + ; After the chief of a country; PN. [< Ratna ?].

Rāghavāpura (Guṇ 40/1320, 149/1417); Skt + Skt; N + N; After the God Rāghava; RN. ~ Rāghapura (39/1507); [Another name : Gommaṭahaḷḷi (Guṇ 40/1320)]).

Rājāpura (PP); Skt + Skt; N + ; Rājā + ; After a king; PN. ~ Rājūru (Nan); Rājanabeḷaguli (PP); Rājēgowḍanahuṇḍi (Heg).

Rāmanahaḷḷi (Mys); Skt + Kan; N + Suf + ; Rāma + (n)a + ; PN/RN. ~ Rāmapaṭna (Huṇ); Rāmapaṭṭana (16/1124, 17/1342); Rāmāpura (Koḷ); Rāmasamudra (CRN); Rāmaseṭṭipura (Nan 302/1512); Rāmayyanapura (Guṇ); Rāmēgowḍanapura (TNP); Rāmēnahaḷḷi (Huṇ); Rāmpura (KRN, Nan 158/15th); Rāmanapura (KRN 49/1548).

Rāmanāthapuradahuṇḍi (TNP); Skt + Skt + Skt + Kan; N + N + N + Suf + ; Rāma + nātha + pura + (d)a + ; After the god's name; RN. ~ Rāmanāthatunga (PP).

Rāśimaraṭikāvalu (PP); Skt + Kan + Kan; N + N + ; Rāśi + maraṭi < moraḍi + ; A village where there is a heap of rough soil, a hillock; GPN.

Rāyanahaḷḷi (Huṇ); Kan < Skt + Kan; N + Suf + ; Rāya < Rāja + (n)a + ; After a king; PN.

Rāvandūru (PP 71/1586, 125/1383, 130/1417); Kan < Skt + Kan + Kan; N + PAP + ; Rā < Rāma (?) + Vand(a) + ; A village to where Rama came (?); RN. ~ Rāundūru (107/1299); [It is Rāmandūru in Śivatattva Chintāmaṇi].

Rēchambaḷḷi (CRN); Kan < Skt + Kan; N + N; Rēcham < Re Chamma < Rājamma ? + b(h)aḷḷi; A village after this name; FPN.

S

Śambhugowḍanahaḷḷi (Heg); Skt + Kan < Skt + Kan; N + N + Suf +; Śambhu + gowḍa + (n)a + ; (Śambhu = Śiva); A village after this name; PN.

Śankahaḷḷi (Heg, Huṇ); Kan < Skt + Kan; N + ; Śanka < Śankha + ; A village where conch-shells are available; MN.

Śāgya (Koḷ 65/11th, 66/18th); SX; Skt ?; < Śākya (?).

Śāntipura (Heg); Skt + Skt; N + ; Śānti + ; A village which is peaceful/ of after Śanti; FPN.

Śānubhōganahaḷḷi (Huṇ, PP); Skt + Kan; N + Suf + ; Śanūbhōga + (n)a + ; After a village clerk; PN.

Śeṭṭihaḷḷi (PP, Huṇ); Kan <Skt + Kan; N + ; Śeṭṭi < Śrēshṭi + ; A village consisting of a tradesman; CN. ~ Śeṭṭahaḷḷi (Nan, Guṇ, Koḷ, TNP 107/1602); Seṭṭihaḷi (Guṇ 178/1488); Seṭināyakanahaḷḷi (Mys).

Śirāmahaḷḷi (Heg); Kan + Kan; N + ; Śirama < Śiruma + ; ? PN.

Śivakahaḷḷi (Yaḷ); Kan < Skt + Kan; N + ; Śivaka < Śiva':ka + ; Feminine form of Śiva; The village after her; FPN. [= a post, a stake, a plug ?].

Śivapura (Guṇ, CRN 5/1828); Skt + Skt; N + ; Śiva + ; RN.

Śīḷavantapura (Guṇ); Skt + Skt; N + Suf + N; Śila + vanta + ; After a man possessed of good qualities; PN.

Śīranahaḷḷi (Huṇ); Skt + Kan; N + Suf + ; Śīra + (n)a + ; After a plougher/a farmer [= the Sun ? ~] Śīra-nahuṇḍi (Heg).

Śravaṇanahaḷḷi (Huṇ); Skt + Kan; N + Suf + ; Śravaṇa + (n)a + ; After a Buddhist or a Jaina mendicant; RN.

Śrīrāmapura (KRN, Mys); Skt + Skt + Skt; N + N + ; Śrī_+ Rāma +; After the epic hero of Rāmāyaṇa; RN.

Śrīrangapura (CRN); Skt + Skt + Skt; N + N + ; Śri + ranga + ; After the god Śri Ranga; RN.

Śyābāḷu (KRN, Gaz); ? + Kan; ? + N; Syā (?) + bāḷu; (?).

Śyāḍanahaḷḷi (Mys); Skt + Kan; N + Suf + ; Śyāḍa < Śyāda + (n)a +; A place consisting of green grass ? MN.

Śyānādrahaḷḷi (Guṇ); (?).

Sabbanahaḷḷi (Huṇ); Kan < Skt + Kan; N + Suf + ; Sabba < Sarva + (n)a + ; Śiva; RN.

Sakkare (KRN); SX; Kan < Skt; < Śarkarā; Sugar (?).

Sambaravaḷḷi (KRN); Kan < Skt + Kan; N + ; Sambara < Śambara +; The village noted for a kind of deer. [The name of a demon]; FAN. ~ Sambravalli (87/1606).

Sampigēpura (Guṇ 91/1610, 150/1521); Kan < Skt + Skt; N + ; Sampige < Champaka + ; Michelia Champaca; FLN.

Saṇabinakuppe (KRN, PP); Kan < Skt ? + Kan; N + Suf + N; Saṇab(i) < Śaṇa + (n)a + kuppe; Village known for Sunhemp plant; FLN.

Saṇṇēnahaḷḷi (Huṇ); Kan + Kan; N + Suf + ; Saṇṇē < Saṇṇaya + (n)a + ; After a little man; PN [May be from Śaraṇayya].

Sangaraseṭṭihaḷḷi (PP); Kan < Skt + Kan < Skt + Kan; N + N + ; Sangara < Śankara + Seṭṭi < Śrēshṭi + ; PN. ~ Changāḷva Seṭṭiyahaḷḷi (137/1097, 138/1524).

Sankanahaḷḷi (KRN 82/17th); Kan < Skt + Kan; N + Suf + ; Sanka < Śankha + (n)a + ; PN. After a conch-shell. ~ Sankahaḷḷi (Huṇ).

Santemaraḷḷi (CRN); Kan < Skt + Kan + Kan; N + N + N; Sante < Samsthā + mar < māṟu + (h)aḷḷi; A gathering of buyers and sellers; CN.

Sanyāsipura (KRN 117/1741, PP 114/1568); Skt + Skt; N + ; Sanyāsi + ; After a recluse, PN.

Sappayanapura (CRN); Kan < Skt + Skt; N + Suf + ; Sappayya < Sarpayya + (n)a + ; After a snake god; PN. ~ Sapainapura (295/1337).

Saragūru (Nan 124/1663, Heg 84/1569, 116/1655, 123/1079, KRN 77/1377; Koḷ 32/15th, 37/10th, CRN); Kan + Kan; Sarg + ūru; A village famous for hunting; MN. [Saraku + ūru = A village where merchandise is availble]. ~ Haḷesaragūru (CRN 197/1762).

Sarakāri Uttanahaḷḷi (Mys); Hin + Kan + Kan; N + N + Suf + ; Sarakāri + utta < hutta + (n)a + ; Government village named after an anthill; MN.

Satyāgāla (PP, Koḷ 30/1321, 31/1720); Skt + Kan; N + ; Satyā + ; A village in memory of truth; MN. ~ Sattēgāla (Koḷ).

Savve (Heg); SX; Kan < Savi < Saviha ? That which has taste, flavour [< Sousava = small, fragrance].

Sāgaḍe (CRN 318/1273, 319/1273); SX; Kan; The village where the forest trees Sleichera trijuga grow; FLN [< Sāgu = cultivation, tillage].

Sāgare (Heg 123/1069, 149/1379, 120/1861, 118/1829, Nan 142/8th (?); SX; Skt; Ocean ? MN.

Sāligrāma (KRN 48/725, 58/1878); Skt +Skt; After a blackstone worshipped as sacred to God Vishṇu; RN. ~ Sālagrāma (79/1667, 50/1628); Sālugāve (92/15th); Sāligāve (51/15th) [< śaligrama: A village known for paddy cultivation].

Sāṇegāla (CRN); Kan < Skt + Kan; N + ; Sāṇe < Śāṇa + ; A village where whet stones are available; MN.

Sātagaḷḷi (Nan, Mys); Kan < Skt + Kan; N + N; Sāta < Sānta < Śānta (?) + g(h)aḷḷi; A peaceful village; MN. [Sāta < Śāta = sharp].

Sātigrāma (KRN); Kan < Skt + Skt; N + ; Sāti < Swāti + ; Named after an auspicious constellation; NN. [< Sāvitri ?].

Sāvukanahaḷḷi (Guṇ, Gaz); Kan < Skt + Kan; N + Suf + ; Sāvuka < Śābaka (?) + (n)a + ; After a young animal; FAN. [Sāvuke < Śrāvaka = Jains].

Sēnāpatihaḷḷi (TNP); Skt + Kan; N + ; Sēnāpati + ; The village founded by an army chief, a general; HN.

Siddalingapura (Mys); Skt + Skt; N + ; Siddalinga + ; **After** a saint; PN.

Siddāpura (Heg, Guṇ, KRN); Kan < Skt + Skt; N + ; Siddā < Siddha + ; The town after him; PN. ~ Siddayyanapura (Koḷ, Guṇ).

Siṇḍēnahaḷḷi (Heg); Kan + Kan; N + Suf + ; Siṇḍē < Siṇḍayya + (n)a +; After a disagreeable person (?) PN; ~ Śiṇḍenahaḷḷi (Heg); Śiṇḍayyanahaḷḷi (CRN); Śiṇḍinahaḷḷi (Huṇ); Siṇḍanapura (Guṇ).

Sindhuvaḷḷi (Mys 199/1434, Nan 348/1106, 349/1334); Skt + Kan; N + ; Sindhū + ; After a stream or river; NN.

Singānallūru (Koḷ); Kan < Skt + Kan + Kan; N + Adj + ; Singā < Simha + nal(l) + ; An excellent village after a man-like lion; PN. ~ Singaṇa nallūru (Koḷ 56/1408, 62/1354); Singanapura (CRN 142/12th); Singapaṭṇa (Heg).

Singaramādahaḷḷi (Huṇ); Kan < Skt + Kan < Skt + Kan; N + N + ; Singara < Śṛngāra + māda < mahadēwa + ; Named after Māda who has been adorned; PN.

Siragōḍu (Koḷ); Kan < Skt + Kan; N + N; Sira < Śiras + g(k)ōḍu; A village near the peak or top of a hill; GPN.

Siriyūru (Huṇ); Kan < Skt + Kan; N + N; Siri < Śrī + (y)ūru; Wealthy village; MN.

Sīgavāḷu (KRN); Kan + Kan; N + ; Sīga + ; A village where climbing prickly shrub the pods of which are used like soap, grow; FLN. ~ Sīgevāḷu (79/1667); Sīgevāḍi (Heg); Sīgavāḍi (Guṇ); Sīgōḍipuura (TNP); Sīgūru (PP).

Sollāpura (Heg); Kan < Skt + Skt; N + ; Sollā < Sonnalige < Swarṇa + ; A golden town; MN.

Sōmanahaḷḷi (KRN, Huṇ); Skt + Kan; N + Suf + ; Sōma + (n)a + ; After a person who has moon as his name; PN. ~ Sōmanapura (CRN, Guṇ); Sōmahaḷḷi (Guṇ 75/1576); Sōmasamudra (CRN 404/993, 405/1569); Sōmēgowḍanahuṇḍi (Heg).

Sōmanāthapura (TNP 88/1276, 89/1300, 90/1326, 91/1281); Skt +Skt + Skt; N + N + ; Sōma + nātha + ; Śiva; RN. ~ Sōmēśwarapura (Mys).

Sōmavārapēṭe (CRN); Skt + Skt + Kan; N + N + ; Sōma + vāra + ; Named after Monday; MN.

Sōnahaḷḷi (Heg, Huṇ); Kan < Skt + Kan; N + ; Sōna < Swarṇa + ; A village where goldsmiths live; EN. [Sōne = A thin, light but long continued rain ?].

Sōsale (TNP 105/1521, 107/1662); SX; Kan; V + Suf; Sōsu < Śōdhisu (?) + ale; (?) The place where the sedimentry soil is deposited; GPN.

Sowtanahaḷḷi (KRN); Kan + Kan; N + Suf; Sowta < Savute + ; A village where a kind of cucumber is grown; PN/FLN.

Sugganahaḷḷi (KRN 86/1606); Kan + Kan; N + Suf; Sugga + (n)a + ; After a person who celebrates feast during harvest season; PN.

Sujjalūru (TNP 16/1749); Kan + Kan; N + ; sujjal [Chujjal] + ; After a kind of tree whose leaves are used along with soapnut powder; FLN.

Suḷagōḍu (PP, Gaz); Kan + Kan; N + N; Suḷa + g(k)ōḍu; A village near a turning peak; GPN.

Suṇḍāpura (Heg); Kan + Skt; N + ; Suṇḍa + ; After a musk rat; FAN. ~ Suṇdavāḷu (PP).

Sunkadahaḷḷi (PP); Kan < Skt ? + Kan; N + Suf + ; Sunka < Śulka ? + (d)a + ; A village where toll is collected; CN.

Suragahaḷḷi (PP, Gaz); Kan + Kan; N + ; Suraga < Suragi + ; A village where trees with fragrant flowers grow; FLN. [< Kshurike = a dagger ?]. ~ Suraguvaḷḷi (25/1598); Suruguvaḷi (110/1586).

Suttūru (Nan 213/1015, CRN 216/1593, Guṇ 61/1126); Kan < Skt + Kan; N + N; Suttūr < Sottiyūr < Sōttiyūr < Śrōtriyūru; A village famous for learned Brahmaṇas. [A rent-free village to Brahmans]; RN.

Sūlvāḍi (Koḷ 79/1580); Kan < Skt + Kan; N + ; Sūla < Śūla + ; A village where sharp, pointed weapons are manufactured; CN.

Sūḷekere Kāvalu (Huṇ); Kan + Kan; N + N + ; Sūḷe + kere + ; A village after a harlot. ~ Sūḷekōte (PP); Sūḷēripāḷya (Koḷ).

T

Tagaḍūru (Nan 266/1543, Guṇ 53/1546); Kan + Kan; N + ; Tagaḍu +; Metal beaten into a plate; A place where these things are made; CN. ~ Tāgaḍūru (Guṇ 61/1126, 251/1527).

Tagarapura (Koḷ); Kan + Skt; N + Suf + ; Tagar + a + ; A village where rams are reared; FAN.

Taggalūru (Guṇ); Kan + Kan; VN + ; Taggal + ; A low level village; GPN. [A large shrub, Clorodendron plomoides ?]. ~ Taggilūru (40/1320).

Talakāḍu (TNP) Kan + Kan; N + N; Tala + kāḍu; After the two Kirāta brothers named therein ? ~ Taḷakāḍu (195/14th, 198/15th); Taraikkāḍu (150/1293, 164/1180); Taḷekkāḍu (200/935); Taḷekkāḍu (207/726); (Another name Rājarājapura); [Taḷai + k + kāḍu; The forest which looks like an umbrella]; MN.

Taḷale (Guṇ); SX; Kan; V + Suf; Taḷa + le; To bud, to sprout; FLN.

Taḷūru (Mys); Kan < Skt + Kan; N + N; Taḷa < sthala + ūru; A settlement; MN.

Tammaḍahaḷḷi (Huṇ, CRN, PP); Kan + Kan; N + ; Tammada(i) + ; After a temple priest; PN. ~ Tammaḍihaḷḷi (CRN 381/15th, 382/1135, PP 146/15th); Tammaḍipura (TNP).

Taṇḍasīpura (Heg); Kan + Skt; N + ; Taṇḍasī + ; A town where thorny trees flourish; FLN.

Tandre (KRN); Kan + Kan; N + N; Tand(a) < taṇḍa (?) + (a)re; A village where a heap of stone lies; GPN. ~ Tandare (89/1492); Tandari (79/1667); Tandre Ankanahaḷḷi (KRN).

Taradele (Nan); Kan + Kan; N + N; Tarad(gu) (?) + ele; After dried leaves; MN.

Taraganahaḷḷi (Nan, Guṇ 113/1638); Kan + Kan; N + Suf + ; Taraga + (n)a + ; A broker's village; PN. [A person given to vain talk; a commission agent].

Tarikallu (Huṇ, PP 9/1620); Kan + Kan; N + N; Tari + kallu; A village around which rough stones are found; GPN. ~ Tariyakallu (Huṇ 24/1162, 32/1669); [Another name : Kaṇṭhīravasamudra].

Tāṇḍavapura; (Nan); Skt + Skt; N + ; Tāṇdava + ; After the divine dancer, Śiva; RN.

Tātanahaḷḷi (PP); Kan + Kan; N + Suf + ; Tāta + (n)a + ; After a grand father; PN.

Tāyūru (Nan 204/10th, 208/1586, 257/1286); Kan + Kan; N + ; Tāy +; Mother's village; FPN.

Tenakallu (Heg); Kan + Kan; N + ; Tena(e) + ; After the top of a rampart. [A spike, an ear of corn ?]; HN.

Telugaramasahaḷḷi (Heg); Tel + Kan + Kan; N + Suf + V + N; Telugu(a) + ra + masa + haḷḷi; A village established by Telugu people, where whetting stone is availble; EN.

Terakaṇāmbi (Guṇ 113/1504, 142/1310); Kan + Kan; V Adj + N + ; Tera + kaṇambi < kaṇive; The town located in the open valley; GPN. ~ Terakaṇāmbe (27/1559, 40/1320, 75/1596, 93/1553; Nan 138/1332).

Tērambaḷḷi (Koḷ); Kan + Kan + Kan; N + N + N; Tēr(u) + am(ma) + b(h)aḷḷi; After a chariot; FPN.

Timakāpura (PP); Kan + Skt; N + ; Timakā < Timmakka; After a lady by name Timmakka; FPN.

Timmaṇihosahaḷḷi (Heg, Gaz); Kan + Kan + Kan; N + Adj + Noun; Timmaṇi + hosa + haḷḷi; A new village after Timmaṇi; FPN.

Timmarājipura (Koḷ, Gaz); Kan + Skt + Skt; N + N + ; Timma + rāji + ; FPN.

Timmēgowḍanapāḷya (CRN); Kan + Kan < Skt + Kan; N + N + Suf + ; Timmē < Timma + gowḍa + (n)a + ; PN.

Tippalāpura (CRN); Kan + Kan; N + Fem.Ind. + ; Tippa(e) + lā + ; After a hill goddess, Pārvati; RN.

Tippūru (KRN 110/1102, 109/16th; Huṇ 24/1162); Kan + Kan; N + ; Tipp(e) + ; A village on a hillock; GPN.

Tirumakūḍlunarasīpra (TNP 1/1725, 4/855, 8/1089); Kan < Skt + Kan + Kan < Skt + Skt; N + N + N + ; Tiruma < Śrīmahā + kūḍ(a)lu + narasi < narasimha + ; A confluence of river where Narasīpura is situated; GPN.

Tirumalāpura (PP); Kan < Skt + Kan + Skt; N + N + ; Tiru < Śrī + malā(e) + ; After the sacred hill; RN.

Toṇḍāḷu (Huṇ); Kan + Kan; N + N; Toṇḍ(e) + (h)āḷu; After a kind of creeper; the gourd Momordica monadepha Rextb; FLN. ~ Toṇḍeyahāḷu (9/1167, 12/12th); Toṇḍavāḍi (Guṇ 59/975, Nan 322/1148).

Toravaḷḷi (Heg, Nan, Guṇ 58/10th); Kan + Kan; N + N; Tora < Tore + v(h)aḷḷi; A village on the bank of a small river; GPN. ~ Toravaḷi (Heg 17/15th, Guṇ 61/1049); Toremāvu (Nan).

Toreyanakāṭūru (Mys); Kan + Kan + Kan; N + Suf + N + N; Toreya + (n)a + kāṭ(a) + ūru; The village after an huntsman by name Kāṭa; May be fisherman also.

Toṭṭavāḍi (TNP 258/1527, 259/1621); Kan + Kan; N + N; Toṭṭa < Tōṭa + vāḍi; A village of gardens; KN.

Tōḍipura (Guṇ); Kan + Skt; N + ; Tōḍi + ; a village by the side of a water course; MN.

Triyambakapura (Guṇ 34/1513, 149/1417, 146/1654); Skt + Skt + Skt; N adj + N + N; Tri + (y)ambaka + pura; After the God, three-eyed Śiva; RN.

Tumbula (TNP 40/1180, 42/1556); SX; Kan; the sluice of a tank, the nave of a wheel; [< tumuḷa, a combat ?].

Tumbusōge (Heg); Kan + Kan; N + N; Tumbu + sōge; After the full, blooming peacock's tail; FAN.

Tummanēraḷe (Nan); Kan + Kan; Adj + N; Tumma < Tumbu (?) + Nēraḷe; After blooming Eugenia jambolana Lam; FLN.

Tunga (PP 30/16th, SX; 60/16th); High elevated lofty place.

Tuppadakoḷa (Huṇ); Kan + Kan; N + Suf + N; Tuppa + (d)a + koḷa; A ghee tank; A village where ghee is produced in plenty; MN.

Turuganūru (TNP); Kan + Kan; N + Suf + ; Turuga < Turukāra + (n)a + ; a cowherd's village; FAN.

U

Uḍigāla (CRN 315/1551); Kan + Kan; N + N; Uḍi + gāla; The village known for the growth of ugly trees ? FLN (DIPṆ).

Uḍuvēpura (Huṇ, Gaz); Kan + Skt; N + N; Uḍuve + pura; A place filled with bushes a jungle.

Uḍḍibāgūru (TNP); Kan + Kan + Kan; N + N + N; Uḍḍi < oḍḍi + bāg(e) + ūru; A village where Sirīsha trees are in large number (heap); FLN.

Udbūru (Heg, Mys); Skt + Kan; Udb + ūru; A villge that has come up ?; MN.

Uddanūru (Koḷ); Kan + Kan; Extended village (?). ~ Uddūru (Huṇ 24/1162).

Uganēdahuṇḍi (CRN 311/16th); Kan + Kan; N + Suf + ; Uganē < ugani + (d)a + ; After a shrubby creeper, the heart-leaved moonseed, cocculus cordifolius dec; FLN. ~ Uganiya (Koḷ, Nan); Uganai (Koḷ 42/12th); Ugune (30/1321); Uguneya (312/1322).

Ukkalagere (TNP); Kan + Kan; N + Suf + ; Ukkal < okkal + a + ; After a tenant, a husbandman; MN.

Ummattūru (CRN 99/11th, 92/1473, 200/1527, 89/1531, 102/1589, Huṇ); Kan + Kan; N + ; Ummatt(a) + ; After the thorn apple, Datura metel and fastuosa [intoxicated ?]; FLN.

Uṇḍavāḍi (Huṇ, Mys); Kan + Kan; N + ; Uṇḍa < uṇḍe + ; After a round mass or ball of anything; MN. [< uṇḍige = A stamp, an impression ?].

Uppanahaḷḷi (Nan); Kan + Kan; N + Suf + ; Uppa(i) + (n)a + ; A village where salt is sold; CN. ~ Upinahaḷi (391/17th, 35/1662); Uppinamōḷe (Yaḷ, Koḷ 7/1512).

Uttambaḷḷi (Koḷ); Kan + Kan; N + N; Uttam < Huttamma + b(h)aḷḷi; A white ant hill, a goddess after such a hill; RṆ. ~ Uttēnahaḷḷi (PP); Uttavaḷḷi (CRN).

Uyigoṇḍanahaḷḷi (Huṇ); Kan + Kan < Skt + Kan; N + N + Suf + ; Uyi < uy + goṇḍa < gowḍa + (n)a + ; After a man who deals with the husk of rice or corn (?); PN. [Uyyāle = a swing ?].

Uyyambaḷḷi (Huṇ); Kan + Kan; N + N + N; Uy + am < amma + b(h)aḷḷi; After a woman who deals with rice husk; FPN. ~ Uyyamapaḷḷi (260/1368); Uyambaḷḷi (Heg 133/1497); Uyyamahaḷḷi (390/1482); Uyyambaḷi (401/1531).

V

Vaḍagere (Yaḷ 182/1582); Kan + Kan; N + ; Vaḍa < Oḍḍa + ; After a stone cutter; EN. ~ Vaḍagere (Guṇ 61/1126); Oḍḍagere (168/1497); Oḍagere (Heg 36/1497). Vaḍḍambāḷu (Heg); Vaḍḍaraguḍi (Heg); Vaḍḍarahaḷḷi (Hun); Vaḍḍarahōsahaḷḷi (PP); Voḍḍagalpura

(CRN); Voḍḍagere (Guṇ); Voḍḍarabyalakuppe (PP); Voḍḍarahaḷḷi (Guṇ, CRN).

Vaḍakānamāḷa (Heg, Gaz); Kan < Skt + Kan; N + Suf + N; Vaḍaka < Vaḍakāṛa < vāṭikā + (n)a + māḷa; A gardener's village.

Vaḍērahaḷḷi (Heg); Kan + Kan; N + Suf + ;Vadēr < oḍeyar + a + ; After a master, a ruler; MN. ~ Vaḍērahosahaḷḷi (Huṇ); Voḍeyanapura (Guṇ).

Vaḍeyonḍanahaḷḷi (TNP) ?

Vaḍlimanuganahaḷḷi (Huṇ); Kan + Skt + Kan; N + N + Suf + ; Vaḍli < Oḍḍaṇa + manuga + (n)a + ; A collection of villages one of whose name is Manu ? PN.

Vagarapura (CRN); Kan < Skt + Skt; N + N; Vagara < Vāgure + pura; A village where nets are made; CN.

Vaḷagerehaḷḷi (KRN); Kan + Kan; Adj + N + ; Vaḷa < Oḷa + g(k)ere +; A village near the tankbed; GPN. ~ Voḷagere (Nan).

Vallahaḷḷi (Heg); Skt + Kan; N + N; a place full of thickets (?); FLN. [A species of pulse].

Vallāmbudhi (KRN); Skt + Skt; N + N; Valla < Vallabha (?) + ambudhi; After the Vallambudhi tank created by a superior person; MN.

Varakōḍu (Mys 123/1236, 124/17th, 130/1109); Skt + Kan; Adj + N; Vara + kōḍu; The village in the vicinity of a high peak of a hill; GPN.

Varahaḷḷi (Nan); Skt + Kan; Adj + N; Vara + haḷḷi; An excellent or gifted village; MN.

Varuna (Mys 166/1828, 168/10th); SX; Skt; The village dedicated to the god of rains; MN. ~ Vāruṇa (Gaz).

Vastillinganapura (Guṇ); Kan < Skt + Skt + Skt; N + N + Suf + ; Vasti < Vasati + linga + (n)a + ; Linganapura where there is a Jaina monastery; PN.

Vājamangala (Mys); Kan + Skt + Skt; N + ; Vāja < _Ōja < Upādhyāya + ; After a carpenter, a goldsmith; EN. [A teacher, a guru]. Ōjamangala (122/17th); Vōjamangala (121/1277).

Vāranchigurupura (Huṇ) ?

Vāṭāḷu (TNP); Kan + Kan; N + N; Vāṭ(e) + (h)āḷu; After a large jungle reed; the Mysore gamboge tree; FLN. ~ Ōṭehaḷu (16/1749, 295/14th); Vāṭahaḷa (296/1196); Ōtehāḷu (298/15th).

Venkaṭayyanachatra (CRN 249/1676, 250/1733); Skt + Kan + Skt; N + N + Suf + ; Venkaṭayya + (n)a + ; PN. Venkaṭapura (KRN).

Vijayāpura (TNP, Guṇ 46/1549, 17/1372); Skt + Skt; N + ; Vijaya +; Victory town; HN. ~ Vijayapura (18/1374, 23/1546); Vijāpura (146/1654).

Vijayaśrīpura (Mys); Skt + Skt + Skt; N + N + ; Vijaya-śrī + ; A town famous for victory and prosperity; MN.

Vīranahosahaḷḷi (Huṇ); Skt + Kan + Kan; N + Suf + Adj + N; Vīra + (n)a + hosa + haḷḷi; A new village of Vīra, the powerful man; PN. ~ Vīranapura (CRN, Nan).

Vīradēvanapura (Nan); Skt + Skt + Skt; N + N + Suf + ; Vīra + dēva + (n)a + ; After a hero god; PN.

Y

Yaḍadore (TNP); Kan + Kan; Adj + N; Ya(e)ḍa + d(t)ore; A town on the left side of the river; GPN. ~ Yaḍatore (Heg, KRN, Guṇ); Yaḍahaḷḷi (Mys, TNP, Nan, KRN 117/1741); Yeḍehaḷḷi (TNP 55/1541); Yaḍakoḷa (Mys); Yaḍapura (CRN); Yaḍeyūru (CRN).

Yaḍavanahaḷḷi (Guṇ); Kan + Kan; N + Suf + ; Ya(e)ḍava + (N)a + ; After a left hander (?); MN.

Yalachagere (Nan); Kan + Kan; N + N; Ya(e)lacha + g(k)ere; The village where jujube, a kind of fruit tree grows; FLN. ~ Yalachahaḷḷi (Nan, Guṇ); Yalacheṭṭi (Guṇ); Yelachagere (CRN); Yelachanahaḷḷi (Huṇ).

Yalādahaḷḷi (KRN); Kan + Kan; N + Suf + ; Yalā < elava (?) + (d)a + ; After the Seemul or silk cotton trees; FLN.

Yalakkūru (CRN); Kan + Kan + Kan; N + N + ; Yal < ele + akk(a) + ūru; A sister's village where betel is grown; FLN. [< ēlakki = cardamom plan ?]. ~ Yalakūru (5/1828); Yalehaḷḷi (Nan); Yalehaḷḷi

(329/17th); Yalemuddanahaḷḷi (KRN); Yalamattūru (Heg); Yelehuṇḍi (Heg).

Yaḷandūru (Yaḷ 5/1244); Kan + Kan < Skt + Kan; Adj + N + N; Yal < eḷe + and < vandu < indu + ūru; After the rising (young) moon; NN. ~ Yaḷavandūru (10/1775, 100/1566); Eḷeyandūru (1/1654); [Alternative names : Bālachandrapura; Chōḷēndra simha chaturvēdi mangalam].

Yamagumbha (Huṇ); Kan < Skt + Skt; N + N; Yama < Yamaḷa + gumbha; After a pair of naves of a wheel; [A place where big pots are made ?]; MN.

Yaragambaḷḷi (Yaḷ 199/1500); Kan + Kan; N + Suf + N; Yaraga < eṛega + m + b(h)aḷḷi; The village of a master; MN. ~ Yaṛagambaḷḷi/ Aṛagambaḷḷi (200/1556); Yaṛagambaḷi (207/1527); Yaraganahaḷḷi (Mys, TNP 15/1621, 16/1749, 27/1736); Eṛaganahaḷḷi (CRN 239/ 1289).

Yariyūru (Guṇ, Yaḷ); Kan + Kan; N + ; Yari < ere + ; The village which has dark red soil; GPN. Yareyūru (Guṇ 148/17th, Yaḷ 20/ 15th); Yeṛeyūru (Yaḷ 36/16th); Yeremanuganahaḷḷi (KRN); Yerehaḷḷi (Heg).

Yāṇḍahaḷḷi (Mys); Kan < Tam + Kan; N + ; Yāṇḍa < āṇḍi (?) + ; After a religious mendicant of the Śaivas; RN.

Yellemāḷa (Koḷ); Kan + Kan; N + ; Yelle + ; a plain which forms the border of the village; GPN.

Yeṇagumba (CRN); Kan + Skt; N + N; Yeṇa < eṇṇe + g(k)umbha; Oil pot; The village where oil is sold; CN. ~ Yeṇṇegumbha (302/ 1526).

Yēchagaḷḷi (Nan 167/1685); Kan < Skt + Kan; N + N + ; Yēcha < ēcha < āditya + g(h)aḷḷi; After the person who is named after the Sun; PN.

Yēnagahaḷḷi (CRN); Kan < Skt + Kan; N + N; Yēna(ga) < ēṇa + haḷḷi; A village where deer are found (?); FAN.

Select Bibliography

English

List of village names published by the Government of Karṇāṭaka
Karnāṭaka Gazetteer (Mysore district)
Epigraphia Carnatica (Mysore district)
Armstrong G.H. : Origin and meaning of place names
Ekwall, Eilert : The Oxford dictionary of English place names
George K.M. : Place names of Southern India
Kittel F. : Kannada-English dictionary
Mawer A. : Problems of place names study
Taylor, Isaac : Words and places
Thurston : Castes and tribes of Southern India (7 Vols.)

Kannada

Kēśirāja : Śabdamaṇi darpaṇa
Gōpālakrishṇa V. : Sthaḷanāma adhyayanagaḷu
Jōśi, Śambā : Eḍegaḷu hēḷuva Kannāḍa kathe
Raghupathi, Kematūr : A glossary of place name elements in Tuḷu and Kannāḍa

Telugu

Kētu Viśwanātha Reddy : Kaḍapa ūrlapērlu